The Afterlife is to Die for

Amazing Possibilities Await Us All

By John S. Weiss

Copyright © 2015 Johns S. Weiss All Rights Reserved

This book or any portion thereof may not be reproduced or used in any manner whatsoever without the express written permission of the publisher except for the use of brief quotations in a book review.

Printed in the United States of America.

ISBN: 978-1517789343

First Edition, December 2013

Cover design by Rebecca Swift
Author's Consultant: Christine F. Anderson

www.JohnSWeiss.com

Dedication

This book is dedicated to those with a very open mind who believe or want to believe that this life is just the beginning of a long and wonderful journey.

TABLE OF CONTENTS

Preface: Life after Death? 1
Chapter 1: Pleasant Dreams 7
Chapter 2: Up in the Air 17
Chapter 3: The Awakening 23
Chapter 4: Lyle Comes Clean 29
Chapter 5: Proof. Well, Almost 39
Chapter 6: My God, Proof 49
Chapter 7: To Hell with Heaven and Vice Versa 61
Chapter 8: Miracles at Mohonk 71
Chapter 9: Bundles of Answers 83
Chapter 10: Smitten By a Snake 97
Chapter 11: Titanic Revelations 111
Chapter 12: Bundles of Mysteries 121
Chapter 13: Mysteries in an Emerald Twilight 139
Chapter 14: Dangers on Omaha Beach 163
Chapter 15: Banquet of Horrors 169
Chapter 16: Mind Surfing 183
Chapter 17: Preparing for the Preposterous 197
Chapter 18: The Observance 205
Chapter 19: Flying Back In Time 219
Chapter 20: The Qumran Conundrum 233
Chapter 21: Bewilderment in Bethlehem 247

Chapter 22: Perplexed In Paradise.. 263

Chapter 23: Boggling the Mind 279

Chapter 24: The Hoax and the Moonlight Sonata. 285

Chapter 25: Brain Drain 295

Chapter 26: Through Unborn Eyes. 319

Chapter 27: Rocking Chair Revelations 337

Chapter 28: Destined to Dream.. 349

Chapter 29: The Rebirth.. 363

Chapter 30: Happy Trails 371

About the Song... 377

About the Author... 379

PREFACE
LIFE AFTER DEATH?

"He's a liar. He's delusional." That's what many people will be saying about me when they read this book. Honestly, I can't blame them. I'm even quite skeptical about all this myself. The mere notion of a life after death experience appears to be a massive stretch of my imagination. But it's all true; at least I think it is.

If this profound, let alone confounding, experience of mine is true, then life is even more of a miracle than it already is. To me, life is now more precious than I ever suspected and, as I have now learned, must be experienced to its fullest every moment of the day.

Of course, there's nothing new about the concept of life after death. The whole idea has been around as long as, well, civilized people have been around. It's part of most peoples' most intimate belief systems. But not mine. I fervently believed that when you died, that was it. Adios forever. That's probably why I'm still having trouble fully accepting my awakening.

What I'd like to do now is take a moment and tell you a few more things about myself that may help you form an opinion. First of all, I don't drink. Not a drop. I'm diabetic, and alcohol conflicts with my drugs. Speaking of drugs, I'm clean in that department too, unless you consider insulin, aspirin and Tylenol substances of abuse. Now I have to come clean about coffee. I'm seriously addicted. I'll have to admit the same for tobacco. I smoke a pipe. It makes me look like a professor, but that's not a valid excuse.

I don't believe in UFOs and little green men. I don't see or believe in ghosts. I think the horoscope industry is a scam. I'm not into conspiracy theories. I think that people who are against gun control should be shot. I'm not a member of any cult. And I've never been religious, even for the sake of tradition.

I'm, fortunately, a cancer survivor. I was diagnosed about six years ago and had to endure very major surgery and months of chemotherapy. It was horrible. Even when I was at my worst, I never gave a moment's thought to the comforting notion that maybe, just maybe, there was something after this life. However, during my hundreds of hours of chemo torture I perfected the art of meditation. Thanks to this, I was able to experience the awakening you're going to learn a lot more about.

The science of it all

Science is an integral part of understanding (and maybe even believing in) the survival of death. But the theories can be very difficult to understand. So, I've tried to put everything I've learned into the simplest possible terms, precisely as it was related to me. At one point during the writing of this book, I seriously considered leaving the science out, but it's just too important and too fascinating. I also considered having a science-only chapter, but it wouldn't have complemented my experience. So, I'm reporting the science in the same sequence as it was explained to me and in virtually the same words.

Religious connection?

Christ no, I don't want anyone to think that this is a 'religious' book. Indeed, some may perceive it to be because of the overall implications. The book may actually reinforce the concept of faith with many who seek assurance. It may also make the most devout atheists think twice about their staunch convictions. All I can say is that it should be read with an open mind. A very open mind. If you get goose bumps, great. If you get pissed off, that's your right.

Not so funny

The concepts presented in this book are of a very serious nature. In fact, few things in the world could be as serious. And during the time I experienced the events you're about to read, I was very nervous. And when I'm nervous, I attempt to take the edge off it with humor. It calms my jangled nerves. So, you're going to find a degree of humor throughout this book. Please don't be put off or offended by it. Likewise, do your best to overlook any language you deem to be offensive. There's nothing like a foul four letter word to express an emotion.

"Death—the last sleep? No, the final awakening."
—*Walter Scott*

"Memories are all we really own."
—*Elias Lieberman*

"Memory is the treasury and guardian of all things."
—*Marcus T. Cicero*

"Memory is the scribe of the soul."
—*Aristotle*

"Memory is the mother of all wisdom."
—*Aeschylus*

"Yesterday is but today's memory, and tomorrow is today's dream."
—*Kahill Gibran*

"Life is all memory except for the one present moment that goes by you so quickly you hardly catch it going."
—*Tennessee Williams*

"Dreaming permits each and every one of us to be quietly and safely insane every night of our lives."
—*Charles William Dement*

"Death may be the greatest of all human blessings."
—*Socrates*

"Our memory is our coherence, our reason, our feeling, even our action. Without it, we are nothing."
—*Luis Bunuel*

"As death, when we come to consider it closely, is the true goal of our existence, I have formed during the last few years such close relations with this best and truest friend of mankind, that his image is no longer terrifying to me, but is indeed very soothing and consoling! And I thank my God for graciously granting me the opportunity of learning that death is the key which unlocks the door to our true happiness."
—*Wolfgang Amadeus Mozart*

Chapter 1
Pleasant Dreams

It had been a long, tiresome January day. And I was glad to curl up with a book before I went to sleep. I was about half way into a really gripping World War 2 story about Iwo Jima, and I just had to read one more chapter. That's what I always tell myself, 'just one more chapter.'

World War 2 history books have fascinated me for years. From the battle strategies to the weaponry to the human drama, it's all beyond exciting to me. What's more, if I've had a bad day, reading about all the terror and misery that millions of people endured makes me feel as though my problems are rather trivial.

When I finally put my Iwo book down and turned off the light, I began a ritual I practice that thoroughly relaxes me: meditation. It's the best way I know to fall soundly asleep. *Most importantly, it opened the door to the unbelievable world I'm going to tell you about.*

I tried meditation many years ago, but was unable to concentrate or focus my mind. But when I was in chemotherapy, I perfected it and became sort of an expert. During chemo, I spent countless hours sitting in a comfortable chair while the poison slowly flowed through my veins. Sure, you can read, but even that becomes tedious, especially when you get dizzy and nauseous.

So, I learned to completely relax, and remove just about everything from my mind. It's not easy. I didn't chant a mantra, but simply focused my mind's eye on an acorn and buried all my thoughts. Why an acorn instead of a leaf, a mountain, a bicycle or a raspberry pastry? An acorn was the first thing that popped into my mind. They're pleasing to look at, and there's really nothing about them that will lead your mind to other thoughts.

After my drooping eyelids told me to put the damn book down, my mind was racing with very vivid images of the tumultuous Iwo Jima battlefield, and it took the passive little acorn a few minutes to help me eliminate them. As usual, meditation sent me off to dreamland, but, this time, to a land that has profoundly changed my life. The next thing I remember was the annoying sound of my Casio alarm clock welcoming me to a new day, a hot shower and a short walk to breakfast.

By the time I strolled the seven blocks to my favorite breakfast spot, the Juan Valdez Café, I was literally craving my next wakeup call: a nice, hot cup of coffee. So I ordered a Café con leche and my usual almond croissant. After about three bites, a dream from the previous night popped into my consciousness. It was about Iwo Jima.

Well, not just about Iwo Jima.

I was there.

In the middle of a real shit storm of a battle.

At first thought, it all made sense. After all, I was entrenched in a rather intense book about the subject. So why not dream about it?

But what a dream this was.

So realistic.

Too realistic.

It's very rare that I ever remember a dream. And when I do, it's usually murky and surreal. Sometimes I'm trying to run, but my legs are as heavy as lead. Sometimes I have the ability to fly. On rare occasions I have a classic nightmare that scares the crap out of me, and I always wake up. But my Iwo dream didn't wake me up, although it could be considered a nightmare.

This was like a real memory — something I actually experienced. All my senses were completely tuned in. There I was, trying to flatten myself into a large depression on the edge of a beach. The sand was very fine and darkly colored. Ugly. Everything was ugly.

My ears were pierced by a thundering wall of sounds: huge explosions, rifle and machine gun fire, bullets buzzing by like hornets, soldiers yelling, screaming, and crying, mechanical clinking and clanking; the only normal, pleasing noises were the sounds of a pounding surf. That seemed out of place in this hellish arena.

The smells were like nothing I've ever experienced. My nose was assaulted by the stench of sulfur, gun powder, burning flesh, blood, superheated metal and charred rubber. My mouth was completely dry, but I seemed to taste everything I smelled. I felt intense heat, perspiration and the sand.

But what I felt more intensely than anything else was fear. There were constant blinding flashes, followed by all sorts objects sailing through the air: stones, charred wood, twisted chunks of metal, rifles, helmets, pieces of blood soaked uniforms, all manner of body parts and geysers of sand. What I saw on the ground was pretty much the same.

In my immediate vicinity, sharing my crater, were two soldiers. The guy on the left of me kept peering over the edge of our shallow crater. Then he'd raise his gun over his head, a Thompson submachine gun, and fire blindly. What a sound that thing made. And the hot, ejecting shell casings kept raining down on me, stinging my face and hands. I didn't see his face. Yet.

The soldier on my right was nearly in the fetal position.

But he appeared calm.

Almost like he was enjoying this nightmare.

He looked right at me and said with a smile, "The fellow next to you, Shorty, is going to get shot. You know, wacked, zapped, wasted, plugged, blown away."

At that moment, I felt a searing pain on the side of my neck. Shorty, had dropped his Thompson, and the hot barrel brushed my neck. I quickly turned, only to closely view this poor guy on his back, eyes and mouth wide open and blood trickling from a hole in his temple. I saw his face and will never forget it.

Over all the explosions, I barely heard a voice from my right say, "See, I told you so. He never knew what hit'em."

The guy was grinning. I vividly remembered being incensed at his total lack of empathy. It was as though he was completely detached from the tragedy.

Then he spoke again. "Shorty and I went to high school together. He wanted me to relive his death with him. He's watched me get mine on Omaha Beach. A real bummer. I never even got to kill any krauts."

I remembered being very confused by this banter. But I distinctly remembered everything he said — like it was *really* said.

Like it wasn't a dream.

Pondering all this nonsense while I savored my almond croissant, I remembered the last thing I heard him say, with a broader grin than before.

"Hope you're enjoying this as much as I am."

That's where the dream clicked off. Too bad. I actually wanted a couple of more seconds so I could have slammed this asshole in the mouth. But this was a dream. How could I, honestly, give a damn?

No matter how hard I tried, I couldn't get this stupid dream out of my head. Every moment of it kept coming back, and I couldn't help from analyzing every aspect of it. As far as I could remember, I had never read this sequence of events in any of the many Iwo books I've had over the years. Of course, all the action and sensory information was a compilation of things I've read. Even the way Shorty had been killed.

The rest of my day was thoroughly uneventful. Not even the staccato sound of a machinegun or the scent of a burning tire oozed into my consciousness. Once again, I was very tired, but after fluffing up my pillow, I instinctively reached for my book. As soon as I saw the cover, I winced. 'Could reading more of this now regurgitate my dream?' I asked myself. No, I couldn't let myself become a victim of my own dreams. With that solved, I got comfortable and jumped back into the book.

The next thing I remembered was waking up at around 3:00am with my reading light on and the book resting on my chest. I had dozed off in the middle of a good chapter. Didn't even have a chance to meditate. Just shows you how zonked I was. I didn't even remember falling back to sleep after I turned off the light.

When my Casio once again woke me in the rudest of manner, I felt totally refreshed. All I wanted, craved to be more precise, was my coffee and pastry. When I left my home, it was misty, drizzling and cold, but the walk to Juan Valdez was invigorating. Along the way, I tried to remember if I had had any more dreams. Nothing. My mind was clean. What a relief. That dream had obviously been a fluke.

I have to admit, I did think about my Iwo dream a few times during the day. How could I help it? It was now a part of me. A real, well sort of real, memory. Why deny it? That night I grabbed my book without hesitation, read until I could have sworn I saw sheep in my room, and went to sleep. But not before meditating.

As soon as my Casio gave me a swift kick in the balls in the morning, a new memory hit me.

Another dream.

Iwo again.

Just as vivid.

But weirder.

I was crouched in the same spot, dead Shorty on my left, asshole on my right. Hell everywhere to be seen, heard, felt, smelled and tasted. The difference was that I knew I was dreaming and saw that it was a continuation of my last one. While I was marveling at this anomaly and wondering how it could be possible, I felt a hard tap on my right shoulder.

When I turned, I wasn't even surprised to see that jerk staring at me with his big brown eyes peeking out from a banged up helmet, gobs of grease and soot smeared all over his gaunt thin face. This time, though, he wasn't smirking. With a note of seriousness, he barked, "If you want to experience combat the right way you've got to be in uniform."

That's when I realized that all I was wearing was my usual sleeping attire: a pair of underpants.

Underpants?

On Iwo?

It was embarrassing.

Embarrassing?

"Did you hear me, soldier?" he asked. "Answer me," he demanded.

I didn't know if I could talk coherently in a dream. Thought my mouth might move, but certainly nothing would come out. I also thought that trying to speak might wake me up. But I didn't want to wake up because, believe it or not, this whole thing was intriguing me.

It was just too real.

Too exciting.

Maybe I was going crazy. Maybe someone had slipped some LSD into the insulin shot I took every night. Then I figured, fuck it, I'll talk to this guy. Nothing to lose but my sanity.

"I don't have a uniform. And this is just a stupid dream," I yelled, trying to be heard over all the thundering noise.

Well, the words came out of my mouth. I wished I had said something more astute, more clever. Wow, I didn't even wake up.

He slowly shook his head, while intently staring at me. Then he said more seriously than I could believe, "This is no dream. This is real. You're damned lucky to be a part of it. I'm doing you a favor. Now get with the program."

It took me what seemed like an eternity to fathom what he had just uttered. No, this wasn't real. Seemed like it, but couldn't be. Of course not. It was a dream. And, yes, I was lucky to be having such an absurd experience. They didn't even say 'get with the program' back in the '40s. And he was doing me a favor?

KaBoooommm. An enormous explosion a few yards in front of me brought me back to my senses.

Without thinking, I screamed, "I don't have a uniform you lunatic. I'm asleep. At home. In New York City. In my Fruit of the Loom briefs."

His sand encrusted lips moved, "You've got a uniform if you want one. Just imagine you're wearing one. Think hard about it. And don't forget boots and a helmet."

Without further pondering the absurdity of what I was experiencing, I followed his advice. Why not? I'll go with it. You know, get with the program. What a joke.

All of a sudden — POOOF. I was in a uniform.

He acknowledged my abrupt transformation with an approving nod and said, "How do you expect to kill Japs without a weapon? Roll over, and grab Shorty's Thompson. He doesn't need it any more. And take the pouch of ammo clips off his belt. You'll need 'em."

Once again, I followed his orders while repressing a laugh. I couldn't imagine what his response would have been if he caught me giggling. Not that I honestly gave a fucking damn. With the gun firmly in hand, I wiggled over the edge of the crater, aimed at what appeared to be a small cave opening and pulled the trigger. The noise was deafening.

And the gun was kicking, jumping and spewing expended shells all over the place. How could you hit anything with this heavy piece of junk, I thought to myself. But it was fun. Serious fun. Thrilling, in fact. I've got to admit that. Over the years, Thompsons have been glorified in hundreds of battle stories I've read. They've also been romanticized in numerous movies about gangsters in the 1930s. I've always wondered what it would be like to shoot one. Now I knew. Or did I? Must be my imagination on steroids. He was laughing. At me.

"If you could only see yourself," he said. "That gun nearly hammered you senseless."

"No shit," I answered.

"You gotta get used to it. With practice, you'll see that it's a damn fine weapon. You've always known that, Johnny boy." he said as he took a swig from his canteen.

"By the way, my name's Lyle," he said.

Still flabbergasted by all this, I decided to set aside my disbelief and just go with the conversation. I had nothing to lose. Presumably, I was getting a good night's sleep, anyway. And the dream now seemed like harmless fun.

"How do you presume to know what I've always known? And how do you know my name," I asked.

Of course he knows everything about me. He's an offshoot of me in my own head, I thought to myself. Then I slapped a new clip into the Thompson.

I decided that to actually enjoy this dream while it lasted, I had to skip the conversation and pretend to be John Wayne. Got to have some fun. So I jumped up, held the gun at my hip and let loose with a long, ripping blast. Emptied the whole clip and slapped in a new one. I was getting the hang of it.

After the acrid smell of gunpowder faded in the breeze, I smelled something new. Lyle was smoking a cigarette. With a Camel hanging from his lip, he was shaking his head and laughing again, really enjoying the pathetic vision of me acting like a complete fool, in my own dream.

"Nice shootin'," he said. "Do you really want me to answer your last question? The answer's going to mess with your head."

"Make it quick," I said. "Before this dream is over I want to do some more shooting, and I've got to toss a few grenades. That'll be a blast. No pun intended."

"You're beginning to slip out of this dream space, he said, so I'll be fast, direct and honest. I'm not you. This is not a dream. You're not crazy. Here's a grenade. We'll meet again the next time you meditate and fall asleep."

I didn't listen to a word of that nonsense. 'Not me? Not a dream?'

But I gladly accepted the grenade, pulled the pin with my teeth, just like John Wayne, and tossed it at that cave opening.

Karrrrummmph, KaBooom, ring, ring, ring. Ring?

That's my fucking Casio.

If I still had the Thompson, I'd blow the shit out of that infernal clock. Time to get up. Reality had returned.

I yanked myself out of bed and went through my usual routine. During breakfast, I thought long and hard about my dream. It no longer bothered me; I sort of got a kick out of it. It was certainly strange and disconcerting, but fun, none the less.

Dreaming, in general, was a mystery to me. People analyzed dreams to death, and I was certain there were a million theories. What's a 'normal' dream? I had no idea. And still don't. Yeah, it sure was strange to dream so damn vividly with such a sensory overload. Maybe this was going to be like a mini series, and I'd return to Iwo tonight. I actually hoped so.

Lyle, obviously my split personality, told me we'd meet again the next time I meditated. Maybe he said 'medicated' and I misunderstood him over all the racket. The meditation connection made a lot sense to me. Meditation puts you in a very focused state of mind. Add that to being nearly mesmerized by a book and I suppose it could conjure up the type of dreams I was having. It had never happened before, but there's always a first time for everything. When I first started meditating, a couple of people told me that it could be a direct route to paranormal experiences. What a bunch of crap, I thought.

That night, I was way too tired to read. A long day, followed by a big dinner, will always do that to you. When I turned the light off and got into my meditation mode, I hesitated for a moment. I asked myself if I really wanted another Iwo episode so soon after the last one. Wait a second: no Iwo book, no Iwo dream. I'd have a sane evening after all.

Chapter 2
Up in the Air

When I woke up, I had no idea what time it was and couldn't care less. I didn't glance at my watch, which I always wear while sleeping, and avoided trying to focus on that stinking Casio that I had obviously beaten to the punch. All I knew was that it was pitch black, the city was unusually quiet, I was very secure and comfortable, and I had a lot to occupy my mind. After the brand new dream I had just woken up from, I wasn't sure if I still had a mind. Maybe I was sane and Lyle wasn't. But Lyle was me. Or was he?

I had fallen asleep with nothing on my mind except the view of my acorn. Hey, wait a minute: could this be a hallucinogenic acorn, something Timothy Leary hadn't even known about?

All I can remember, and vividly so, was that my first sense was my freezing cold derriere plunked down on an exceptionally uncomfortable metal railing, a rather telling indication that this was definitely not an Iwo dream. Anything cold would have been welcomed on Iwo.

I was in some kind of a huge metal structure that was seriously vibrating. There were rivets all over the place, about to shake loose, I thought. Instead of explosions and screaming, there was an annoyingly loud droning sound. Couldn't figure it out for the life of me. I also couldn't figure out why the several guys I saw were dressed in large puffy leather coats, wearing equally puffy gloves and hats. Shit, where was I? The smell didn't give me any indication either: it was a mixture of oil, gas and gunpowder. Maybe I was in the bowels of a submarine or something like that.

Shit, where the fuck was I?

Just as I wondered if my old crater mate, Lyle, was inhabiting this dumb dream, I saw him walking towards me, slightly off balance. At first I didn't recognize him because he was all bundled up like the rest of the guys in this strange vehicle.

Laughing hard, he sat next to me on the uncomfortable steel girder, and looked me up and down, seeming to scrutinize every shivering inch of me. Putting his hands over his face, he laughed even harder, like a certifiable maniac.

After regaining his composure, Lyle asked, "Know where you are?"

"I don't have a clue," I said.

"Come on, use your imagination," he said. "I thought this would fascinate you. It does whenever you read about it, and you always enjoy movies of this genre. It should be obvious."

Then it smacked me in the face.

It was obvious, something I should have realized right away. It's just that the transition from my Iwo dream was completely out of context.

This, I never expected.

It was even stranger than the Iwo dream, if that's at all possible, because not one shred of it was on my mind. I hadn't read any books about this in over a year, nor had I seen any movies.

I was flying who knows where on a bomber.

I always loved reading about battle exploits in the sky. It always amazed me how anyone survived, considering the percentage of planes that were literally blown to hell.

Just as Lyle was about to put in his two cents, having obviously read my mind, all hell broke loose. The airman closest to me let loose with a 50 caliber machine gun that I hadn't noticed before. Turned out he was just testing his gun, not zapping some Jap or kraut. The noise made the Thompson sound like a child's cap gun. Incredible. It was almost impossible to hear the tinkling of the spent shell casings bouncing around the steel floor.

Clapping his hands to get my attention, Lyle spoke in his distinctly midwestern accent. "Well?"

"Yeah, yeah, yeah. I know. Took me long enough to get it." I said.

"Well?" he asked again.

"Well what?" I answered.

"Don't you think you look like an absolute moron sitting on a B17 Flying Fortress wearing nothing but your ridiculous underpants?" he chuckled.

"Oh. Right. I know the routine," I said trying not to laugh.

So I did the good old imagination thing, and, kazaam, I was properly dressed. 'John,' I said to myself, 'Just shitcan the common sense and go with the flow.' It was a logical thought in a situation that defied all logic.

I took it a step further and asked, "So, Lyle, what's this all about?"

As seriously as he could, Lyle explained, "Its January 27, 1943, and we're on our way to blow the shit out of a Jerry town called Wilhelmshaven. Right now we're still over the English Channel, just about to fly over the French coastline. In a few minutes from now, all hell's gonna break loose."

"So I guess we're going to see some vicious flak action and probably a swarm of ME109s. Right?" I asked.

"You bet your ass," he answered. "But," he continued, "when you experience this, I want you to seriously think about something extremely important."

"Important? Extremely important?" I asked."

The only thing important to me, I thought, is that I don't wake up before I see one of our gunners turn an ME109 pilot into hamburger meat. Even better, I'd like to be the one doing the shooting."

Lyle brushed his hat back an inch or two over his forehead, put a hand on each of his knees and leaned towards me. Shit, I thought, looks like I'm going to get some God damn lecture.

Of course, this ain't really happening, I thought, so I'll take it with a grain of salt. But it's got to be quick. Can't wake up yet. Got to get an enemy bandit with a 50. I was having a shit load of fun.

Knowing full well every thought in my mind (he is me, damn it), he calmly said, "I know you think this is all bull shit, and I can't blame you. You're also thinking you've got a few screws loose. Let me assure you: you're perfectly normal, this is not a dream and I am neither an aspect of you nor a figment of your imagination. Think about what I just said, what you consider to be nonsense, and, maybe, just maybe, we'll take the next step."

Give me a break, I said to myself. It's just a dream.

And what is this 'take the next step' baloney that Lyle uttered?

Enough thinking — time to bring on the ME109s, duck some flak and turn some jerry buildings into dust. I'm going to wake up sooner or later, I feared.

After plenty of action, I was squinting at a 109 banking hard to my left, trailing oil smoke from its engine.

'No more sauerkraut for you, Fritz,' I said to myself.

Then a cloud seemed to light up with 7:30 AM written on it, and it sounded like it was buzzing.

My Casio brought me down from 20,000 feet to pillow level, as aggressively as ever.

I decided to stay snuggled up in bed for a while so I could reflect on every second of my dream. It was an awfully good one. Just as vivid and real as my visits to Iwo, more like a lifetime experience. In no way was I going to let myself forget any moment of it, as was the case with dreams of my past. They would all get blurry. Quickly.

But these weren't really dreams, not as I had ever experienced, read about or possibly imagined. Of course, they were dreams. Had to be. To say the very, very least, I was confused, perplexed, confounded, concerned and worried. Yes, I was worried about my mental health. But I was also thankful that these weren't terrifying nightmares. A nightmare at this level of reality would be devastating to my nerves.

Before I threw off my sheets and jumped into the real world, I thought hard about anything that could be causing these dreams. Was I taking any new medication? Was my Tylenol way beyond the expiration date? Was I sniffing glue? Was anyone slipping anything into my food? Was I washing my fruit? Did I have a brain tumor? Had I offended a voodoo practitioner? Was there any mold in my pillow?

I couldn't seem to blame it on anything. There had to be an explanation, and I was on a quest to discover it. Screw all the analysis for a moment, I thought, these dreams were fun and terrifically thrilling. I wanted them to continue.

Tonight, I'd love to be back in that B17 dropping bombs. I never got a chance to do that. Maybe all this stuff that's happening to me is 100% normal. Why worry about it? Then I remembered that I had recently been trying a new toothpaste. New toothpaste? Nah, couldn't be that.

On my way to Juan Valdez, I continued to ponder my airborne dream and the prospect of returning to it soon. Hopefully, in fact, tonight. But this time, I hoped for a logical variation. This time, I wanted to be a fighter plane pilot. That's something I've dreamt about since I was a kid, and the written accounts have always knocked my socks off.

The fighter of my choice would definitely have to be a P-51 Mustang. All I had to do, I assumed, was find a combat history book involving this plane, read some juicy passages before meditating, fall asleep, and, kazzzam, I'd be roaring towards an ME-109 or a Jap Zero, with my 50s and 20mm cannons spreading a path of instant death and destruction. Sounds pretty vicious, but, hey, it's only a dream. Right?

Another reason I longed for one of these special dreams to take place in a fighter is simple: They're single seaters. You know what that means: no room for Lyle. Just me. These dreams are screwy enough as it is. But having to talk to some strange variation of myself is just too weird.

It's not that I don't like this apparition, it's just that he freaks me out. Especially all that nonsense he dispenses about these not being dreams. It just wastes valuable dreamtime. And I no longer need him to point out that wearing only underpants is no way to fight a war. If I want to be practically naked in a P-51, so be it, I thought.

Fortunately, the rest of my day was normal. During dinner, I wondered if my dreams could go far beyond World War 2 situations. Stimulation via reading and meditation might take me anywhere.

That evening, I stopped off at my parent's house. My mother had been rummaging through a cabinet and discovered a box of old family photographs. So, I couldn't resist the temptation to look at them all. Honestly, it hurts to see your whole family so young. You really long to bring back the past. To get rid of the wrinkles, trim the waistline, restore a drastically receding hairline, return to a simple, innocent time.

That night, all I could do was reminisce about my wonderful days growing up in Purchase, New York. It was beautiful. We only lived there for fourteen years, but it felt like an eternity. When you're a kid, time goes by very slowly. Too bad you're not wise enough to take full advantage of every second.

My mother had given me a bunch of the yellow tinted photos, every one of which I studied until I couldn't keep my eyes open. After what seemed like a two second meditation, I zonked out.

Chapter 3
The Awakening

Whenever I wake up in the morning before my Casio has had the chance to insult my whole being, I just lie there with my eyes closed, hugging my pillow, feeling the comfort and security of soft sheets enveloping my body.

On some occasions, my top sheet and quilt are missing, the obvious victims of a restless night. That was my first realization when I woke up in what I assumed was the morning. Not only was I uncovered, with no pillow at all, but what I assumed to be my bottom sheet felt mushy and sort of prickly. There was also the sensation of a mild breeze, as though I had forgotten to turn off my fan. My fan? It was January, so that device was safely stored in my closet.

I still hadn't opened my eyes. All this, I thought, was simply my fertile imagination at work. Even the smell of freshly cut grass, or the feeling of the sun on my skin, didn't ring any bells. But when I was startled by a seriously tickling sensation on my face, and scratched a large bug off my cheek, I reluctantly opened my eyes.

'Fuck,' I exclaimed, 'What the fuck?'

I hadn't been snoozing on some bloody sand, or in a B-17, or even in my own damn bed.

I had woken up in a dream on a lawn.

A fucking lawn with fucking bugs.

I sat up, rubbed the sleep out of my eyes and thought to myself, what kind of shit is this? Grass? Bugs? It took about two seconds to focus my eyes and carefully examine the immediate vicinity. I knew exactly where I was: right smack dab in the middle of my old back yard in Purchase.

Then it hit me again:

Before my pre-sleep meditation, I had been literally dreaming about my old home. So this all made perfect sense. Perfect sense? Well, in the scheme of everything that had been happening the last few nights, it did.

Well, enjoy it while you're here, I mused. There was nothing unnatural or dreamlike about anything I saw, felt, touched, or smelled. I knew I was in a dream, but seemed as awake as ever.

I was definitely in Purchase.

In my good old back yard.

Analyzing all this seemed a waste of valuable, fleeting time. I had done that on Iwo and in the stratosphere over Germany, without arriving at any comprehensible conclusions.

Get off it, John, I thought to myself. Going to wake up soon, and it'll all be over. Now it was time to explore. Cover every inch before waking. As far as I could tell, it was midmorning, most likely July. The year? Who knows? Who cares? '54? '59? '62? It always looked the same from this perspective. After a bit more thought, I headed first to our garden.

My parents had always planted a rather large garden since as far back as I could remember. And here it was — with its kaleidoscope of lusciously colored flowers, and row after row of vegetables. As I had done many times before in my past life, I grabbed a few cherry tomatoes, marveled, once again, about this unreal, yet painfully real experience, and popped them in my mouth. Literally shivering with a combination of joy, nostalgia, and total disbelief, I felt the tomatoes bursting in my mouth, releasing a rich flavor that ignited a powerful flood of memories.

Too bad I took this for granted way back then, I thought. Wiping off some juice that was trickling down my chin, I felt that all my senses and emotions were in hyper drive. Shit, this was real.

Shooing away a bee, I looked beyond the garden, past an enormous oak tree, and peered at the side entrance to the house.

I fully expected to see a very young version of my mother, sister, father or grandparents open the door. But that didn't happen, although I was absolutely certain that I could will it to happen.

I also had to see my dog and cats. And could I ride my old bicycle? Drive my Mustang? Start my favorite model airplane engine? It would all be possible; I just knew it. 'Please don't wake up,' I kept urging myself. Please don't.

The sounds of buzzing bugs, chirping birds, a distant lawn mower, highway traffic, and my own chewing were interrupted by a squeaking sound. Not an unfamiliar squeaking sound, though. It was the noise the swings made as they went back and forth on our jungle gym.

Examining it in my right field of vision, I fully expected to see someone from my past. Instead, I saw something that seemed to violate this wonderful experience. It, of course, was Lyle. On *my* swings. Apparently enjoying himself, no less. This shouldn't surprise me, I thought. He was, after all, some kind of projection of myself or maybe someone I knew. Couldn't be. Must be. Confusing as shit.

"Enjoying yourself, John?" he inquired. "Quite a but different from the last few nights, wouldn't you say?"

My honest response: "This place is personal. I'm trying to think you away, but it's not working."

"Maybe you should be thanking me," he had the audacity to say. "I brought you here, knowing full well all the memories it would unleash."

Then, throwing his legs back to gain more momentum on the swing, he laughed.

Why was I bothering to talk to him, or even acknowledge his presence, I wondered. I'm just breathing more life into this imaginary figure — this warped reflection of myself. See if you can intelligently get rid of it, I thought to myself. Absorb it back into yourself.

"You cant," was his response. "I'm not you at all."

After spending a few moments in what appeared to be careful thought, he continued, "I owe you an apology. This is the first time I've ever done anything like this, and I'm sorry I've confused you and gotten you so pissed off."

How am I supposed to respond to this gibberish, I wondered. More to the point, this was the first time I had ever done anything like this. I've never before dreamt with such spectacular clarity, and I've never had an imaginary friend.

A new tactic: "Why are you doing this to yourself?" I pointedly asked him.

Then silence. No answer. He was deep in thought. Thrusting his legs all the way forward while throwing his head back, he seemed to fly on the swing. Just like I always did. For the first time I noticed how young he was, 20 at the most. And his clothing was duller than any I've ever seen. I never really gave a shit about clothing, but I certainly never wore anything remotely like that. God, it was all so strange.

"Remember when I said something about taking the next step?" he asked, intently staring at me.

"Yeah. Whatever." I answered.

"This is important," he said.

"I don't have a clue why I'm doing this to myself," I mumbled.

"Here I am in the middle of the best dream I've ever had, and it's being interrupted by some imaginary vision of myself. It's self-destructive. And now there's a next step that's, of all things, important? Please, just vanish before my mind turns to oatmeal." I yelled.

Well, I figured that would do it. I was waiting for a flash of light or something, and then pooooof, no more Lyle. But no such luck. He just kept on swinging, seemingly lost in thought.

"One more thing I want to say," uttered good old Lyle.

"For Christ's sake make it quick," I stammered. "I'm gonna wake up soon."

"If I vamoose, you'll be able to dream a little while longer, but never again with the same intensity. You're here because of me and me alone. And regardless of what you think, I'm not you. Not at all."

"Horseshit," was my response.

"You're narrow-minded," was his response. "No imagination. No curiosity. Firmly cemented in your own limited way of thinking."

"You win, asshole," I said. "We'll take the important next step, but something tells me I'll have dog shit all over my shoes. My dream shoes, that is."

"Excellent decision," he cried. "Now, you're in for . . ."

I never realized that Lyle had such a ring to his voice.

Ring?

Then it dawned on me (no pun intended): That's not him. It's my fucking Casio. I'm waking up. Leaving my cherished back yard. My dream's over, and I'm left on a hook.

That day, every corner of my mind was consumed by this whole thing. No matter how hard I tried, I couldn't bury it in some dark corner. Still couldn't figure out what Lyle represented in terms of my own subconscious thoughts. But I knew the answer lurked in some crevice.

There was no other explanation.

It occurred to me that it might not be a horrible idea to consult a few close friends or family members. I was itching to reveal this to anyone willing to listen. Maybe I'd get an answer. Or an inkling of one. People would listen kindly, probably break a little sympathetic smile and offer a few empty words of logic. They'd be thinking to themselves: John is seriously fucked up.

Yeah, this was my own personal problem. Or opportunity, depending how you looked at it. If I just went along with everything: you know, conversed with Lyle about who knows what, what would be the downside, I asked myself.

If I could keep my head screwed on, however, there would only be an upside: I could continue having these awesomely spectacular dreams while getting a good night's sleep, and possibly even maintaining some semblance of my sanity.

Lyle, old boy, you win.

After a whole day with all this shit rattling around in my brain, I was overly ready for bed. And did I study my Purchase pictures before meditating? You bet your ass I did. Then I was back in the same spot, like I had never left my yard. Lyle had slowed down his swinging, looking far more serious than before.

I was ready.

Chapter 4
Lyle Comes Clean

"Good to see you again and looking so cheery," Lyle said with what looked to be a genuine smile.

"Let's get on with it and take that 'important next step,'" I said, making an attempt to sound enthusiastic. I don't think I fooled him.

"I know what was on your mind yesterday, and . . ."

"Now how would I have guessed that?" I interrupted. "Sorry. Go on," I added, as sincerely as I was capable of.

He sat there on the swing, staring at his awful looking, mud caked shoes. God damn, they were ugly shoes: shit brown, wrinkled and cracked leather, laces that were broken and knotted in may places, big holes in the soles. Nothing like anything I had ever worn. The same thing applied to his pants: disgusting dark brown, covered with spots and stains; they looked like diarrhea. They were also as baggy as hell.

After what seemed like a minute or so, he looked back at me and shifted his weight on the swing. Once he was comfortable, he spoke quietly, slowly, even sheepishly.

"No. I'm sorry," he said, surprising me. "I've botched this whole thing from the gitgo. Your confusion, anger and disbelief are all my fault and entirely understandable. Let's start from the beginning. Ok?"

That response kind of blew me away.

On the other hand, nothing should have surprised me. Man-oh-man, I thought, do I need help. But I had promised myself to just go with it, so I said, "Yes."

That 'yes' led me to a world that has profoundly altered everything I have ever believed — a paradigm shift of galactic proportions.

"Before anything else," he said, "let's go somewhere comfortable where we can talk without any interruptions."

"Ok," was my response. "Where would you suggest?"

"How about that room in your house where you and your whole family spent so much time: the 'sun room,' as you called it."

"Perfect." I said.

Then I was drowned by a flood of memories.

'The sun room.' I uttered to myself, 'the sun room.' It was where my grandfather used to sit and smoke his pipe, where I used to tease and torment my little sister when we watched television during the evenings of our childhood. When you walked into this airy room, the first door to the left was a smallish closet where my parents kept all their liquor. I loved the cocktail of smells that seduced my nose whenever I opened the door. I've got to admit, when no one was around, I'd steal my way into that closet and quickly take a tiny sip of banana liqueur from a crusty old bottle on the bottom shelf. That bottle stayed there for what seemed like forever, always waiting to send some sweet, forbidden warmth down my young throat.

Lyle asked me whether I wanted to walk there or simply get there instantly by thought. "What if I run into someone in the house?" I asked, without considering how impossibly stupid that sounded.

"If anyone's there," Lyle said, "they won't see or, for that matter, respond to you."

After a nice, slow walk, sucking up as many memories as I could, we got settled in the sun room: he took the couch, I curled up in my grandfather's chair, and swore I could smell his Dunhill tobacco. Before he got to the 'important next step,' Lyle wanted to remind me that I might wake up and vanish at any moment. There was nothing he could do about it. The slightest sound or feeling could alter my dream state.

"When that happens, and it will from time to time," he assured me, "use meditation to fall asleep again the next evening, and I'll be able to get you back. That's critical. Thinking about Purchase doesn't matter any more. Just acorns and meditation."

I nodded a 'yes, I get yuh.' Still looking over every inch of the room, I felt myself relax.

"This isn't going to be easy," said Lyle. "At first, there will be no way you're going to believe anything I tell you. You're going to dismiss it all as garbage, like something rotting in your subconscious. That was my own initial reaction when I first learned about it."

Smiling, I remarked, "Maybe you're going to tell me I died and went to heaven."

"Hold that thought," he said. "We'll get back to it later."

Holy fucking shit, I thought, what's going on here?

"The hard part is figuring out where to begin," he said, as his eyes squinted and his mouth drew back.

Lyle continued, "Oh well, I'll start with something that I know you admire so much about me. My clothing. You know, that shitty stuff you wouldn't be caught dead wearing. Hey, I like what I just said, 'caught dead wearing.' Because you caught me dead wearing it."

"You just lost me," I said. "Please get to the point before I wake up and spend the entire next day in suspense."

"You're right. Here goes" he muttered. "This is the last civilian clothing I was wearing before my induction into the armed services, at the ripe old age of 18. I wore it the last day I saw my own childhood home in Wisconsin. It reminds me of standing in mud at the bus station the last time I kissed my parents and little sister goodbye. It's what I was wearing the last time I kissed my sweetheart good night. I never got to wear this 'disgusting clothing,' as you refer to it, again, because I was killed on June 6, 1944 on Omaha Beach during the D Day invasion." Just like you, I have very dear memories."

Oh, sure, I thought to myself, I'm really supposed to believe this? Then I remembered him saying something about his death while we were on Iwo. Am I actually starting to believe this shit?

"I don't expect you to believe this shit," he said, as he made quotation marks in the air with his skinny fingers. "But I've been thinking about a way to prove all this to you a bit later," he continued.

"Yeah, some proof would be nice," I said. "Something substantial that will make me, somehow, swallow all this stuff."

He closed his eyes, cocked his head back, slowly shook it from side to side, and sort of grunted. "Uhggh. This is hard. And, believe me, it's going to get worse. Lots worse."

"Me? Talking to a ghost? Don't worry, it ain't gonna get any worse," I said, trying to stifle a nervous laugh.

Lyle sat there perfectly still, perfectly quiet, his eyes shifted off to the side. Then, all of a sudden, he swung his eyes back, lurched up at me and yelled, "Boo."

That did it. His idiotic attempt to scare me succeeded. Completely startled, I woke up. A ghost with a sense of humor. Just my luck.

My infernal Casio read 5:45AM. I'd never be able to get back to sleep no matter how hard I tried. All I could do to pass the time and bury all this junk in the back of my mind was to read. So I did. That day was very productive for me. The evening promised to be great because it was my weekly TV and dinner night at my daughter's apartment. She records the shows we both love, and I enjoy playing with her two adorable cats.

The rest of the evening was a blur. Then I went to sleep and woke up back in the sun room, back in the tobacco scented chair, back looking at an embarrassed Lyle. He knew what his little stunt had accomplished and that I was not at all amused. He also knew from reading my mind, let alone my attitude, that I felt like this was an utter crock of shit. But I'd learn differently. In time, a short time, I'd be converted.

"Very sorry," uttered Lyle. "Won't happen again. I just couldn't help myself."

"At least you're a ghost with a sense of humor," I said. Maybe I should call you Casper, 'the friendly ghost.'

"By your very limited definition, I guess I am a ghost. But I never wear a white sheet and never do any haunting. Actually, we 'ghosts' never haunt anything, not on purpose, that is."

For a moment, Lyle seemed lost in thought. I, of course, was completely lost. But ready to listen to more.

Casper continued, "Let's go back to 1944. I had gone through basic training here in the states, then specific invasion training in England. For a boy who had never really gone anywhere in his life, this was all so exciting. After some delays and lots of anticipation, the day finally came — June 6. It was time for me to conquer the world, kick some kraut ass, and find out if everything I had heard about those French girls was true."

Lyle twisted uneasily on the couch, placed his hand on his chest, and nearly whispered, "As guys were being blown to bits in the surf, some of them close friends, I reached the shoreline and suddenly felt like someone had punched me in the chest. No pain. Just a punch. I went a few more feet when my legs stopped working. What a strange feeling. I fell forward, right on top of a severed leg. Then it was all over. I was dead, shot through the heart by some evil kraut, probably hiding in a bunker. What happened next is going to sound like an obnoxious cliché, but I saw an intensely bright light, saw some of my most cherished moments in life flash by, and saw my long gone grandfather holding my hand."

Jesus, I thought, how am I supposed to respond to this?

Still rubbing his chest, Lyle continued, "That's when I began to slowly learn, myself, what I'm attempting to teach you. It would be easier if you were dead."

'Dead?'

Did Lyle say 'Dead?'

I didn't like the sound of that. Not one fucking bit. I knew I was safely sleeping in my bed, but the whole thought of what he said really bothered me.

"Didn't mean to frighten you," he assured me, as he began to giggle. "I know how all this must sound to you, but bear with me. And never forget, if you reach a point where your bullshit meter has had enough, I'll wake you, and you'll never see me again. At least not in this life."

"Are you kidding me?" I asked. "My bullshit meter short circuited quite a while ago. On top of that, I think it was shot to pieces by the same kraut who nailed you. So continue; this is just as good as watching CSI."

"Glad I'm entertaining you," he said. "Now I'll get to the stuff that's really unbelievable."

"You know what I wish?" I asked.

"Of course I do," answered Mr. Dead. "I know everything in your head — everything since a month or so before you were born. I've seen, felt, heard, tasted, and smelled everything in your life. I even know millions of things you experienced that you never even knew you experienced. But I'll get to all that later."

"Nice short answer to my question," I said. Then, all of a sudden, my question was answered. Not in words, but in action.

I wanted to smoke my pipe, and there it was, right in my hand. But it wasn't just any pipe, it was a very special one my mother gave me that had belonged to my grandfather. The pipe was filled with my favorite tobacco, and, believe it or not, was lit."

Lyle looked at me with pride in his eyes.

"See," he chirped. "If you're going to smoke a pipe in your grandfather's chair, you gotta smoke the right one."

He saw that I was at a complete loss for words. Smoking that beautiful pipe seemed so God damn real to me that I nearly choked. Luckily, I didn't wake up.

"By now that shouldn't surprise you," he said.

"Tell me you're kidding me," I answered, a puff of thick, bluish smoke curling over my lips.

"It's simply one of those thought things. You know, like covering up those stupid looking black underpants of yours with a uniform. You've certainly got the hang of it."

"Guess so," I answered. "But . . ."

"But what?" he interrupted. "Absolutely anything you've experienced in life can be materialized by thought. Even if it's something you've never directly experienced, your consciousness can produce a construct."

"You lost me on that one," I said, accidently blowing a cloud of smoke in his face.

He waved it away then blew a cloud into my face. Sure enough, he was smoking a Camel, and I hadn't seen him think it.

"I'll give you an example, although we're really getting off the subject. I haven't even begun to scratch the surface," he said.

"Heard yuh," I said. "Just show me a thought construct of something I've never experienced, and then we can get right back to ghosts, death, bright lights, and all that fun stuff you want to talk about."

"Ok, I've got an idea that's going to turn your head inside out," said Lyle, with a big, shit eating grin. "You'll never forget this."

'Oh fuck,' I said to myself. 'What have I asked for?'

"I want you to think hard about a sexy woman you'd like to meet. She can be anyone: a model, actress . . . anyone. This will work best if it's someone you've seen lots of pictures of in magazines or movies, preferably movies," he said, with an even wider shit eating grin.

"Thinking hard," I said, while closing my eyes and applying full concentration.

When I opened them, I nearly fell of my chair, and probably came damn close to waking up again.

What I saw was too good to be true. Just too unbelievable. Sitting on the couch, right next to Lyle, was none other than Angelina Jolie.

My God, did she look real.

And gorgeous.

And she was smiling. At me.

"I'm dumbstruck," I said to Lyle, watching Angelina run her hand through her hair. "How is this possible? Is she some kind of a hologram?"

"John," he said, chuckling, "She's real . . . so to speak. She's a three dimensional, perfectly articulated, solid construct from a combination of your consciousness and the collective consciousness that pervades every part of the universe. She's a true quantum being, not too much unlike you and me."

"Oh well, thanks Lyle, you just cleared everything up for me. Now what the fuck did you just say?"

Angelina calmly sat there during the conversation, seeming to enjoy every moment of it. She even shook her head in affirmation of the gibberish Lyle was spewing.

"Let me try this again," he said.

"She's as real as those jeans and sweatshirt you thought on. You knew how they looked, how they felt and accepted them as real. It's all in your head. Just think about it: You've seen Angelina in movies, photos and TV commercials. You've heard her speak. You know exactly what the female form is like. Your consciousness cluster puts it all together for you, and voila: Angelina."

AAHHHHHHHHHHCHEW. Angelina sneezed.

"Gesundheit." I said.

"God bless you, dear," sighed Lyle.

"It's all the smoke in here," she purred. "You two morons are polluting the air."

Angelina plucked the Camel from Lyle's lips and stamped it out in the ashtray.

"That was physical action," I gasped. "Does that mean we can interact with her?"

"Haven't you heard anything I've said?" he asked.

Angelina nodded in agreement.

"She's real. Every incredible inch of her." he continued.

As he said that, Angelina stuck her tongue out at me, pulled back her arm, and punched me in the shoulder. It felt real. It hurt. I imagined waking up with a black & blue mark.

After what seemed like an eternity, she was the first to speak.

"John?" she asked, "Could you please think up the heat in here? I'm, uh, freezing my ass off." So I complied. Immediately.

"Lyle," I inquired, "Can you do this sort of stuff every day?"

"Can. And do." he said with obvious pride.

Then I joked, "If that's so, I'm gonna slit my wrists."

Staring intently at me Lyle yelled, "Don't ever say that. I mean it. That's not a joke. It's the worst thing you could do, short of killing someone else. Coming to this dimension is a privilege earned by living as full a life as you can and gaining as many memories as possible."

"Ok, ok. Gotcha. Just kidding. Sorry." I said with as much sincerity as possible, given the whole ridiculous situation.

Jesus Christ, I thought. I'm in a dream. In the house where I grew up. Smoking my grandfather's pipe. Talking to a fucking ghost. Looking at some fucking android version of Angelina Jolie. And I said something wrong? This is priceless.

All of a sudden. My right arm began to feel numb, and I couldn't move it. When I mentioned it to Lyle, he said, "You're waking up; probably see you tomorrow."

The next thing I knew, I was back in my bed, only to discover that the position I was in had put my arm to sleep. Shit. I hate it when that happens. So I used my good arm to throw the numb one off the side of my bed so the blood and feeling, would rush back. While lying there, all I could think about was the whole Angelina experience. But, then again, it's just a dream. I kept trying to reassure myself.

Chapter 5
Proof. Well, Almost

The next day was a disaster for me. I got nothing accomplished and began to fear that this new dream world of mine could be very harmful. 'This is not healthy,' I repeatedly told myself. But it *was* fascinating, thought provoking and just too much fun.

I was getting bored telling myself that this was all some insane, yet spectacular, dream. I should just enjoy it while it lasted; a quirky thing like this would vanish all too soon. Probably. But what if it didn't? What if I kept on meeting Lyle? What if he kept on telling me he was going to explain everything, but continued putting it off like he had been doing all along? I wanted an answer, even though the thought of that, in itself, was fucking utterly ridiculous.

Proof. That's what I needed. Proof that I was experiencing more than a dream. Proof that Lyle wasn't some version of myself. Proof that he was a ghost. Proof that there was some alternate dimension that was permitting this. But, obviously, how could any of this be proved? Any proof would be a product of my own imagination. How could it be anything else? This was all happening in my bed, in my head, in my sleep.

And back to thinking about Angelina. Dream or no dream, she seemed just too real. Of course, Iwo Jima, the B-17 and my old home were very real, as well. But she was human and had her own personality. I couldn't wait to get to sleep that night. So I hit the sack earlier than usual, skipped my reading, and breezed into a meditation. The next thing I expected to see was Lyle's wise-ass expression, through a thick haze of cigarette smoke.

All I saw was my ceiling when I opened what I hoped were my dream eyes. My nefarious Casio read 7:10AM, roughly five minutes before ringing. I had slept the whole night without dreaming. Shit. Could I have dreamt and forgotten about it, I feared? No way, I assured myself. Could these amazing dreams be over with? The realization of that distinct possibility made me feel terrible.

Fast forward several hours: Had a late dinner and decided to watch a movie in bed on my laptop. So I popped in a DVD, "The Ninth Gate," with Johnny Depp, Frank Langella and Emmanuelle Seifert. By the end of the movie, I was good and ready to catch some zzzzzzs. Off went the light, and I meditated to sleep.

When I opened my dream eyes, I was, believe it or not, happy to see Lyle. I had made it back. For the first time since I had met him, Lyle actually went to shake my hand. He had a solid grip. A ghost with a solid grip?

"Welcome back. Or should I say 'welcome home?'" he asked. "Missed you yesterday. You weren't in a deep enough sleep to pull it off. Meditation won't help if you're not in the proper sleep cycle."

I decided to get right to the point, "Lyle, I've been doing some thinking."

"I know," he responded. "And you're right, you need some proof — as I promised. And please don't think of my mind reading as an invasion of privacy. It's the way of the world: mine, that is."

"Nothing should surprise me any more," I said with resignation.

Before continuing, Lyle fished in his pocket for a butt. Lit it with a thought, and looked back at me.

Then he actually had a productive thought. "This whole area we're in is just too filled with your memories. It's interfering. We've got to change our location. Now let's think of some place to go so I can explain how this proof is going to work." He began to pace the floor. "Got an Idea." Lyle looked like he had just reinvented the wheel. "I thought of a place where you used to be very comfortable, and the memory trace won't be overwhelming. The views are spectacular and the old lodge serves hot apple cider with a natural cinnamon stick. It's ambrosial."

"As far as I can recall, there's only one place that fits that description," I gushed with excitement. "It's gotta be Mount Lemmon."

"Yup," he said, taking a big drag on his Camel. "The perfect place to bat the breeze."

"Can we go right now? I haven't been back since my days at The University of Arizona."

"Of course," he answered. "Why don't you just think us there."

I closed my eyes, brought back all my memories of the place, and, kerplunk, we were sitting right in front of the fireplace. On an old wooden table beside us were two steaming mugs of that infamous hot cider. And from the window, the view was precisely as I remembered: huge, gnarly evergreens, twisted by snow, wind and time, and a bright blue Arizona sky, providing an azure cast over the Santa Catalina mountain range. Wow. It was impossible to imagine that this whole place and surrounding area had been burned to the ground a few years ago. I remembered how forlorn I felt when I read about it.

Mt. Lemmon, which proudly stands 9,000 feet above sea level a short 25 miles North of Tucson, was one of my favorite destinations for numerous reasons. With a temperate climate, it provided a very welcome refuge from Tucson's oppressive desert heat; The beauty of the entire area was startling; It was a great location for studying and doing papers; the drive up and down, through twisty mountain roads, allowed me to fully exploit the capabilities of my British sports car, a Triumph TR-4A.

It was a small, two-seater, with large blue racing stripes over its pearl white body. With the top down, and its engine emitting a throaty scream, I'd blast around precarious turns and corners the whole thrilling way up — only to be repeated on my way down. Getting back to reality (reality?), Lyle and I both took a few sips of cider, he lit up yet another Camel. For a few long moments, nothing was said. Then it began.

"Proof." I asserted.

"Proof." He agreed.

Taking a long, pensive puff, he began, "Been doing a lot of thinking about this. I had to arrive at an idea that would provide at least a little tangible evidence. The problem is, it all has to be accomplished in your head, while you're fast asleep. Even if I did something like reunite you with your grandparents, you could claim it's all in your imagination and subconscious mind. So . . . I discussed the matter with some of my, uh, colleagues here."

"More ghosts, huh?" I quipped.

"Promise me something: for now, no more wiseass remarks and no more jokes. I'm trying to make some sense out of all this for you. Comprendo?" Lyle seemed agitated.

"When you're right, you're right," I said, savoring my cider.

"The only way for this to be done is for me to come into your world with you and have you experience something that's not in your subconscious mind — something you couldn't even create in your subconscious mind. Here's how it's going to work. I want you to pick a spot in Manhattan that you know well, but haven't visited in a while."

It didn't take me long to nail that one. I used to live up on 82nd street and East End Avenue, and know the area, every inch of it, like the back of my hand. But I hadn't been there in nearly a year.

"That'll do just fine," said Lyle, slyly reading my mind.

"I can't wait to hear what we're going to do. And how you're going to pull off whatever it is," I said.

"Tomorrow night, we're . . ."

"Tomorrow night?" I interrupted. "What's wrong with right now?"

"For this to work, it has to be done directly after you meditate. You need a full charge, so to speak. What we're going to do can be a little rough on you, and there's a good chance it might wake you up."

"Explain," I asserted, raising my eyebrows and shaking my head.

"Although time is an illusion, but a necessary one, you're going to step back into your real time, while remaining in dream time. The two times are incompatible. A world you're used to . . ."

"What the fuck?" I interrupted.

"I told you this stuff isn't easy. Since I haven't really explained anything yet, be prepared to be confused. You'll learn all about the time differential later."

"Why is everything 'later?' I asked.

"I've never educated, or should I say 'enlightened,' a real live person before. So cut me some slack. Just go with it." He said.

Once again, I promised myself to be calm and patient. I had nothing to lose. At this point, I had little confidence that there was going to be any proof I would believe. How could there possibly be proof, I thought.

Regaining his composure, my spectral friend continued: "You know what real time is; it's what you experience all day long. But it shifts gears when you come here. A couple of hours in dream time can equal a couple of seconds in your real time. Dreams fly by in a fraction of time, usually creating distortion. When you're with me, your consciousness is both condensed and heightened — way more than in a normal dream, as you now know through experience."

"How do you know all this?" I asked, realizing immediately that it was a dumb question.

"This is my world. Not yours. Everything's different here, and everyone learns the ropes when they, uh, get here. I know the basics and maybe a little bit more because I have a passing interest in science. Listening to real scientists, however, even confuses the shit out of me. 'Just learn the new rules and know how to apply them.' That's what every one says and does here."

"I promised to keep on track with you, but you just said something that prompts a question," I asserted.

"That's ok," he said, with cider dribbling on his shirt.

"You mentioned the word 'rules.' I was wondering how you could be permitted to educate me about your world, exposing me to many of the hidden wonders. Don't you have 'rules' that prevent you from doing this?"

"Rules?" he laughed. "There are no rules here. There are no cops. No judges. No practicing lawyers, thank God, and no jails. I'm not exposing you to anything that millions of people don't already believe. People have always believed in an afterlife and always will. It's one of the fundamental concepts in all mass religions that give people hope and security."

"I know, I know," I answered. "That's a no-brainer. But . . . you are personally giving me this education, well before I pay you a, uh, permanent visit. This is drastically different from common belief."

"No problem with what I'm doing," he assured me. "Since the beginning of recorded history, many people have claimed to have had similar experiences. You've no doubt heard of out-of-body experiences, near death experiences, channeling, clairvoyants . . ."

"Of course I've heard of that crap," I interrupted. "It's all bullshit. Mumbo-jumbo. Idiots sitting around Ouija boards or attending séances. They're the same types of fools who see ghosts, fairies, leprechauns, UFOs, Big Foot, the Loch Ness Monster, Jesus' image on a piece of toast, and, and, and I could just keep on going."

"For the most part, you're absolutely right," he agreed. "At least ninety nine percent of all those claims and experiences are pure bullshit. People are born liars, publicity seekers, attention junkies, the victims of brain washing, alcoholics, delusional lunatics . . . and the list goes on and on."

"Seriously," he added with authority, "A tiny fraction of one percent of that 'mumbo-jumbo' is entirely authentic. It's purely natural for some people to slip back and forth between both worlds."

I found that impossible to argue about. I mean, the whole thing was impossible to begin with. But what the fuck; Lyle had my attention.

"Once you understand how all this works, you'll clearly see what I mean," claimed Lyle. "But, like I've been telling you, it's not going to be all fun and games."

"Whatever," I said.

Lyle blew a smoke ring, and then blew another right through the middle of it.

"Now that's what I call a miracle." I said.

I got the feeling that there was one more thing he wanted to add to the conversation. Lyle's body language gave his intent away.

"Since you asked about 'rules,' I want to finish the topic." Lyle was fishing for words. "As I mentioned, there are no rules and no punishment here."

"You made that very clear," I said.

"But," he continued, "I wasn't completely clear about that."

"Aha," I exclaimed.

"There has always been an agreement, not a rule, that we'd never reveal anything that could in any way alter the future of discoveries and resulting memories. The human experience is just too valuable to everyone — on both sides."

"Please explain," I responded.

"I could tell you where trillions of dollars worth of buried treasures are hidden all over the world. I could reveal the location of Jimmy Hoffa's remains. I could direct you to a complete and incredibly well preserved Tyrannosaurus Rex fossil. And so much more."

"Now you're torturing me," I said.

"My spectral lips are sealed," he said, grinning. "That and so much more is for humanity to discover. Those experiences will be incredible and richly memory laden."

"You mean nothing has ever been revealed? No slips of the lips?" I asked.

"This nature of information has been revealed many times. There's no way to successfully prevent it," he declared. "But I, for one, would never reveal anything. So don't get any funny ideas."

"Show me where I can dig up a few thousand pounds of gold, and that will suffice as all the proof I need," I said, drooling.

"No way, Jose," was the response I expected from Mr. Goody Two Shoes.

"Ok, fair enough," I dejectedly responded. "But it wouldn't screw up the fate of humanity if you told me where I could find one lousy stinkin' diamond. Just a little one: maybe four carats? Or even two carats?"

Lyle blew a smoke ring in my face.

"End of subject," he laughed.

"You haven't heard the end of this from me," I assured him.

"End of subject," he repeated.

"For now," I uttered reluctantly.

"On the subject of 'now,'" he said, "Let's finally get back to the proof I've been trying to tell you about. You have to be prepared."

Oh shit. I had a bad feeling that I was going to wake up soon. I had to hold off until I knew what all this 'proof' baloney was about.

Lyle was about to think himself another mug of cider, when it was pretty apparent that he had a change of heart. An ice-cold bottle of Rolling Rock appeared in his hand. At that moment, a steaming hot café con leche appeared in mine.

Lyle raised his bottle to me and said, "Salute."

I returned the gesture and said, "Proof."

One big sip and he began: "Let's backtrack to your old stomping grounds over on East End Avenue. Tomorrow night, if you get here, you'll land on the corner of 82nd street. I will have already thought us there. What we'll do is look for a couple of things that are not in your memory: A broken window, some new graffiti, anything that stands out. The following morning, you'll go up there as soon as possible, and see if you recognize the things we picked out. Obviously, whatever we choose will be very recognizable. If, for some inconceivable reason, it doesn't work, we'll try it again."

"I've got a smarter idea," I declared. "If it doesn't work, just point me in the direction of some buried treasure. Then I'll be a huge believer. Your noble deed will create a whole new religion for me."

"Nice try, asshole," he said, slurping some beer.

Lyle's lecture continued: "This will work. The only obstacle we'll face is a time conundrum. You're going to find the time differential very disorienting. I was told that it could make you nauseous, and, at the worst, cause you to puke."

"Would it be a dream puke, or would I blow chunks in my bed, for real?" I asked with concern.

"In your bed. For real." He answered.

"Are you fucking with my head, Lyle?"

"Look, it probably won't happen. But be prepared. Before you meditate yourself to sleep, put a plastic cover over your bed and a large bowl on the floor nearby. You'll be fine. Trust me." he said with a wink.

As I wondered about that I sensed something strange.

"You're waking up now. See you tomorrow night, and try to . . ." Lyle said, fading out, as the whole place disappeared.

In two seconds, Mount Lemmon was just a memory. Again.

Chapter 6
My God, Proof

Well, that was certainly a lot to digest. Getting through the next day seemed to take forever. Towards the end of the afternoon, I went to my local Home Depot to buy a plastic painter's drop cloth to put on my bed, as per Lyle's suggestion. Lyle's suggestion? What? Was I taking this crap seriously? Although this was light years beyond my belief system, I knew I couldn't fight it.

Even if everything was a crock of shit and I was just experiencing some perplexing, let alone astonishing, dreams, I honestly didn't want them to end. And I knew that once I had some closure about this 'proof' thing, I'd be able to have my remarkable dreams at night, and get on with my life during the day. What if I got my proof? What if Lyle wasn't a figment of my imagination, but an honest-to-goodness spook? What if this dimension of the dearly departed really did exist and I was being given a sneak peek? First of all, why me? Second of all, could I handle it?

That evening, I opted for a very bland dinner. After all, if there was even the slightest chance that this quantum-conundrum-time-differential thing Lyle was warning me about could upset my stomach, I didn't want to tempt fate. Maybe I could think a few Rolaids into my mouth tonight on East End Avenue.

That night, I leafed through a few bland mail order catalogs. Nothing in any of them that could pollute my mind. Then I turned off the light, turned on my meditation and, the next thing I knew, I was on East End Avenue, with Lyle insisting that I keep my eyes shut tight for a moment.

While I was waiting for his words of wisdom, I noticed that there were unearthly sounds assaulting my ears. Never heard anything like that before on East End.

Lyle commenced. "Before you open your eyes, remember that you've entered real time in dream time. That means that everything, including sound, will be in slow motion. Ridiculously slow motion. This is what's so damn disorienting and can get you nauseous. You're going to see people, dogs, cars, bikes, and even some snow in an almost mystical way. When you open your eyes, reality will be in the toilet. Now open them, staring first at the ground, then slowly raise your head. Once you get used to the time distorted views, we'll start looking for something for you to commit to memory. In case you're wondering, it's about one in the morning, but there are plenty of people out and about."

Before I looked at anything other than my shoes, I asked Lyle a single question.

"If this is such a problem, why aren't we here in real time? It would be so much easier."

"Yes and no," was his answer. Then he explained. "It's easy to travel around in real time, but I didn't want you to wake up during the time it could take to thoroughly look around. As I told you, dreams usually last a very short time, although you feel as though the clock is ticking by normally. Your first Iwo Jima dream was just about two seconds."

As he spoke, I slowly raised my head, and viewed a scene I'll never forget as long as I live.

"Holy shit," I screamed.

"Warned yuh," he laughed, steadying me with his arm.

What I saw was beyond comprehension.

Fascinating? Yes.

Scary? Not at all.

Nauseating? Not yet.

It was impossible to take it all in at once, so I had to concentrate on individual elements. I was definitely on 82nd Street and East End Avenue. That was for certain. All the solid things were perfectly normal. But everything else? WOW. It was the ultimate definition of slow motion.

The snow caught my attention first. There were large flakes suspended in the air, almost frozen in time. Just big white puffs as far as I could see. It was gorgeous. Mesmerizing. I waved my hand through a few of the flakes, and they appeared to pass clear through. I was there. And I wasn't there.

The next thing that riveted my concentration was a woman walking a small dog. She was frozen in a pronounced mid step, just coming off the curb: one foot on the ground, the other hanging in the air. Her arm was suspended at an unnatural angle as she held tight to the leash. The puppy had just jumped up, its head, legs, and tail all splayed out comically, as the puppy hung in the air. Her right arm was lifted high, hand wide opened as though she were waving at someone across the street. The wind, which I had no sensation of, was blowing her long blond hair and green scarf over her shoulder, both frozen at parallel angles.

"How are you feeling?" he asked.

"Fine," I said, as I studied the woman's face.

It was grotesque. Most of her features were horribly distorted. It looked like one of those terribly embarrassing candid photos that you tear to shreds the instant you see it. Her mouth was wide open, and her lips were perversely warped back over fully exposed teeth. One eye was wide open, the other half shut. And her nose was crinkled up. Phew. Not what I'd call a 'Kodak Moment.'

"We've got to start looking for something that you'll recognize tomorrow morning," said Lyle with a note of intensity.

"In a second," I answered, understanding his concern.

My gaze had fallen next on a man caught mid stride, crossing the street. One leg up, one down. He was smoking a large cigar and had blown a billowing cloud of smoke through the side of his mouth. It hung nearly motionless in the air, blocking most of his face.

"Ok, I've seen enough," I said to Lyle. "Now let's see what we can find."

There was nothing out of the ordinary from our point of view, so we walked North to 83rd street. Nothing out of the ordinary there either. So it was on to 84th street, where Lyle said "Finally."

"What do you see?" I eagerly asked.

He pointed to a lamppost with a paper sign taped to it. The sign, which measured about 7 x 10 inches, displayed a cliché photo of a Pug wearing a Santa hat. The caption read 'Dog Walker,' and at the poster's bottom were tear off tabs with a name and phone number. Across the photo, in large, red letters, someone had scrawled 'Dog Shit Suks!' with a broad-nib magic marker. Yup, the moron had spelled it 'suks.'

It was very common to see dog walker advertising in this neighborhood. After all, we were right at the entrance to Carl Schurz Park, an absolutely gorgeous area that ran adjacent to the promenade overlooking the east river. This park was the dog capital of the upper East Side.

"Great find," I said to eagle eye Lyle.

"We need something in addition to this," he said. "And here it is."

Lyle was pointing at a generous amount of smashed up red glass strewn for roughly six feet along the curb. Some poor slob is now missing a rather large tail light, I thought to myself.

"Even if one of those street sweeping trucks happens to come by later this evening, they'll never get all this glass. You'll find some in the morning," Lyle assured me.

"I wish there were something more concrete than what you've identified, but I guess the combined glass and poster will do," I said, only partially convinced.

"I'd like to give this a try," he urged. "But if none of these things are here in the morning, promise me you'll give it another try."

"It's no secret that I continue to believe that this is all bullshit, just a figment of my imagination. But, yeah, if nothing's there in the morning, I'll give it another try."

"We're done tonight," he uttered. "But before you wink out on me, I have a few more things to say. First of all, when you get your proof tomorrow morning, I'll know it. Then we're not going to meet again for a week because you've got something important to do before we take the next step. I want you to get your hands on a couple introductory books to quantum mechanics, and, if you can bear the thought, a book on metaphysical studies."

I winced.

"You don't have to read any of the books from cover to cover. Just familiarize yourself with the basics. That's all I ask. Believe me, it'll help you swallow some of things I'm going to reveal to you."

I didn't like the idea of taking a week off, but I saw Lyle's point and understood his concern. I was just about ready to ask him if I really *had* to read about metaphysical crap when I found myself lying on my side, staring at my repugnant Casio. It was still relatively early, so I was able to fall back to sleep. When the alarm went off at 7:30AM, the moment of truth had arrived: the morning I had been waiting for. The morning that changed my life forever.

The big question was this: Should I have breakfast first? Or proceed directly to East End Avenue? East End first was my decision. As I walked to the bus stop, I noticed that there was a layer of frost on the ground; to my delight, last night's snow hadn't stuck. Or maybe that snow was only in my dream. There was a fucking shit storm raging in my head.

On one hand, I didn't want to find the broken glass and 'suk' sign. I hoped they wouldn't be there. That would have made everything so damn easy. I would have gotten all the proof I needed — proof that everything I'd been exposed to was, as I suspected, a complete figment of my imagination. Maybe I'd have a few more wonderful dreams. Then, one night, the dreams would vanish as quickly as they had come. I'd chalk it all up to one of life's little mysteries.

On the other hand, what if I found the things Lyle had pointed out? What if I found proof? Proof of what? An afterlife? That none of this was a dream? That Lyle really was a dead dude wasted by some Jerry on Omaha Beach? Was I ready to concede this? Would I become a believer? Was I prepared to have my mind completely blown?

Absolutely, no.

Absolutely, yes.

It would change my point of view about absolutely everything. And, Lord knows, I was in dire need of a new point of view. Even if it meant turning my whole belief system on its head and kicking out its teeth.

Enough thinking. The time had come. The moment of truth.

I was there.

And I had a perfectly clear view of the lamp post, but there was no sign to be seen. Holy, holy, holy shit. However, when I got real close, I saw that it had been torn down, but the tape remained, gripping a few shreds of paper. Then I saw the broken red glass exactly where it had been last night. Holy, holy, holy shit.

My mind and everything else was spinning. I was in a frenzy. One part of me sort of wanted to find the sign. Another part was frantic to find it. Another part was scared to find it. But persist I did.

It was nowhere to be found on the ground. Then it hit me. I had overlooked the most obvious place of all: the trash can right in front of my friggin' nose. Peering over the rim with considerable suspense and apprehension, I spied a few AA batteries, some empty water containers, two drained Snapple bottles, a crumpled up Coke can, and a suspicious looking, crumpled up piece of paper.

Then, with all the drama in the world, I retrieved it and slowly unrolled it.

Holy, holy, holy shit. The pug was just as cute as the night before.

Suddenly, I felt like I had to sit down. Right away, in fact. My legs felt like Silly Putty. This was no longer some stupid, funny joke. Lyle had shown me the proof he had promised. And in a way, it made sense. I couldn't have imagined any of this. None of it, at all. This was real.

Now what was I supposed to think? What was Lyle, really? A ghost? A spirit? A poltergeist? A wandering soul? A God? A guardian angel? He didn't have wings. Or a halo. He wasn't accompanied by trumpets or harp music. He didn't speak in a bold, booming voice, saying words like 'thee' and 'thou.' He didn't wear a beard and white robe. There was absolutely nothing heavenly about him. Lyle was just a ghost. That's all, just a ghost. Just a ghost? That was amazing enough. It was all beyond comprehension.

The rest of my day was a blur. Lost in thought, I accomplished nothing. My mind was racing, and I knew I couldn't make it stop, let alone slow down. What made it all even worse was the fact that I couldn't see Lyle again for a week. There was his assignment to contend with. I couldn't just blow it off. Had to spend some quality time at Borders, reading about quantum mechanics and metaphysical something or other. Instead of, God forbid, buying the books, I'd peruse them right in the store. 'Tomorrow,' I said to myself.

Tomorrow arrived faster than I expected. Science was one of my favorite subjects in high school and college, so I assumed this shouldn't be too much to take.

Metaphysics was a different story. That topic worried me. Having not so much as a shred of respect, let alone interest, in this horse manure, I pictured myself falling fast asleep in the store. As far as I was concerned, metaphysics was the domain of weirdoes: people who had a profound interest in bending spoons with their mind,

ESP, levitating stuff, healing people with the wave of a hand, palm and crystal ball reading, time traveling, talking to dead relatives and other disembodied spirits, and a myriad of other shadowy, highly questionable endeavors.

To exacerbate my feelings, the people browsing this book section at Borders looked like they were from a necrophiliac's wet dream. In fact, two painfully skinny women — both attired in all black and accessorized with thick necklaces that clanked like cow bells — were seriously discussing the coloration of auras. They looked at me and moved away, apparently having read my mind. The term, 'para abnormal' seemed to fit the occasion.

Oh well, getting back to reality, if that applied any more, I made the wise decision to begin my assignment with quantum mechanics. A few of the titles struck me as introductory, so I whisked them off the shelves.

Immediately, the subject fascinated me. I knew why Lyle wanted me to familiarize myself with this incredible field. The mind blowing concepts fly in the face of nearly everything common science, and common sense, have led us to believe. And unlike the confounding, hazy world of pure theoretical physics, the discoveries made by quantum scientists have been proved through experimentation, observation, and utilization.

The unbelievable quantum world is real.

In the immortal words of Niels Bohr, one of the most preeminent physicists of the 20th century and the founding father of the subject, "Those who are not shocked when they first come across quantum theory cannot possibly have understood it."

Score one for the Neilsmeister.

To put it simply, although simply does not apply . . .

Quantum science deals with the smallest of the small, the elementary particles that rule in the micro world. Everything in the known universe is composed of these particles: you, me, your car, the sun, almond croissants, acorns, cowboy boots, and even politicians.

They are nature's basic building blocks, presumably created at the instant of the big bang.

Einstein, the E=MC2 guy, also provided a foundation for quantum theory without intending to do so. It sort of oozed out of his theories. Like Newton before him, Al was a classical physicist who devoutly believed that order and rationality were nature's bedrocks, no matter how strange things got. But quantum proved him to be wrong.

Chaos ruled.

So did unpredictability and irrationality.

Einstein was pissed.

He hated the idea that, in the dastardly quantum world, particles could pop in and out of existence, seemingly at their own will. They could occupy two separate positions at the same time. Some could even travel back in time. And get this, photons, the particles that compose light, travel as a wave and collapse into a particle when a person observes them. You heard it right: human awareness has a direct affect on teensy tiny particles.

These revelations inspired one of Einstein's most famous quotes: "God does not play dice with the universe." Well, it seems God also plays poker and the horses. Einstein's theories insisted that nothing could travel faster than the speed of light. Nothing.

Once again, Quantum theory gave him a painful kick in the family jewels. The culprit is called quantum entanglement. He called it "Spooky action at a distance." Simply stated, once two particles have been in a system relationship with each other, even a platonic one, they will instantly act in accordance with each other, no matter how far they've been separated, whether they're ten feet or one hundred billion light years apart. They always know what each other is doing. So, how can information travel that fast?

No one has a fucking clue.

But they've got proof that's too confounding to explain. Scientists have observed entanglement with highly sensitive equipment.

So... Lyle, that sly bastard, knew that I would now be more open to hearing about the seemingly impossible. That my own fortress of disbelief would have some major cracks in it.

He was right.

And that was even before I tackled a few of the metaphysical books.

The next day arrived with little fanfare. I wished my Casio were a quantum particle so I could collapse it with observation. No such luck.

Then I was back at Borders, in the metaphysical section, hoping no one would recognize me.

For this occasion, I wore all black. 'When in Rome...,' I figured.

Since there were literally thousands of books in there, with some of the most obnoxiously stupid titles I've ever seen, I had some trouble making a selection. I was hoping to find *Metaphysics for Dummies*, but it didn't appear to exist. Or something called *Metaphysics 101*. Didn't exist either.

Fortunately, I found a few titles that didn't sound like they'd bring back my breakfast. So, with a pack of Rolaids and Tums close at hand, I began reading. After grimacing through a few chapters, I reluctantly came to a conclusion. Lyle was right again. The stuff I was reading was fascinating. Impossible to believe, but, none-the-less, fascinating. Luckily, it was very basic metaphysics and paranormal lite, not hard-core shit about auras, dowsing, telekinesis, time travel... etc.

I learned that human beings, all human beings, possess extraordinary capabilities that very few of us know about, and far fewer can access. We are truly unique creatures with minds that can achieve everything from the most minor to the most spectacular miracles.

You really have to read this crap with an open mind. Whether you believe it or not (usually not), our consciousness is purportedly connected to a universal field of knowledge that empowers us in really astonishing ways.

My belief system was stretched beyond its limits, but . . .

They don't just feed you all this malarkey and expect you to take their word for it. The books are filled with real life justifications and common situations that make perfect sense.

Serious, seemingly competent researchers at seemingly respectable institutions have been conducting sophisticated testing for many, many years. And test subjects come from all walks of life. Even if their findings are 99% crapola, that remaining 1% is enough to knock your argyles off.

Now, let's see if you can guess what field of science was included in practically all the metaphysical books I perused? You don't need to read my mind to guess this one.

Quantum theory.

Quantum theory helps metaphysicians (doctors of the absurd), explain their own strange world of science. It appears that quantum mechanics is the foundation for everything.

Once again, I hated to admit it, but Lyle had softened me up. After all I had learned, nothing he could say would throw me for a loop.

Well, almost nothing.

Chapter 7
To Hell with Heaven and Vice Versa

Boy, what a week that was.

Tons of things on my over-burdened mind.

I had gotten my proof . . . if I wanted to believe it.

My arguments and negativity had been defused.

Many of the doubts that had been plaguing me had been thoroughly trounced by my formal introduction to quantum mechanics and metaphysics. I was, by no means, an expert in either of these fields, but I had learned enough to be receptive to nearly anything Lyle was going to tell me.

He knew what he was doing. And his idea to take a week's reprise from dreamville made perfect sense. To jump right back either before or directly after my 'education,' would have been counter-productive. A few days of thought, consideration, and acceptance got me good and ready for what was shortly going to split my head wide open.

It still occurred to me that someone could be spiking my café con leches with some mushroom-derived potion. Or my insulin could have been hallucinogenic. Or it could have been a delayed reaction to all the chemo that polluted my brain. Nothing more than that.

NO. It was something more than that.

I was eventually able to put all this shit on my mind's back burner, but as the days, hours and minutes ticked by, and the week drew to an end, the suspense was murdering me. On my final day, I got myself good and tired, did a nosedive into bed, and meditated myself to sleep.

And . . . I was back.

Where in the fuck am I now, I thought to myself. There was crashing surf, a less than gentle sea breeze, and a breathtaking, panoramic view of a gorgeous beach. From a porch, where I sat in a large, overstuffed chair, I watched two little kids doing handstands on the sand, then I did a 180 degree sweep with my eyes.

Everything I saw said 'exotic' resort in some very exotic part of the world. And there he was, sitting adjacent to me, studying my every reaction — Mr. Exotic himself, sipping some intense green drink, with a tiny umbrella stuck in a piece of fruit.

He broke the silence. "Miss me?"

"Honestly," I said, I've been looking forwa . . ."

"I know. I know," he interrupted. "I was firmly in your head when you found the proof, firmly there when you consumed the quantum info, and holding on for dear life when you dipped into your favorite, the metaphysics. I'm also very glad that you're ready to take the next step."

"You've got to make me a promise, Lyle: stop reading my mind. It's unfair and really freaks me out."

"I didn't think it bothered you so much. It really cuts through lots of extraneous shit," he explained.

"If that's what you thought, then you're not so good at it."

"Ok, ok," he said. "I'll do my best to avoid your thoughts. I do it without thinking."

"Needless to say, you already know that I have millions of questions to ask you."

Lyle blew a smoke ring and said, "Yup. And you're ready to take the quantum leap."

"Sounds like something I'd say."

Lyle laughed, "I've been wanting to tell you that I enjoy your humor. It makes things very natural and easy. I also want to say how glad I am that you're not a God fearin' man. You're basically religionless, so you're going to have more of an open mind, and challenge me less."

"Jesus Christ, you're God damn right about that, Lyle."

"I don't want you to hit me with tons of questions that aren't in some logical order. So, let me explain things in an order that will make sense, and you'll slowly but surely learn what you need to know."

"What I 'need to know' first is where in the hell we are."

Lyle looked from left to right, broadly smiling. "I assume you've gathered that we're not on Mount Lemmon any more."

"That crossed my mind. The ocean was sort of a hint."

"Brace yourself," he said, "We're in Hawaii."

"Yeah," I intoned. "And I bet you've been here all week with either Angelina or some other incredible babe."

"Sorry to disappoint you, but the answer to that is a definite no," he exclaimed. "Honestly, I'm a one woman man. I've got a girl who I'm tight with. I certainly look at others, but . . . I never cheat on her. Never. Ever."

"So who's the lucky lady," I asked.

"She's my sweetheart. From Wisconsin. The beautiful gal I left when I went overseas to become a war hero. She's all I ever wanted and all I'll ever want."

"I'm a little hazy about all this, Lyle. Explain."

"We had promised each other that we'd get married as soon as I got back after the hostilities ended. We were just two kids, madly in love. Now she's here with me as a mind construct, just like Angelina, exactly as she looked on that fateful day when I kissed her goodbye. Actually, she's still alive by your definition, a cute little old lady whose health is fading. When I visit her in your dimension, she has no idea I'm there."

"How often do you visit her?"

Lyle continued, "John, I've visited her every day since the day I died."

"I hate when you say that."

Lyle continued again, "She's everything to me. We had planned our lives together. We knew what we wanted our house to look like; we even knew what we were going to name our kids. Then I got yanked out of the picture by some slimy kraut. And then she got dealt a bad hand with life. To say the least, her life has not been a bed of roses. Believe it or not, she has thought about me every single day. She always wishes we were together. Pretty soon her dream, no, both of our dreams, will come true."

I wasn't certain, but I could have sworn that Lyle wiped a tear from his eye. Suddenly, I began to see a whole new person in him. There was a lot more going on here than I had imagined, and the reality of it all was beginning to sink in.

"Let me get this straight," I said. "In your thought construct of her here . . ."

"Her name's Betty. Bet, for short," he interjected.

"As I was saying . . . in this dimension, Betty is exactly as you remember her. But eternally ageless. And the both of you can communicate and react to each other as though you're really together, all enabled by your deep memory of her. But the real Bet has aged normally, completely unaware that you spend lots of time thinking about her."

"Basically, that's it in a nutshell, John."

"What happens when she dies?" I asked with some trepidation.

"My thought construct of her might vanish, and the real Betty and I will resume our lives as we left off in June of 44."

Changing the subject, I asked,"What is this place?"

"We're in Waikiki on O'AHU island at the Halekulani Hotel."

"The . . . what? . . .hotel? Say it slowly," I requested.

"The H a l e k u l a n I," he said, pronouncing each syllable.

"Never heard of it."

"You also have no idea what the word, halekulani, means, do you?"

"No doubt I'm gonna find out right now," I said.

"In native Hawaiian it means 'house befitting heaven.' Bet would have loved that."

"I'll admit, we certainly are in heaven. Right?" I asked.

"Not exactly," answered a pensive Lyle. "Let me clear something up while we're on the topic. Heaven does not exist. Hell does not exist. Purgatory does not exist. Angels do not exist. Demons do not exist. Santa doesn't exist. The tooth fairy doesn't exist. All these myths and many more have been created by humanity."

"Something's bothering me." I declared. "Do you mean that everyone, no matter what they've done in their life, ends up in the same place?"

"Yup." He said, slurping a chunk of pineapple off a tiny plastic sword.

"What about a guy like Hitler? Or Jeffry Dahmer? Or Vlad the Impaler? Or Dick Nixon? Do you mean to tell me they end up in the same place with everyone else?"

"They do. They're just people being people, like you and me."

"Somehow, I find that entirely unacceptable. They don't have to pay for all the miserable shit they've done? All the suffering they've caused?"

"You've been brainwashed into thinking that they do, and you're not even religious. Scientifically, they're just people. That's all that matters."

"This is fucked up." I said with conviction. "There should be a hell."

"In a way, there is a hell," he said. "Your dimension, with all its inhumanities, certainly qualifies as one Hell of a place. In fact, the more you learn about my world, the more you'll think it really is heaven."

But I continued to wonder why their next life should be a good life.

Changing the subject again, I asked, "Lyle, something has been bothering me more than anything else."

"Something? Just something?" he asked, laughing.

"I mean, uh, what are you?"

"For starters, I'm not a 'what.'"

Lyle got himself very comfortable in his chair. He took another long, luxuriating sip from his mermaid shaped glass, and blew a cloud of smoke that was whipped away with the sea breeze.

"Everyone up here . . ." He began to say.

"Up here?" I interrupted. "I thought there was no 'up here'."

"There isn't. We never use that expression, but I must in order to avoid confusion. If I said 'here,' I'd mix up the dimensions. I'm right *here* on earth, as solidly as you are."

All of a sudden, Lyle's face began to change. What the fuck, I thought. What's happening now? His eyes were fading to numbers.

Numbers? Oh shit. It was happening.

I was waking up. What a merger: his face, my Casio. At least it wasn't blaring yet. Once again, I had beaten it to the punch.

My alarm clock from hell. Could I still say that: 'alarm clock from hell?' Yep, I assured myself. It was probably made in China by child slave labor. So it qualified.

With conviction, I jumped off my bed, jumped into the shower, and ran to Juan's. Couldn't wait to inhale a large latte, and devour a heavenly blueberry scone. I'll always refer to them as 'heavenly,' regardless. Once I was fully satiated, and had begun to daydream, it occurred to me that this might be the perfect time in my life to do something I had always thought about: write a book. And now, I had the perfect story to tell. I'd write about this, my evenings with Lyle in the land of the dead. I wouldn't have to invent anything. Just tell it like it is, I told myself.

Yeah, right. 'Tell it like it is.' The book would, no doubt, wind up in the metaphysical section, read by the same jerks who talk to their plants and practice aura sex. I made a mental note not to dismiss the idea entirely, though.

Hours and hours flew by, and that night, firmly in bed, I picked up a new book I had just begun. I found that I couldn't concentrate on it at all because my thoughts kept veering off to that heaven and hell conundrum. What if, somehow, the world were to have definitive proof that heaven and hell didn't exist? There would be sheer pandemonium. People from all walks of life would be grief stricken. With their belief systems completely shattered, they would probably not be able to cope with life.

One thing's for certain, the Church would be in ruins. And that's big business. Thousands of people would be out of jobs. Nuns would be giving lap dances in confession booths, and the whole Vatican could well become an enormous mall. People would, at least, remain religious shoppers.

There was one other thing bothering me. When Lyle mentioned all those things that didn't exist, he failed to include God and Jesus. I wondered why. 'I've got to remember to ask him about that,' I firmly told myself.

Finally, I had tired myself out. Completely. Meditating was a snap, because my mind went blank in a second.

I went from the warmth of my little heater to the warmth of the Hawaiian sun and a pacifying, salty breeze. Waking up while fast asleep never ceased to amaze me.

Lyle was sitting there, staring off into the distance.

"I don't want to be here any more," he sputtered.

I knew right away that something was rotten in Denmark. Lyle was not at all his usual self. Something was deeply troubling him. I was going to ask him if he had seen a ghost, but thought better of it. This was no time for humor.

"What's wrong?" was all I could think to ask.

"This place reminds me too much of Bet," he said.

"But I thought that was a good thing," I responded.

"It is, but not right now."

He continued, "My Betty, the one in your world, is very sick. While you were gone I spent the whole time with her in the hospital."

"I'm sorry to hear that."

"She's in pain, and there's nothing I can do for her. I tried kissing her forehead, holding her hand, giving her a hug, and telling her how much I love her. And for a single moment, as she let out a breath, I thought she felt my presence. I can't explain it, but I think she knew I was there."

"But couldn't you read her mind?"

"For those fleeting moments, I wasn't trying. I was just lost in my own thoughts and memories."

"What's she suffering from?"

"She's had a series of small strokes. She's still recuperating from a bout of pneumonia, and she's got a painful blood clot in her left leg. And being 83 years old makes in that much harder. I really doubt she's going to last much longer."

"But when she goes, you'll have her here with you forever. That must provide at least a little consolation."

"To a certain degree, it does. And it would release her from a deteriorating life. Being with her forever is a beautiful thought, but, although we'll be together again for a very long time, it won't be forever. I'll get into that with you later."

"Look," I said, "If you'd feel better being alone right now, just say the word. We can continue all this when the time is right for you."

"Thanks for the understanding. But talking to you will help lessen the burden on my mind, and I could use a little humor. And, remember, you're only here with me for a few seconds in dream time."

"Lyle, honestly, I'm not too much in the mood for humor right now."

"If I tell you I've got a 'confession' to make, will that remind you of a thought you had before you went to sleep?"

"You've lost me. Completely."

"I had promised to stop eavesdropping on your mind, but when I was trying to escape my own thoughts for a moment or two, I picked up a couple of yours."

"I'll overlook the transgression. What did you hear?"

"John, sometimes you've got a fucking sick sense of humor. The thought crossed your mind that nuns would be doing lap dances in confession booths if the religion industry went belly up."

I couldn't help laughing. Maybe it was nervous laughter, but it felt good. It provided a release from my drastically serious talk with Lyle.

"Sort of remember that," I said, still laughing.

"I couldn't imagine anything in poorer taste." He said. "Funny? Yes. Socially acceptable? Not in a million years."

"Lyle, that's one of the luxuries of being alive. I can think absolutely anything I want, and no one's the wiser."

"If you could read my mind," snickered Lyle, you'd know that we're going to one of your favorite places in the world. It's jammed with your memories, but I don't think that will interfere with anything. We'll both be very comfortable there, which is important, considering where our discussion is headed."

"And where would that be?" I asked, fully knowing the answer.

"The truth," he said, without smiling. "Now we're ready to go."

I closed my eyes.

Chapter 8
Miracles at Mohonk

What an incredible change of scenery.

"Lyle," I said, "This time you've really outdone yourself."

We both took a seat in antique leather chairs, overlooking a glorious view that I had enjoyed on many occasions.

"Kinda thought this place would be right up your alley," he said.

I got out of my chair and walked around, basking in the memories.

Perfect, I thought.

He had brought us to the Lake Lounge, an enormous, magnificent room at the Mohonk Mountain House. Built in the late 19th century, this renowned national historic landmark is located about ninety miles north of New York City, nestled smack dab in the middle of the Shawangunk Mountain Range — known affectionately as the 'Gunks.' Now I was going to learn all about death in the very place where my family and I had the time of our lives on many occassions. Go figure.

"Just one question, Lyle," I said. "Why don't I see any people? This place is always crowded, especially in the middle of the day."

" You're here on a pure memory construct of only the physical place, not the people," he answered.

"Well, that really cleared things up," I said with a sarcastic tone.

"But . . . uh . . . we're not alone," he added.

"Huh?" I grunted.

"There are plenty of us afterlifers roaming around, but you can't see them and they can't see you."

"Now you're fucking with my mind, as usual."

"I have full control over who you see and who sees you. If you saw all the 'ghosts,' as you say, you wouldn't be able to concentrate."

"Then tell me this," I said. "When we were in Hawaii, presumably in dream time, I saw those two hand-standing kids on the beach, but not in slow motion. How'd you pull that one off?"

"Actually, they were two 'ghosts,' twin brothers who had drowned in rough surf right there a few years ago. I just allowed you their memory traces."

"You're freaking me out. That's horrible." I declared.

"No," he answered, "That's life. By the way, did you happen to notice that guy in the red bathing suit sitting on the sand off to their right?" he asked.

"I did." I remembered.

"He's their deceased grandfather who welcomed them 'here' after their unfortunate accident."

"Grandfather? The guy didn't look a day over twenty one."

"John, you'll soon see, that is when I really open your eyes, that nearly everyone 'up here' looks young, no matter how old they were when they died."

I just looked at Lyle, shook my head, and rolled my eyes.

"John, if you wanted to pick a time in your life when you looked your best, how old would you be?" he asked.

"Twenty-one or there about," I said.

"Then that's how you'll look in your afterlife if you want to. Or let's say you were at your happiest when you were forty. You could also project that age, if you desire. As you'll learn, everything is memory. You are what you remember."

It was all nonsense that was beginning to make some strange sort of sense. Now, that certainly makes sense, doesn't it?

"Just one more thing about this, and then I want to get into the good stuff with you," he said. "The same memory projection also works with your clothing. I could be wearing anything I want. But I choose this 'garbage,' as you call it, because it's what I wore during some of my final, precious moments. It's how Betty and my family remembered me."

"I get it," I said. What else could I say?

"Get comfortable," said Lyle. "I've decided that the best way to do this is for me to lecture you like a professor. You just sit there and listen until I open the floor to questions."

"Will there be a quiz?"

"Yes. And if you fail, you're out of here. Honestly, the only failure I'm worried about is my own, John. I've never tried this with a live, flesh and blood person. I could make a mess of it."

"When you die," he began, "all your organs cease to function — all but one, that is, and we'll get to that shortly. Now remember your quantum mechanics. Your entire body, everything, from your heart to your brain to your toenails, is composed of the same basic particles, just configured differently. As your body rots away, these particles are reclaimed by the universe as pure matter and energy. Some of it, though, is lost to radioactive decay, but even these particles released through the 'weak force,' are recycled, so to speak.

Following me so far?" he added.

Lyle continued. "Getting back to that other organ, the one that continues to function . . . well . . . that's the answer to everything."

"An organ continues to function?" I asked, quite confused.

"First of all, we refer to it as an organ for the lack of a better description. But no living person knows about it. You haven't discovered it yet for two main reasons: It's so far beyond comprehension that you'd never even think of looking for it, and if you did look for it, you'd never find it."

Readers: This is very important . . .

"This organ," Lyle continued, "technically known as the *particle bundle,* is not flesh and blood. It's infinitely small and composed of four fundamental particles that attract each other by an exceptionally strong electromagnetic or gravity wave force that is yet to be understood. It's even been postulated that a pinpoint black hole is holding the particles together. Honestly, the whole thing is still in the theoretical stages.

Although there's space between the four particles, they are infinitely fused and contain an unimaginable amount of energy. If one could somehow be split, the release of energy would be catastrophic. This bundle, which happens to reside deep within the brain is neutral in charge, does not spin, and has just a tiny bit of mass. The bundle is fully conscious and contains every single memory we've ever had and the capacity to absorb all the memories that have ever existed in the universe.

It also has the ability to fully access the knowledge field that pervades all space, including the space within us. It's like a processor and memory chip with infinite capacity. This almost frightening anomaly is the essence of intelligent life, and we feel it is alive itself. And just as startling, all particle bundles are, physically, precisely the same. It's as though they've been duplicated on an assembly line. I'm going to go into more detail about the bundle later. As you can imagine, there are many theories — from the sublime to the religious."

"Getting back to death," he continued, "the instant your brain shuts down completely, the bundle is released. Thanks to its quantum characteristics, it tunnels into what is believed to be a parallel dimension, better known as heaven, hell or whatever you choose to call it. You should know that this dimension, if that's what it is, is completely indistinguishable from the original one. There's just some electromagnetic variation.

Now remember, this particle bundle is you. The new you. Everything but your body. And it takes a dead relative, close friend, or volunteer transition trainer to explain what has happened to you upon your arrival. It's been that way since the first conscious human. By the way, the instant your bundle has tunneled through, every single consciousness knows of your arrival. Sounds incredible, but its taken for granted here. Turns out, everything is related to quantum entanglement.

Now, if you've paid attention to what people say about near death experiences, this should sound familiar. When the bundle first leaves your brain, it appears to be disoriented and out of phase with the new world. That's why many people see 'their lives flashing before them.' Remember, the bundle contains trillions of memories and can compute at the speed of quantum entanglement. More on that later.

Many people who have endured a near death experience also claim to have witnessed a bright light just before seeing a relative. Very true. For the first time, the bundle is being bombarded by photons, so it takes an instant to get acclimated.

As an aside, if you're wondering how NDEs are possible, listen to this. If your brain is somehow tricked into thinking that life is history, the bundle can be released and tunnel to the other dimension.

If you're somehow revived, and your brain regains some electrical activity, it's possible for the bundle to be recalled. Interestingly, though, no one who has experienced NDE has ever reported the 'events' in reverse. We've also heard that on extremely rare occasions — I mean one in every 20 billion — the wrong particle bundle has reversed itself into the wrong brain. You can only imagine the results from that.

How are you doing so far? Completely lost?" he asked.

"I'm getting the gist of some of it, but I'm gonna have loads of questions. You do have to clear up one thing for me as soon as possible." I asserted.

"What's that?" Lyle asked.

"For starters, I can't understand for the life of me how this knowledge was acquired. What the fuck am I missing?"

Lyle continued, "I was going to get to that. The problem is that any angle from which I attempt to explain this creates even more perplexing questions. But let me see if I can answer this one without adding to the confusion.

Once the particle bundle is acclimated, it assumes its role as a fully functioning person in this strange new world. It communicates with everyone in this vast community, and interacts with the other world: yours. Of course, the bundle is exactly the same person it was prior to death. There are no identity alterations.

With that in mind, picture a group of particle bundles sitting with each other in dream time, in a thought constructed lab at Princeton University, for example. They're still infinitely small, but resemble their former selves in every detail. Think hard and imagine them having a long, heated debate about the topics that defined their former lives: theoretical physics, molecular biology, neuro physics, astronomy, quantum engineering, computer science and so on.

Can you see where I'm going with this, John?"

"Shit. Incredible. I know what you're going to say. Every fucking genius who has ever existed can be attending that debate. The greatest minds in history." I exclaimed.

" You're ninety nine percent right," Lyle assured me. "Einstein would be in attendance. Neils Bohr would also be there, as well as many more men and women who helped make this world a better, or worse place, depending upon how you look at it."

"I'd love to watch Einstein, Freud, Newton, Copernicus, DaVinci and Plato in a heated debate," I beamed.

"John, that opens up another can of worms for me to explain. That incredible gathering you just imagined could never entirely happen. Simply stated, this dimension is not forever for anyone. After roughly one hundred and fifty years, us particle bundles vanish. In a sense, we die.

'Where do we go when we die,' you ask? No one has been able to figure that out, and it's the subject of constant debate. There are as many scientific explanations as there are religious ones. Sound familiar to you? We'll get deeper into this later, as well.

Back to what we were talking about before, Einstein, Freud, Bohrs and other top thinkers who died within the past one hundred fifty years could be in that debate as current particle bundles. They would be able to contribute real thinking and be able to gain integrated access to the universal field of knowledge.

John, your eyes are rolling again. Do you want . . ."

Lyle's lips were moving, but there was no sound.

Fuck no. I'm awake. Back in the real world. When I was able to think rationally again, I started to get confused. Before this past evening, most everything I had experienced had been touchy-feely stuff, nothing with much substance, nothing that required deep thinking — and even deeper understanding.

I had to admit to myself that the fun and games were over. But, hopefully, not for good. Lyle had a lot to say, and I had a lot to listen. That much I owed him. The more I got to know him, the more I began to like and respect him. He was slowly allowing me a glimpse of his personal life, which confirmed that he definitely was not a shadow of my subconscious. I couldn't possibly be imagining or constructing this stuff.

For that matter, I had finally come to the conclusion that there was a lot more than dreaming going on in my head. Between the proof I had been shown, and the bewildering science I was being exposed to, there's no way I could be pulling any of it out of my ass.

With that settled, I could concentrate.

This particle bundle stuff was a lot to swallow. And death after death? Give me a fucking break. Was there life again, after the second death? I wondered. I couldn't wait to hear what all the 'dead top minds' had to say about that.

I also wondered what thought memories Jesus had left there, that is, if he existed in the first place. If He didn't know the truth there'd be some serious shit on the debate table. I couldn't wait to ask about that. What about the particle bundles themselves? Where did they come from? Could anything as powerful and complex be formed in our brains? And how could they all be the same if some people are brilliant and others are retarded?

What's more, how does reincarnation fit into the picture? If a child dies at birth, where does the particle bundle go? Does the manner in which we die have an effect on the bundle? What if someone is electrocuted? Or vaporized by a missile or even an atomic bomb? What if you kill yourself or OD? What about abortion? At what stage of pregnancy is the bundle formed? Do animals like gorillas, dogs, dolphins or even hamsters have a different type of bundle?

But my biggest question of all was about me. Exactly how the fuck did I manage to get into this dimension or whatever the hell it is? Did I fall through a tunnel? Is this like Alice in Wonderland?

I just wanted to get back. So after a late night meditation I got my wish in an instant.

Wow, Mohonk again and a smiling, pensive Lyle.

"I've got lots of questions for you, but one is more important than anything," I said. "How's Betty doing? I assume you've been with her at the hospital."

"Very thoughtful of you to ask," he said, with true sincerity. "Not much has changed. She's very weak and has to be fed intravenously. Just looking at her is heartbreaking. There was a huge bouquet of flowers on her nightstand that her daughter had sent. I wish I could get her some, as well. Now let's get back to our conversation before you so rudely wake up again."

"I'm eager," I said with enthusiasm.

"I'm going to begin with a quick review. So far, you learned that everyone has a particle bundle embedded deep within their brain. This quantumly small unit is composed of four particles, tightly bound by some immensely powerful, unknown force. This bundle is the seat of all consciousness, self-awareness, memory creation and retrieval, and access to an infinite pool of information — in short, everything that makes us human.

While the bundle is in your brain, it is controlled, to a large degree, by the brain itself. But when our brains die, the bundle is no longer a 'prisoner' of our bodies. I say 'prisoner' because the brain severely restricts most of its true capabilities. The brain also creates many problems, because it is a seriously dysfunctional organ.

Getting back to when you die, the termination of electrical activity in your brain releases the particle bundle. It then tunnels into the dimension of the dearly departed, and begins a new, breathtakingly fulfilling life. But after roughly 150 years, it vanishes to, uh, . . . well, that's the big question."

"Nice summary." I said.

Lyle continued, "Yesterday, you were wondering how this particle was discovered. Before I say anything more, you've got to remember that all this is theoretical. Over the next several million years, the theory will probably undergo countless revisions. Sorry about the deviation, but it was necessary.

Since day one, our scientists, philosophers, alchemists, and so on have wondered about how and why they arrived here, where they're going, and, most significantly, what they're composed of. These very same questions have been endlessly pondered on *your* side of the tracks as well. And you know as well as I do that there are theories galore. Always will be.

But there has never been a time in all of history when (dead) people like Einstein, Bohrs, Heisenberg, Jung and many others of that stature have been able to pool their minds. Unlike Newton, DaVinci and other geniuses from the more distant past, these new thinkers are armed with formidable knowledge that has been completely unknown.

Remember, these people developed all the theories that have led to the understanding of space-time, consciousness, quantum mechanics, and so much more. That's an unprecedented knowledge base.

Up here, in my dimension, they have spent countless hours of dreamtime devoted to the challenge of deciphering the most mind-boggling riddles of all time. And let me remind you that hours of dreamtime are equal to many years of your own real time. Just think about it."

"Question," I interjected. "Can they actually see this particle bundle? Or was it discovered purely through mathematics?"

"We are all particle bundles. You just have to look within. That's . . ."

"Sorry to interrupt," I said, "but couldn't Newton, for example, observe the bundle?"

"Of course," Lyle answered. "But, to put it into your own scientific terminology, he didn't know what the fuck he was looking at. He new zilch about modern nuclear theory, particle physics, and quantum mechanics. He was at a complete disadvantage.

What's more — and don't ask me for details on this — Einstein and company also had the privilege of studying the results from particle colliders. They actually think their way into these God damn machines and study, first hand, the results of atom smashing."

"Wait a second," I said. "If they, being particle bundles themselves, got in the way of a proton beam, couldn't they get smashed to shit? It would be suicide."

"Very very good thinking, John. What you said makes perfect sense. But they're not dumb enough to jump in, so to speak, in real time. Even if they did, the bundle's extreme strength would probably protect it. Thankfully, no one's ever been hurt."

"When I was getting quantumized at Borders book store, I read that particles are affected when they're observed. Unless I completely misunderstood what I was reading, they're somehow aware of our own consciousness. Is this a factor to be taken into consideration when observing particle bundles?"

"Absolutely. The only thing that can observe a bundle is another bundle. That's the essence of human interaction. To get more . . ."

At this point, I had to interrupt. "Ok, ok. Enough. Enough. I get it."

"No you don't," he said. "But let's get on to something else."

"Lyle," I said with conviction. "You've got to explain how I got here. I can't figure that one out for the life of me."

"I'm getting to that," he answered. "I understand how important this is to you, but you need just a little more background. Be patient. Please."

Patient? Be patient? The one thing I really wanted to know seemed like it was going to remain a mystery. How much more do I have to learn before that is revealed to me, I wondered? At least I had accepted the unbelievable fact that, yes, I was really here.

"John," he resumed, "I'm going to skip as much as I can. But there's just a little more for you to learn before I can provide an understandable answer to your most troubling question. Why don't we resume this conversation somewhere else? A change might do us both some good. And I've thought of the perfect spot — a spot where I can really relax."

"Fine by me," I readily agreed, expecting another exotic or memory jammed location.

On that last thought it happened . . . instantaneous location change.

Chapter 9
Bundles of Answers

We were there.

There?

Where the hell were we, I wondered.

I must say that Lyle looked very proud of the location he had chosen. He was swaggering around, waiting for a response from me. I decided to reserve judgment until I had taken the opportunity to thoroughly explore this seemingly odd place.

We were in a medium size living room, and my first impression was 'early Ramada Inn guest relaxation area,' if you get my gist. All the furniture appeared to be pre Eisenhower era, Sears Roebuck originals. The carpeting was a dung brown shag; the walls and ceiling were an interesting shade of nicotine stained mint green. The whole place was lovingly well worn and immaculately clean.

Then I saw it.

What a beauty. An ancient, pre-war radio in pristine condition. You could almost picture a squeaky clean, all American family huddled around it enjoying one of F.D.R.'s fireside chats. Suddenly, I knew precisely where we were. And I was fucking relieved that I hadn't made one of my trademark disparaging remarks.

After drooling over the radio, I had walked over to the fireplace to investigate a few framed photos on the mantle. The first was a typical family on the front-lawn portrait taken in the late 1930s, or so. Mom and Pop looked proud as all hell. Sitting on pop's lap was a very young girl, with one waving arm almost completely blurred. She had long braided hair and a puffy dress decorated with what I think were embroidered birds.

Mom's face, frozen in the middle of a hearty laugh, was also blurred, but not beyond recognition. Lying on the grass in front of her was a boy in his early teens with, you know, one of those awkward, coming-of-age looks. Obviously distracted by something outside the photo area, he wasn't staring into the lens. None the less, you could easily see the boy was a young Lyle. The next picture? Lyle again. This time, he was considerably older, very much the same Lyle I knew — the Lyle who was with me, now, in his good old family living room.

The yellow-tinted photo showed him in basic training: He was in a crouching, ready to attack position, holding an M1 Garand rifle. His fatigue hat was at a very cocky angle on his head. He looked capable of conquering the world. I don't know why, but the last picture sort of sent a chill up my spine. It was Lyle again, but this time he was standing in front of a battered Ford cruiser, with one arm around a very attractive, young girl.

It must have been Betty — the Betty with whom he wanted to spend the rest of his life — the Betty whom he had anonymously adored through every stage of her hard existence — the same Betty whom he now visited every day in the hospital.

"Well?" asked Lyle, breaking the silence.

"Thanks," I answered, with a lump in my throat.

"Thanks for sharing this with me." I continued.

"I'm here at least once a day with Betty, sitting right over there." He pointed at a maroon velvet love seat in front of a window with cream-colored curtains. I walked over and instinctively peered through the dusty glass. And there it was — sitting in the driveway, that vintage Ford.

"Time to get on with it," said Lyle. "Lots more to discuss. Lots of questions to be answered."

I couldn't quite understand why he wanted to discuss this 'death/bundle' shit in a place so dear to him — a place with such vivid, highly personal memories. But, if he was ok with it, I was game.

"If you don't mind," he said, "I'm going to sit over here. It's my father's chair, where he always sat, reading the paper, smoking his gigantic cigars. Why don't you take the couch, and, by all means, feel free to put your feet on the coffee table."

"I'm trying to remember what you last told me. Something to do with Einstein?" I asked.

Lyle took it up from there. "I had finished explaining how recently deceased mega scientists discovered the 'true' nature of the particle bundle. (Lyle chuckled) Actually, I only scratched the surface, but I think you got the basic point."

"Quick question," I said. "How do you know all this stuff?"

"All this 'stuff,' as you say, is available to all of us ghosts. All we need to do is pay attention to the memories: old ones and those being created as we speak. It's all an open book for anyone interested. I just wish more of us were interested."

"You mean you can access anyone's thoughts and memories at will? Without their permission?"

"Like I said, 'it's all an open book.' You want it, you got it. But you gotta want it, gotta think about wanting it. Those of us who don't give a shit about anything scientific don't have to seek anything out. You look dumbfounded, John."

"More like pissed off." I ranted. "You ever heard of invasion of privacy?"

Lyle shook his head and laughed. "It's the way of the world. It's the way things were meant to be."

"Meant to be?" I asked. "That has religious overtones to it. Like fate and destiny."

"We'll get to all that later."

"Later, later, later, later, later, later, later." I mumbled.

"Everything in our world is memory," he continued. "And it's that way in yours too. If someone punches you in the kisser, by the time you feel it and get ready to punch the chump back, it's all memory. 'Now' is something you can only experience 'later.' When you're sitting there twiddling your thumbs thinking, it's either about memories or future memories."

"Future memories? What the fuck . . . ?" I interrupted.

Lyle cut in, "If you think about getting a hair cut, for example, you're creating a possible future event. It becomes an instant memory. If it didn't, you'd never get to the barbershop. Everything's memory. It's a no brainer."

"You must mean a 'no bundle,' don't you?" I asked with a sense of accomplishment.

"Getting back to reality," he snickered, "We learn and share memory. Remember that I said 'share.' It's central to your 'BIG' question. All memories, from the very first one in time, are recorded and passed along. The next thing I'm going to tell you is really going to fuck up your bundle. All memories, even yours, are photographic."

"Bullshit." I said, rolling my eyes. "If I had a photographic memory, I'd know it."

"You wouldn't know it. In fact, you can't know it unless you're lucky enough to be one of the rare few whose brain is slightly defective," he said with a degree of seriousness that was almost scary.

"I'm lost. Totally, absolutely, positively, fucking lost," I readily admitted.

He continued, "Everyone who has ever existed has a photographic memory. And the same goes for anyone who will ever exist. This memory incorporates all your senses — vividly. That goes for sight, taste, hearing, smelling and feeling. The whole shebang. And all for a reason: You're being prepared for your afterlife. You are being prepared to contribute and share your memories."

"You mentioned something about a 'slightly defective brain?'" I reminded him.

"Do you want to learn about how you got here?" Lyle asked, slightly on edge.

"What do you think?"

"Then we'll have to return to the brain conundrum later. And none of your 'later, later' shit please." He spoketh.

I nodded ok, and he continued.

"We're almost there. Just bear with me. In my dimension, or, 'up here,' as you may say, memories rule. They're the most precious things anyone owns. And it's a privilege to share them. In fact, people with the most coveted, original memories are our own version of celebrities."

"That means a bloke like John Lennon must be a big deal 'up there.' Elvis too." I said.

"Absolutely," agreed Lyle.

"There are basically two ways memories can be shared or accessed," he continued. "A particle bundle can sample a memory just by accessing it from someone else's bundle. No communication is required. That's the most simple and direct way. But, by far, the least fulfilling.

The best, and by far the most rewarding, method of memory sharing occurs when two or more bundles lock onto each other and dissolve common memories together."

"Lyle," I said, as I squeezed my head between my hands, "English. Use fucking English. What the hell are you talking about? Locking bundles? Dissolving memories?"

"I'll give you an example," he said with a glint in his eye. "In your realm, John, people get together in special interest or affinity groups. Book groups will read a common book and discuss it. Movie clubs do the same thing with movies. Church groups meet regularly for their mumbo jumbo sessions. Travel clubs take groups to specific locations, and everyone shares the experience. Civil War buffs get together and reenact battles. And so on. Up here, memories are not just photographic, they're also three dimensional. When you add all that to a photographic replication of all sensory stimulation, you end up with a one hundred percent realistic experience."

Lyle continued. "Here's the mother of all examples: Let's say a group of several hundred war veterans who fought on Iwo Jima got together for a reenactment. If they dissolved all their battle memories, the result would be an Iwo construct, one hundred percent real from every perspective. They could relive this horrible experience exactly how it was, down to every detail. And I mean every last detail.

What's more, if other 'ghosts' wanted the full Iwo experience, they could tag along as dissolved observers. They'd become part of the group, and see, feel, hear, smell, and taste all the horrors of the battle. If they wanted, they could even participate without interfering with the authentic memories. Is what I'm telling you beginning to sink in? Beginning to ring a bell?"

I nodded with a look of astonishment and understanding.

With a 'here's your answer' attitude, Lyle charged on. "You remember my good old buddy, Shorty? He really was killed on Iwo, exactly as you witnessed. Being a war aficionado and a concerned pal, I have gladly relived this tragedy with him on numerous occasions.

Likewise, Shorty, also a war nut, has invaded Omaha Beach with me a bunch of times, and has viewed my demise from several different perspectives..

Now brace yourself. While I was waiting for Shorty's immortal moment on Iwo several days ago, I sensed an unfamiliar presence, the signature vibration from a partially obscured bundle. This bundle, still imbedded in a live person, was attempting to create its own Iwo Jima memory construct, and join the one it sensed, which just happened to be mine. The bundle was in a hyperactive state because the person had been meditating.

That person, of course, was you."

"Amazing." I said.

He continued. "There's probably a less than one in ten billion chance of that happening. For us to cross paths like that at that instant is nearly impossible."

"How did I end up 'invading your territory,' so to speak," I asked.

"I immediately realized that this was an extremely rare situation: a pre-death bundle attempting to temporarily cross the threshold, in order to share Iwo Jima memory constructs. Simply unprecedented.

So, I decided to let it (you) participate, which entailed the establishment of a resonance link, synching with your vibration and establishing temporary control of your bundle."

"What in the damndest fuck did you just say?" I asked.

"You mean that doesn't sound like a simple explanation to you?" asked Lyle, staring into the distance.

I just shook my head in disbelief.

Lyle continued, "If you didn't have a history of reading World War Two books, and weren't deeply engrossed in a very explicit account of Iwo, this would never have happened. What's more, if you hadn't meditated directly after reading, this would never have happened. What's even more, if you didn't have such a hyperactive bundle, this would never have happened. What's even more than more, if I wasn't in an Iwo construct at the 'preeeeecise' moment your bundle attempted contact, *this* would never have happened.

Last but not least, if I wasn't such an inquisitive, nice fucking guy, I wouldn't have allowed this to happen. This is why you should be kissing my ass," roared Lyle.

"Well, I guess I owe it all to you, your royal highness." I said, chuckling.

"Your gratitude is overwhelming," he said in resignation.

"Just kidding, Lyle, and I'm sorry. Right now I'm in a state of utter shock and complete disbelief. I mean, I do believe it, but . . . uh . . . I fucking don't believe it."

"Understood." Said Lyle.

We both let a few minutes breeze by without saying a word. Lyle knew I was overwhelmed, and he was giving me some breathing room. I was just beginning to calm down when a voice from behind surprised the shit out of me.

"Mind if I join you guys?" asked a young, perky female voice.

I was so startled, I woke up.

It was around four thirty in the morning, and I was wide awake. But I was actually glad to be awake. In my own bed. What a relief. I needed the time to think. And think I did . . . until my Casio belched its evil tune. A tiny bit later, while drowning myself in a large coffee I reviewed everything I had learned over and over and over again.

It was all too fanfuckingtastic. Everything was pretty difficult to understand, but I got the basics. I knew that Lyle was responsible for these wonderful, exciting, touching experiences. And I realized that he, and only he, had complete control of my mind in his dimension.

I still had so many questions that needed answering, and I knew that all the answers would be as startling as anything I had ever read in a science fiction book. For instance, he talked about particle bundles vibrating. Vibrating? What was that all about?

And getting back to another lingering question on my demolished mind, where the hell did these bundles come from? How were they created? Another thing that was gnawing at me was the voice that woke me up. Who was she? What was she doing at Lyle's first and last home? Then it hit me. I knew exactly who she was. She was Betty, exactly as she appeared when Lyle shipped off to England. But now she was a fully articulated, completely lifelike thought construct. For all I knew, she had always been with us, but Lyle had kept her invisible. I wondered why he had decided to finally reveal her to me. I couldn't wait to find out.

The rest of my day sped by. Fortunately, waking up that early in the morning had made me extremely tired. Meditating myself into a very deep sleep took only a few short moments.

The next thing I knew, that Marquis DeSade alarm clock of mine was painfully yanking me into consciousness.

What?

No dream last night?

I was heart broken.

To say the very least, that was one hell of a long day. I made a feeble attempt to stop thinking, stop torturing myself over all the possibilities that could have prevented my dreaming. All that's important to mention about that long, dreary day is that I tired the shit out of myself, read until I couldn't see the pages, meditated carefully, and passed out cold.

• • •

Back to my impossible dreamland.

I was right. It was Betty. Not exactly in the flesh, but definitely her.

Lyle, who happened to seem tired and slightly withdrawn, proudly introduced her to me. She smiled politely and shook my hand.

"I just wanted you to meet each other," he said. "Betty has known about you since your first moments on Iwo. And I've certainly told you about her."

Something was wrong. I could feel it. Lyle was cordial, but way too reserved. At least Betty was bubbly. She was sort of what I had expected: attractive in a 40s, mid-western kind of way. She had long, wavy, dirty blond hair, hazel eyes, full lips, and enormous, pearly white teeth that blinded you whenever she smiled, which was very often.

She wore a green scarf in her hair; her blouse was a multi-hued, window pane flannel; her pants were, uh, an ugly shade of plum, and I didn't notice her shoes. What I noticed the most, was the sincere warmth she exuded. Lyle was lucky. Or maybe I should say 'would have been lucky.'

Then there was too much silence.

"What's the matter, Lyle?" I asked.

"I'm thinking about Betty, the original, old, hospitalized Betty," he answered, as I kind of expected.

"Is the situation worse?" I felt awkward talking about the real Betty in front of the constructed Betty. But neither of them seemed to mind.

"She's been in a coma since yesterday," he said. "She's hooked up to a breathing machine and a heart monitor. This is very difficult for me to handle."

"At least she's not in any pain I hope."

"Not really, but she's frightened. She may be in a coma, but she's got full brain activity, and she's aware of herself."

"Sorry," was all I could think of saying.

Betty was conspicuously absent from the conversation. I couldn't blame her.

Lyle shook his head and said, "I know everything that's on her mind, but although I know it's almost impossible, I think she knows I'm right by her side. It's like she's almost trying to say something to me."

Betty was examining her fingernails. She was uncomfortable.

"I'd like to leave this topic for now," resumed Lyle. "There's nothing I can do, and it's dragging me down. One thing you should know: If at any time you suddenly wake up with no explanation, it could be because I had to rush to the hospital. If I feel even the slightest change in her vibration, I'll have to run."

"Don't think twice about it," I added.

Betty looked like she wanted to hide beneath the cushions.

"Now let's change the subject," he suggested.

It only took a few seconds for Lyle to pull himself together. His whole body language changed. The old Lyle had returned.

"I've been doing some thinking," he said. "We've covered lots of the science, but, although there's tons more to discuss, let's take a break and have some fun. I've got two options for you."

"Look, that's great, Lyle. We definitely need some R&R. But . . . you just mentioned something before that reminded me of a question I've got to ask. It probably won't take you more than an hour to answer it."

Finally . . . Betty laughed.

"Fine," quipped Lyle. "I hope whatever you ask doesn't require a very lengthy answer. If it does, I'd prefer to put it off."

"I don't think it's so bad," I said. "You got me intrigued about particle bundles, and now you're saying they vibrate?"

"There's a two hour answer to that or a five minute one," he said.

"Guess what?" I announced enthusiastically. "Let's do the five minute version."

"Excellent choice," he happily declared.

Lyle continued, "Yes, bundles do, indeed, vibrate. All bundles, which means all people, have their own specific vibration. And it differentiates everyone exactly like a fingerprint or DNA. I can instantly recognize anyone I've ever met this way. And it doesn't matter how distant they are. Vibrations travel at the speed of quantum entanglement. Still with me?"

"So far, so good," I honestly answered.

"Great." he continued. "Now it gets a bit more tedious. Everyone's bundle, including yours, is affected by your mood, situation and health. It's still your signature vibration, but it's slightly altered. In a way, you can compare it to . . . uh . . . you're not going to like this."

"Give it a shot," I said, intrigued.

"It's similar to an aura."

"An aura?" I asked. "I thought that was total horse shit, a pile of bat guano."

"Sorry to inform you, but aura's are real. Most people in your dimension who claim to see them are full of shit. But there are some who actually can."

"Some?" I asked.

"That will be answered at another time," he said in a 'don't dispute' tone.

"An aura," he continued, "is a sort of colorful cloud that surrounds you in roughly the shape of your body. If there's anything wrong with you, the colors will shift in accordance to your problem — whether it's a headache or a kidney stone. Sensitive people can look at an aura, and tell you what your problem is, even if you've got no idea. At a later time, I'll talk about sensitives and why they are that way."

I nodded, rolling my eyes.

"Back to vibrations," he urged. "When I pick up someone's vibration, no matter where they are, I know how they're feeling, and if they've got something to discuss. Live people all have a very distinctive bundle vibration that also communicates health. That's how relatives know exactly when a loved one or close friend is getting ready to tunnel. That's how I constantly know Betty's condition. Once you're here, it becomes second nature and is taken for granted."

"Do unborn babies give off a vibration?" I asked.

"Yes," he answered. "But human memory does not begin until late in the seventh month of pregnancy."

"When does a bundle begin to vibrate?" I asked.

"There are theories, but no one knows for certain. It's a mystery of nature that we'll discuss later," he said, with no room for me to argue.

"Later, John. I'll answer that later," he replied.

After a moment, he continued. "Like I tried to say earlier, I've got two options for you in the fun department. Of course, you'll get to experience both of these and many more, but you've got to choose one to start."

"For Christ sake, Lyle, what are the options?" I asked.

I cursed. Betty blushed.

I was just about to apologize for my slight indiscretion when Lyle chimed in.

"Don't give it a moment's thought. Be yourself. Curse all you want. She's heard it all. Remember, I'm no angel. No halo. Can't play a harp. Don't sit on peoples' shoulders. Never flown through the Pearly Gates."

I added, "Yeah, but, at least she looks like an angel."

"Ok, here are the two experiences. One is a simple memory trace that goes way back into history. Everyone eventually does it. It's a very interesting, memory, but, at the same time, it's disgusting. Absolutely revolting. People, I mean ghosts, sometimes puke.

When I really think about it, the other experience is more up your alley at this time, because you'll find it even more fun and thrilling And, I hate to say it, educational."

"Will you get to the fucking point. Sorry, Betty." I yelled.

"Getting there at my own pace, excuse me." He continued, "This experience combines just about all forms of memory sharing. You'll be accessing the works. What I want you to do is think of the car of your dreams, and you'll experience it at the ultimate level of reality, more so than if you actually drove one in real life. And I know precisely which car you're going to choose."

"Try me." I challenged.

"Your numero uno choice is a 1963 Studebaker."

"Over my dead body," was my immediate response.

"Well, then, how about a competition-ready, vintage Shelby Cobra?"

"Lyle, you're a genius."

Chapter 10
Smitten By a Snake

Was I excited? Enormously.

Something was telling me loud and clear that this was going to be an absolutely incredible experience. The word, 'Cobra,' has always made my blood run hot with magic and passion. Since my high school days, Cobras have always represented the ultimate driving machine.

While all these powerful visions were accelerating around my mind, I noticed that Lyle was deep in thought. He wanted to make this a dream come true, perhaps even for the both of us.

"Here's how I think we should do this," he said. "I'm going to generate the basic car, and you're going to alter it to meet your own specifications."

"Sounds good to me." I said, with incredible enthusiasm.

"First of all, where do you want to take your drive?"

"Colorado." The word rang from my mouth before I even had a chance to think.

All of a sudden . . .

• • •

We were there. Standing on a wide country road at the base of some foothills that led to a higher mountain range, no doubt the Rockies. It was a scene almost too beautiful to describe. Between the strong smell of evergreens, a blue sky with huge puffy clouds, a damp, refreshing breeze, and a temperature of around sixty five degrees, I was in heaven.

"Now for the part we've all been waiting for," Lyle said, as he spread his arms.

The Cobra appeared. It was sitting on the road directly in front of us.

"Go ahead," said Lyle, "Kick the tires."

As I ambled up to this lusty apparition, I jumped in surprise. Almost woke up, in fact. The passenger side door abruptly opened, and out stepped Betty.

"Didn't think I'd miss this, did you?" she asked.

"Glad you're here." Lyle and I both said simultaneously.

"You've got a lot of work to do on this car, John. As you know, all too well, it's not really a Cobra yet."

Lyle was right. It was a very basic A.C. Bristol, just as Carroll Shelby had imported them from England, beginning in the early '60s. Once they arrived at his sprawling workshop in California, they began the long journey from tame sports car to vicious Cobra. Pure alchemy.

Lyle walked up to the car, took Betty's hand, and said to me, "Before we get started, it's important for you to know how this is all being made possible. Lot's of memory functions are being dissolved into one another."

Lyle cleared his throat and continued. "We're going to combine several aspects of memory to create a fully articulated, precise replication from a full 360 degree perspective, including the car and driving location.

All your senses will be hyper activated. The conjoined, fully dissolved memories will begin with your own driving experience. You've aggressively driven some very hot cars on mountain roads, including many in Colorado. You know the sensations of rapid acceleration and hard cornering, and you can double clutch and power shift with a manual four speed.

You've read numerous Cobra road tests; you've seen Cobras in action in Tucson; you've seen authentic road racing movies that featured Cobras; you've built scale model Cobras; and you've been fantasizing about Cobras for years. You will also be sharing memories with actual racing legends who have campaigned Cobras all over the world. All this information is out there and it is now in here."

Lyle tapped my head with his finger.

He continued, "When you put all this together, it adds up to the ultimate Cobra experience — more vivid and realistic than even the real thing. And don't forget, there are no cops, no radar, no speed traps, you can't blow the engine or tranny, can't get a flat, can't burn out the clutch or brakes, can't run out of gas or oil, and if you really fuck up, you can't get yourself killed."

"I'm still trying to come to terms with everything you said, Lyle. It's all really too hard to swallow."

"You'll get back to semi normal when you select an engine. Speaking of which, you have two choices today: a very hot, stroked and bored 289 or a ferocious 427."

"No contest," I panted. "It's gotta be the 427."

A moment after I said that, clanking noises came from the car, the hood bulged slightly, and a scoop appeared. The car also sank down a couple of inches in the front from the added weight of the enormous engine.

"Christ." I commented.

"Now how about a transmission?" he asked. "You might need one."

Without a moment's thought, I oozed,"A close ratio four speed with an exposed gate and a competition clutch."

"I forgot to ask you if you want two four-barrel Holleys on the engine. Or maybe even Webbers if we can get them to fit." Lyle added.

"I'll stick with the Holleys," I said.

"Smart choice," he added.

"Lyle, I've been wondering about something. You seem to know a little about Cobras, but how much car experience have you really had?"

Lyle rubbed his chin and said, "Experience?"

"Yeah. Have you ever gone over fifty miles an hour, even in a memory merger?" I snidely asked.

"Tell me if this qualifies," he answered.

"I drove with 'Big Daddy' Don Garlits in a Double A Fuel Dragster."

"Hmmm," was my response.

"I dusted the Autobahn with a Ruff Twin Turbo."

"Hmmm," was my response.

"I've raced at Le Mans three times in a monster Porsche, and a Ferrari 365GTB."

"Hmmm," was my response.

"Burned a hole in Sebring in a Grand Sport 'Vette.

"Hmmm," was my response.

"Was with the Beach Boys when they recorded Little Deuce Coupe."

"OK, OK, OK, OK, OK, OK. Enough. Enough. I get the point, Parnelli."

"I wasn't finished," said Lyle.

"Oh yes you were," I answered.

"But I was just getting warmed up," he bragged.

"OK, Mario, let's get back to my Cobra," I almost pleaded.

"We've done the drive train. How about wheels and tires?"

"I'll need Goodyear Blue Dots, the fattest available."

The tires appeared, and the fenders flared out to accommodate them.

I continued, "They have to be mounted on magnesium alloy wheels, with spinner hubs."

"What's next?" asked Lyle, with excitement.

"The exhaust system," I stuttered. "It's got to be free breathing, with next to no restriction. And, although they're tacky, I want side pipes so I'll be able to hear every last pop and wheeze from the engine."

My God, I thought, those pipes that suddenly appeared look evil.

"This car is getting more frightening by the minute." said Lyle, approvingly. "What else do you want to do with it?"

"The suspension," I said, "has to be perfect."

"That's done," nodded Lyle. "What else? Aren't you missing something? It's right in front of your nose."

Even Betty knew what I was missing. She sheepishly approached me, and whispered it in my ear.

"Holy shit." I exclaimed. "How in the fudge did I miss that?"

'That' just happened to be the paint job. My beautiful Cobra was a very unbeautiful shade of dark puke green.

All I had to do was think and . . .

The car was now a wicked metal flake blue, with extra wide, white racing stripes. Just way too phenomenal, I thought.

We all stood there drooling over this God almighty creation.

"Well, what do yuh think?" I quietly asked.

"Sweet." said Lyle.

"Awesome." said Betty.

"Now I believe the devil really does exist." admitted Lyle.

I just continued to stand there completely dumbfounded. Trying to grasp the sheer, insane wonder of what I was intently staring at, I thought of how far I had come in the last few days. From utter disbelief to giddy acceptance. When I finally snapped out of it, I noticed that Betty had walked over to a nearby pond, and Lyle was sitting in what could now be officially called a Shelby 427 Cobra.

"Now that I've got the chance, there's something I want to ask you," I said to Lyle.

He just sat there with his imagination in overdrive, one hand on the steering wheel, the other on the shift knob.

"It's about Bet," I said. "She's so quiet, and I'm getting weird vibes from her. Is she somehow against my being here? Learning all these secrets?"

Still starry-eyed, he twisted his head towards me." The only problem she has with you is the fact that you're alive. Ironic, ain't it? She's a little nervous, but she'll get over it."

"Weird," I said. "A ghost afraid of me. Priceless."

"You've got your car, now here's the plan," Lyle continued. "You're not going to like this, but I'm going to disconnect you in a second."

"What?" I belched.

"I want you to enjoy your drive while your fast asleep. And, as of now, you're just about out of dream time," explained Lyle.

"Just one thing," I added. "Make sure you roll up the windows before you leave because it looks like it might rain."

Then the car began to shrink and assumed the shape of my pillow. And instead of a throaty exhaust, I heard the obnoxious scream of my Casio. Damn, if I could only run it over with my Cobra, I yawned to myself.

When I rolled out of my bed, I discovered that I was in an incredibly good mood. And that was even before I had devoured an almond croissant and flushed it down in a tidal wave of coffee. My day was entirely unproductive because my mind kept shifting to the Cobra. The damn thing seemed larger than life, almost spiritual in being. It was waiting for me in another realm, another dimension. Somehow, that didn't seem so strange to me anymore. The whole premise of 'impossible' was slowly but surely vanishing from my personal reality.

Getting myself as tired as possible had become one of my daily rituals. Of course, I overdid it, and nearly fell asleep during dinner. Reading was out of the question. And I almost nodded off before meditating. Perish the thought. The next thing I knew . . .

I was back.

My stunning car was waiting for me, but where was Lyle, I wondered. Could he be under the car adjusting the brakes? Could he be shooting some lube into the bearings? Just then, the passenger side door opened, and Betty leaned out. After a heroic yawn and a tendon yanking stretch, she withdrew herself from the car and hopped up and down until the blood had rediscovered her feet. Is all that really necessary for a fucking thought construct, I asked myself.

I was fully expecting Lyle to emerge from the other side of my Cobra, but no such luck. I knew he had to be around somewhere. Without him, there'd be no me, no Cobra, no Rockies . . .

"Lyle couldn't make it. So . . . you're stuck with me," said Betty.

"How soon will he return from where ever the hell he went?" I asked, assuming she had an answer. Fortunately, she didn't appear to be afraid of me. Maybe Lyle had had a little talk with her. I certainly hoped so.

"I haven't the slightest idea," she answered. "He's with Betty now. The other Betty. She took a real bad turn for the worse a few hours ago. He'll stay with her until she's stabilized. 'If she's stabilized,' I should say."

"Do you feel odd saying 'the other Betty,'" I asked. I fully expected to hear a squeaky, computer-synthesized voice say, "Sorry, I'm not programmed to answer that question."

"Not at all," she confidently answered.

She stared me directly in the eye and said, "I am Betty."

"Yes, of course you are," I replied, very uncomfortably.

"John, you don't have to patronize me," she strongly asserted. "There's an awful lot Lyle hasn't explained to you, and that includes my unique presence."

I didn't know how to respond. If I started asking questions would I be overstepping my bounds, I asked myself. And I was wondering, I mean seriously wondering, how I could be here without Lyle's presence. Without his particle bundle, I was a bundle of nothing, and I assumed the same applied to Betty.

"John, I know how anxious you are to drive the Cobra," she blurted.

"But how can I drive, or even be here, without Lyle's presence?" I asked.

"There's a short explanation, and a long one," she said. "I'll try the short one, so you don't run out of time and wake up in the middle of a hairpin turn."

"Excellent thinking." I said, and meant it.

"Let's talk in the car," she said. "You can lean back in your seat and try to absorb what I'm going to tell you."

"If it's ok with you, I'll take the driver's seat." I said.

We both got comfortable.

I was dying to start the engine.

Betty was dying to start talking.

"Lyle and I were childhood sweethearts, and planned to spend our entire lives together. Back then, that really meant something. Then the war came along, and we lost each other. Just listen. Please don't interrupt.

When Lyle's brain stopped functioning on that miserable French beach, his life flashed before him, and many of his most precious memories included me. He had no idea what he was doing, but he accidently thought constructed me while his particle bundle was tunneling its way to this dimension. When he entered this realm and adjusted his new eyes to the blinding light, the first face that came into focus was mine. His grandparents were there to help bring him across, but it was my face that welcomed him. They helped both of us adjust.

"This is quite a . . ." I tried to speak.

"Shhhhhhh," she urged. "Just listen. During that fleeting moment while he was tunneling, I received every single memory he had of Bet. And as soon as he was able to access all her life's memories, which was almost immediately, they were added to me. Since those first unique moments, Lyle and I have spent just about all our time together, but Lyle also spends a lot of time with the original

Bet. As he has watched her age through every stage of her difficult life, he has accessed her continuing memories for me.

I am Betty. All her memories, all her happiness, all her sadness, all her problems, all her pain, all her joy, all her never-ending love for Lyle."

"That's a heart-warming story," I said, quivering. "But it still doesn't answer my original concern. If you don't have a particle bundle, which I'm sure you don't, how can you let me access all this?" I motioned towards the car and surroundings.

"Of course, I don't have a naturally occurring particle bundle, but I get by very well with the next best thing."

"You've really got my interest," I added.

" I told you I'm unique. What you'd probably call an anomaly. I may not have a bundle, but I have an unexplainable vibration — my own identity. My vibration is now in synch with Lyle and with you. That's why I can do what I can do — without Lyle. End of story."

"One last thing," I said, letting the magnitude of this sink in. "Does this mean you're a scientific wonder 'up here?' How is this accounted for? I mean, it just can't possibly be taken for granted."

"Lots of questions. No satisfactory answers. But, we're all waiting for the big event," she proudly said.

"The big event? What's that?" I almost demanded.

"I don't want to talk about that now, and I'd appreciate it if you'd just leave it alone. I shouldn't have opened my big mouth in the first place," she said.

"There's a lot you and Lyle aren't telling me. A lot. I can feel it, and it's getting on my nerves."

"You don't know the half of it. You don't even know the real reason why you're here. This is a bit more than just an accident. I promise that Lyle will reveal everything to you later."

"I can see now, I said, that you're far more than a typical thought construct."

I needed to learn more. I needed to know if I, as in *me*, was in some sort of danger.

"Don't be a baby," she urged. "You've got nothing to worry about. If you want to put an end to these experiences, Lyle or I could release you at any time you please. Or, you could stop meditating. But . . . we hope it won't come to that. You may become an important part of our future."

"Jesus Christ," I yelled. "This just keeps getting crazier and more unbelievable by the second."

"And you've only heard a small part of it," she added. "It may seem nuts to you, but it's no crazier than life itself. Absolutely everything is a miracle. What happens 'up here' is no more 'impossible' than what you experience 'down there.' If anything, my world is far less amazing than yours. Don't worry, we understand and respect your bewilderment and disbelief."

"Betty, I said, here I am, fast asleep in my bed, and at the same time wide awake in a dream. But it's not a dream, as I'm told by two seemingly normal human beings who are anything but human. But . . . you claim to be as human as I am, and want me to accept it. I mean Lyle is, for all intents and purposes, a ghost. And you? A real-life imaginary person? A replicant? This is all, uh . . . nuts."

"Well, I'm not at all surprised," she said. "In fact, if you easily accepted everything, I'd know that you were about two blades short of a Swiss Army knife."

"Honestly, Betty, you're easier to talk to than Lyle, you've got a better understanding of what I'm going through, and you explain things with more clarity."

She laughed and gave me a simply sincere "Thanks."

"Can I ask you a very personal question?" I said.

Bet gave me an affirmative nod.

"It's probably none of my business, but what's going to happen to you when the hospitalized Betty dies? Will you both be here? Will you vanish? What will become of your, uh, vibration?"

"John, it is your business, and probably the most important reason why you're here. Now I'm going to turn your mind into strawberry jello: you're here so you can ask that very question and provide a quantum state observance. Confused? I hope so."

"You just left me so far behind, that I could never catch up, even in this Cobra," I said.

"Do you know why 'people' are here?" she asked.

"Yeah, I answered, to drive Shelby 427 Cobra's."

Betty grabbed the shift lever, made a long vrooming noise with vibrating lips, and giggled.

"The universe, itself, is a conscious entity. And we're here to acknowledge its presence by asking the simple question, 'why are we here?' and by observing."

"What the F are you talking about?" I said through my clenched teeth.

Betty slanted her head and peered at me with one piercing eye, the other obscured by her hair.

"Just a theory, John. Just a theory. When I was young, I was taught to believe in God, Judgment Day, the love of Jesus . . . you know . . . all that fun stuff."

Staring at the Snake logo in the center of my steering wheel, I jerked out a response. "Listening."

She continued. "When I got here, I quickly learned that most of that was a myth. But, like the majority of people here, whether they were devout holy rollers or staunch non-believers, I believe in some form of a creator. There's just too much going on for all this to be just a dumb coincidence. This was all planned, not just haphazardly blasted out with the Big Bang."

This was fascinating. And if there was so much as a thread of truth to any of it . . . wow.

"Hmmmmm, observer," she whispered.

"Reading my mind? Like Lyle does? I asked, jarring her.

"Oh . . . ah . . . just one word," she answered, a bit startled.

"What's so special about 'observer?'" I asked.

"That better describes what you're doing here," she admitted.

Only one word made its way to my dry mouth: "What??????"

Betty closed her eyes, gently smiled, and said very softly, "You're the observer."

I'll admit it again, I was confused, but I had a confident feeling that it would all be spelled out for me, along with all the other mysteries I was certain to encounter. I sensed that Betty understood my confusion and sympathized with me far more than Lyle did. She was filled with compassion. God, I was glad she was here. I then felt her remove my right hand from the steering wheel and hold it palm up.

With a mischievous smile she said, "I'm going to read your palm."

"Betty," I answered, "I was just beginning to believe that you were down to earth . . . well, as much as you can be, that is."

She laughed very hard as she began to trace a line down my hand with her fingernail. It tickled. "I'm going to tell you your immediate future. Hold still for a second. I see you fulfilling a dream."

"What dream?" I asked nervously.

She brushed some hair from her eyes, looked intently at me, and said, "It's right here. See for yourself."

With that, she slapped a key into my palm that featured a bold, Cobra logo.

"Betty, I said, you can read my future any time you like. Want to come along for the ride of your life? Or death?"

She answered my question by securely fastening her safety belt.

I put the key into the ignition. Held my breath. And . . . the Cobra instantly sprang to life with a hearty shake and a ferocious roar. It was almost like kicking a sleeping Grizzly in the gonads. I was intently watching the tach needle dance back and forth between 1000 and 4000 RPMs. The tank was full, the oil pressure was perfect, and the engine temperature was creeping out of the green.

Shivering with anticipation, I stepped on the brake, depressed the massive clutch, clunked the shifter into first gear, and watched the revs hit 2500. Just as I was about to launch the beast, Lyle appeared out of nowhere, casually sitting on the left fender of my car. That did it. The asshole jolted me. Literally scared the living shit out of me.

• • •

The next thing I knew I was wide awake, gripping my pillow instead of that beautiful, mahogany steering wheel. Shit. Shit. Shit.

'Come to think of it, I said to myself, this is all for the better.' I had spoken to Bet for such a long time that I would have certainly woken up during my drive.

During this rather boring day, I began to wonder about Betty's comment. 'I was the observer?' What the fuck did that mean? And, this whole thought construct thing was way beyond amazing. By using the power of collective memory, you could create what appeared to be a flesh and blood human being that you could interact with in every possible way.

And then there was the Cobra. Was this my thought construct? Or did Lyle do it over my shoulder? This must be the case. That evening while I was meditating, I kept seeing a ghosted image of the Cobra logo on my acorn. That did the trick.

When I opened my dream eyes, I was right back where I was when I had left. The only change was that Lyle had removed his ass from my fender, and was standing beside my open window. I smiled at him and revved up the engine a bit. Betty made a bunch of additional vrooming noises, as her hands were turning a phantom steering wheel.

Once again, I put the car into gear, and said to Lyle, "Sorry. I'm stealing your girl for a little while."

He smiled.

I popped the clutch, and the Cobra jerked and roared.

And I felt acceleration in the pit of my stomach as I had never felt it before. Now I had to figure out how to control this monster, so *I* didn't look like an asshole to Bet. She was sitting there, pinned to her seat, one hand gripping the seat corner, the other holding on to the door handle for dear life.

The Cobra tore ahead, literally eating the asphalt in big gulps. The rear tires were smoking through each gear shift. When I hit fourth, I had to quickly apply the brakes and downshift, because I was approaching a corner. With the tail hanging out, and the car in a controllable drift, I slid through the turn. Betty held tight, catching her breath as the G forces slowly decreased. Then I gave it all the gas I could, and the car accelerated out of the turn, sending up a shower of gravel. Betty put one hand over her eyes.

Fortunately, I was able to enjoy a nice long workout with my Cobra. I didn't want it to come to an end. All I could think about was how much I'd love to have this car in real life. Unfortunately, real, vintage Shelby 427 Cobras in good condition bring down around $4 million at auction. Oh well, only in my dreams.

And this dream was over. Instead of the sounds of a massive V-8 belching fire, I was hearing my stinking Casio belching out a very rude 'good morning.'

Chapter 11
Titanic Revelations

What an evening that was. I hoped I'd get another shot with the Cobra, but I wasn't about to hold my breath. With my eyes shut tight, I could picture that wonderful car waiting for me in some imaginary garage. That's what you call very wishful dreaming.

Bzzzzz. My Casio went off again. Time to really get up and get my ass over to Juan's. My whole day was boring, compared to where I had been the previous evening. It became very obvious to me that this dream stuff could get quite dangerous. Things were far more fun and interesting on the other side.

I couldn't help but wonder what was next. Where was I going to go? What seemingly impossible new things was I going to learn? That night, I crawled into bed feeling like a kid on his way to Disney World.

...

Once my meditation took effect, I sensed a rocking sensation.

Then I felt . . . dizzy?

Where the fuck was I now?

Where had Lyle and Betty taken me?

And where were they now? I couldn't see them.

I woke up standing at the entrance to some extraordinary lounge. All my surroundings were far more ornate than anything I've ever seen. Every inch of wood, from the furniture to the moldings, was intricately carved and highly polished. There were windows in the walls made of beautifully cut glass, and I was standing on a richly textured, multi-patterned Persian carpet.

Lighting was provided by brass and cut crystal sconces, and hanging in the middle of the ceiling was an enormous, crystal chandelier. I could have sworn that it was gently swaying. Weird, I thought.

What struck me as the most interesting of all were the people, a conglomeration of regal looking men and women, mostly middle aged and over. They were all elegantly dressed in what I initially thought was formal attire from the late 19th or early 20th century. Maybe, I thought, this was a costume party in some incredible mansion.

But why was the chandelier swaying? And why was I getting dizzier by the moment? Finally, I spotted them in the corner of the lounge, sitting on a grandiose, over-stuffed couch, drinking from heavily-cut, crystal goblets that glistened in a rainbow of colors. I made a beeline towards them.

"Would it be too much to ask where the hell we are?" I stated.

Lyle whispered something to Betty, and she shook her head affirmatively. "John, she said, we're going to put some music into your head that'll answer your question."

"Will it also tell me why I'm so damn dizzy?" I asked.

I looked at Bet, and she closed her eyes, gently swayed her head back and forth, and traced her hand through the air like a conductor. I began to hear a sickeningly sweet Celine Dionne song that was immediately recognizable.

"We're on the Titanic. The freakin' Titanic," I blurted. "What's next? Are Kate Winslet and Leonardo DiCaprio going to run by?"

"You want them to?" asked Lyle.

"Why did you choose this, of all possible places?" I asked.

Bet answered, "It's beautiful. It's romantic. It's history. It's a vivid part of thousands of memories."

"Yeah, tortured memories," I added.

They reluctantly agreed with me. And asked what I wanted to do. I told them I had to get the hell off the boat before I started puking.

Lyle became lost in thought. Betty asked me if I got seasick often.

"Seasick? Often?" I responded. "All I have to do is think of a God damn boat and I start retching. I've been that way my whole life."

Thankfully, we changed locations faster than you can say 'iceberg.' And what a change it was. We were sitting on a mountain ledge overlooking a silvery lake. It was magnificent. Totally peaceful. A far cry from the Titanic. I just enjoyed it all, without asking where we were.

"Something has been deeply troubling me about this 'no heaven, no hell' thing," I stated in a sorrowful tone. "I've never given heaven or hell so much as a second's thought. But now that I know that a form of life continues after death, It seems unfair that people like Hitler get to enjoy all the unlimited pleasures. It's terrible."

Betty jumped in. "In this universe, there is no concept of fair or unfair. Or good and bad. Or kind and evil. It's all pure science, pure physics, pure mathematics, pure consciousness. In short, the universe doesn't give a damn about how we've conducted our lives. In human form, we simply accrue memories, and they become part of the human record. Of course, no one knows if we go anywhere after our 150 years here. Maybe there's another existence that takes 'good and bad' into account."

I hesitated, then brought up something I had been thinking about. "Lyle, Betty told me that she's a unique specimen in the world of thought constructs. Something about having a vibration . . . her own identity. Is this . . ."

Lyle interrupted, "No one has been able to explain how or why this happened. It's directly related to the fact that I unknowingly constructed her while my particle bundle was tunneling here.

Obviously, I didn't know what I was doing; I didn't even know I was coming here . . . didn't even know I was dead."

"But . . ." I was cut off again.

"Please let me continue," urged Lyle. "As you can imagine, Betty is the subject of lots of speculation, and somewhat of a celebrity because of it. Thanks to this implausible vibration of hers, she's an independent thought construct."

"What . . ." I was cut off again, as I should have expected.

"Please, please let me just say what's on my mind," pleaded Lyle.

"Knock yourself out," I responded.

"What I mean by *'independent'* is that she's free to do as she pleases. Not that I would ever even dream of it, but I couldn't deconstruct her if I wanted to."

"Do you mean to tell me that this has never happened before?" I asked in total disbelief.

"Yes. Never happened before," he proudly answered.

"How's that possible? After all this time and so many people passing into this dimension?" I asked in disbelief.

Lyle looked very surprised. "All what time? In the scheme of things, human consciousness, and our memory capability, are brand new entities in the universe. In true geologic time, the few million years we've been around is like a grain of sand in the ocean. What Betty and I have accomplished could be a normal step in 'Evolution, The Sequel.' And, John, you haven't realized the big picture yet. There's another potential paradigm shift with Betty that won't be realized until close to a hundred years from now."

"Lyle, just tell me what it is. I could be guessing from now until eternity," I said, in desperation.

Betty spoke up. "Just think about this, John. I'm an independent thought construct, so I will not vanish when Lyle's time is up. And since I don't have a particle bundle . . . well . . . that could mean that I won't disappear after 150 years."

"Are you telling me what I think you're telling me?" I asked in disbelief.

"Yes. I may well exist for all eternity. History's first immortal," she said.

"That's incredible," I said, thinking about the implications.

"But there are many problems, John." Betty admitted.

"Please go on," I implored. I was very intrigued, to say the least.

"I better answer this one," said Lyle. "It gets difficult. When my original Betty dies, there will be two duplicate Betties in this dimension. No known physical law prohibits this. The situation will probably be hurtful for both of them, to put it mildly."

I remarked, "I'll say. You'll have to spend equal time with both of them.

Lyle looked down and slowly moved his head back and forth. "And then there's the 'eternity' problem. How's my original dear Betty going to feel about her double being immortal?"

"It gets even worse," I added. I put my hand on Betty's shoulder and said "How is she going to handle this eternity thing? Does she want to be here forever? Without you?"

"We've discussed a potential solution," said Betty. "Close to . . ."

Lyle quickly interrupted. "Now is not the time to talk about this."

Betty quickly added, "No. No. No. Not that solution. The other one."

"Ok," said Lyle, quite relieved.

Once again, I felt as though games were being played, and something very significant was being kept from me. I would have become very persistent about getting an answer, but I realized that it wasn't my business. But, then again, this was some flaky ghost world I was yanked in to, and I had a feeling that I was going to be involuntarily involved in whatever they were bantering about. I had a right to know.

Betty continued. "Sorry we're being so evasive and keeping you in the dark. There's no harm or deceit intended. It just has to do with our strange, ghostly stuff — the stuff you find so difficult to accept."

"Amen," I said, partially under my breath.

Betty explained . . ."There are two solutions. One's possible, the other, a revolutionary idea, may be impossible. The possible one is the one I'm prepared to explain right now. Actually, it's a simple solution aimed at preventing me from facing eternity without Lyle."

"I think I know what you're going to say. Right before Lyle's time is up, you're going to create an exact thought construct of him that will stay with you forever."

"Basically correct," said Betty. "But, as you know, I can't create a thought construct. Someone else with a real particle bundle will have to create the first one and maintain its presence until they pass on. Shortly before they pass on, Lyle's construct will be handed down to the next person who will maintain it and so on and so on and so on."

I could see that Lyle had something delicate to say. "John, my time here will be up in less than 100 years. Shortly before that time comes, Betty and I might ask you to create the thought construct. I'm confidant that we're always going to be close friends, and you may end up knowing me better than anyone."

"Well, that certainly makes perfect sense for something that makes no sense at all," I said. "See how well I'm proceeding with all this crazy stuff?"

My eyelids darkened when a big puffy cloud drifted in front of the sun. I opened my lids, but instead of the cloud I was expecting, I was looking at my murky bedroom lamp as it began to reflect the early dawn streaming in through my windows.

Shit. I had wanted to hang around this dream a while longer. The conversation we were having intrigued me. As usual, it was preposterous, but very interesting. It revealed a set of human problems and emotional issues that no one could possibly dream of.

Well, no one in their right mind, that is. And having that discussion in such an exotic environment made it all the more surrealistic.

And what was the alternate solution they had for Betty's existence? The 'revolutionary' one that was probably 'impossible?' God knows what that one's all about. But I wanted to know. My curiosity was torturing me. I made a quick decision that if it somehow involved me, and could affect my future, I wanted zippo to do with it. If these spirits or, whatever they were, were trying to alter some natural phenomena, it could be dangerous. I sure as fuck didn't want my electrons, protons, and shitrons blasted all over the universe.

I can hardly remember what I did the rest of the day. But it was more apparent than ever that these experiences had taken over my life. How could anything you do in real life compare to what I was experiencing? On any normal day, I don't get to sail the Titanic, tool around in a sizzling Cobra, and have philosophical conversations with a fucking ghost and his absolutely charming replicant.

When I dragged myself into bed, after walking around my block a dozen times listening to music, I tried to imagine where I'd wake up. Lyle was unpredictable. It could be anytime, anywhere in the world. And my ticket to all these exciting places was meditating on an acorn. A fucking acorn.

• • •

Odd.

Very odd.

Very unexpected.

Lyle had taken us somewhere in real time.

Of course, we were there in dream time, so the world was in the slowest of slow motion. But . . . Lyle had made an excellent choice because it was drop dead enchanting.

"Don't you love it?" asked Betty.

"My head's spinning," I answered.

We were in a Rockwellesque suburban park, sitting on a wooden bench by a small frozen lake. Tall, old-fashioned lamps illuminated a late night, happy scene of men, women, and children ice skating and frolicking in the snow. It was very lightly snowing, just a few shimmering flakes frozen in place in the air.

"This place brings back happy memories," said Lyle.

"Where are we?" I quickly asked.

Betty answered. "We're at a skating lake where Lyle and I used to go from the time we were little kids. They always held midnight skatings, and nothing's changed."

"Where's the lake?" I asked, then realized I knew the answer.

"Wisconsin. Just a few blocks from where we grew up," said Lyle.

"I would have expected a memory compilation from the 1930s or '40s?" I asked. "Why are we here in current time?"

"It makes us feel good to know that, although the world has completely changed, something so dear to us is still here — exactly as it was," said Betty, as she turned around and around, absorbing everything in sight.

Then I spent some time looking around. The whole scene was similar to what I had experienced with Lyle that night on East End Avenue. People and their clothing were frozen in wild, ungainly positions as they skated, trailing long plumes of cottony vapor from their mouths and noses. Children, with all their jumping and general crazy antics, were in the funniest positions of all.

I snapped out of my daydream when Lyle handed me a big, steaming mug of lovingly thought constructed hot chocolate. I looked at it and said, "What, no marshmallow?"

"Look again," he said. "And, by the way, I threw in some rum for added warmth."

It was delectable. All three of us were sitting there enjoying the sights, letting that soothing cocoa warm out throats. It was perfect.

I tried to picture Lyle and Betty skating there way back when. They had lived a fairytale American life before Lyle was so cruelly snatched away. At least they still had each other and all their memories. But I couldn't forget the real Betty, the elderly one on her deathbed whose life turned out to be anything but a fairytale. I assumed she was in a hospital probably not too far from where we were.

Then I realized that I hadn't recently asked Lyle about how she was doing. We were all in such good spirits that I thought better of asking about her at that moment. But he's probably reading my mind, I thought, so I may as well spring it on him before I forget.

"Lyle, it just occurred to me that I haven't asked you about Betty's condition. Have there been any improvements?

"Thanks for the concern," he said, as the steam from his mug obscured his face. "No improvements, but she's stable. At this point, I'd be surprised if she gets any better. Oh, and one more thing. I'm just about certain she's aware of my presence. It's nearly impossible, but I could swear I sensed it."

"Lyle, thanks to you, if there's one thing I've learned it's that nothing is impossible."

Out of nowhere, Lyle began to seem tense. "John, sorry about this, but before we get into anything new, we have to find another location."

"Why?" I asked. "This place of yours is beautiful, peaceful, and the bench is reasonably comfortable."

Lyle took a moment or two to respond. "It's because of Betty. The wonderful memories here, combined with thoughts of the original Betty's impending death, are too much for her to take. I've never seen her like this. Never."

"Shit. Is this my fault?" I asked. "Is it because I just asked you about Betty's health?"

"You had nothing to do with this," answered Betty. "Anything and everything reminds me of my life here with Lyle, and where my future may be headed. This place just happens to be extremely intense."

"Anywhere either of you want to go?" Lyle asked Betty and me.

"Away from here," asserted Betty.

"Then I've thought of the perfect place. And you'll enjoy the slight touch of irony when you ask your next question."

"I'm ready." I said with expectation.

Chapter 12
Bundles of Mysteries

What a drastic change.

Once again, it was beautiful.

In a starkly exotic way.

We were overlooking a quiet body of water.

There were patchy green, rolling hills, with rocky outcroppings.

The air was sweet, humid, and hot.

There were buildings here and there.

Many were Church or Cathedral like, and all ancient.

"I give up," I loudly asserted. "I don't have a clue where we are."

Lyle was standing there, hands in his pockets, and Betty seemed more relaxed, not yet very animated, but approaching her old self. She was stretching her legs, perched on her toes, peering at something in the distance.

"Lyle, I asked, are we in real time?"

"No. We're sharing millions of memories that span thousands of years. This is a significant place for people who are deeply interested in history and the modern origins of human faith and belief."

"I still don't have a clue. How long are you going to keep me guessing?" I asked.

Betty walked over to me and pointed to a body of water, off in the near distance.

"John, she said, that is the Sea of Galilee, where Jesus walked and preached to his flock. Right there on those very shores. We're in the heart of the Holy Land, the Promised Land of the Old Testament."

Betty cleared her throat, and took on the part of a tour leader. "Right over there," she pointed, "is the Church of the Primacy of

Peter. It's built on the site where Jesus is said to have appeared to the Apostles after His Resurrection."

She took a deep breath and continued. "See that hill sort of behind the Church? That's the Mount of Beatitudes. It's where Jesus gave His Sermon on the Mount, while overlooking the sea."

Lyle spoke up and politely asked Betty to skip the rest of the history lesson. She acquiesced, fully satisfied that I understood the historical importance of the area. The three of us walked closer to the shore and found a soft place to sit down. I actually felt very good here, very calm and peaceful.

"John, said Lyle, it's your show. Now's a good time to ask some questions."

I flopped on my side, propping myself up on an elbow. "One of the last things I was wondering about the other day is what happens to our particle bundles when we die the second time around. Is it possible that they're recycled . . . as in reincarnation?

Betty hopped on this one. "There has always been plenty of speculation about this, but recent particle bundle science strongly indicates that there's no reincarnation."

Lyle added, "Actually, reincarnation was seriously doubted long before the new physics. There's simply no evidence for it. Particle bundles with memories from multiple lives do not exist. It's one life per bundle and one bundle per life."

There was some logic behind everything Lyle and Betty were telling me. If there were no particles that contained memories from more than one life, there'd be no evidence for reincarnation. Yet another human myth bites the dust.

"Now for my next question," I said, as I stretched my legs out. "Has anyone determined how and when bundles are formed in our brains?"

"Long answer, John. Very long answer with numerous theoretical overtones," said Lyle.

"I'm just going to roll on my back and listen. Take all the time you want, Mr. Professor."

"I'll be adding my two cents too," added Betty.

Lyle began, "When you consider the physical structure of particle bundles and the amount of brutal energy required to create them, it would be impossible for them to form in the human brain."

Betty took over. "From this point on, it gets difficult. I mean really difficult. For everything to make sense to you, I've got to back track a little. Research, in the form of vibration detection, has determined that particle bundles first become active in the human brain towards the beginning of the eighth month of pregnancy. Before that, the primitive brain and body are developing, getting ready to accept the introduction of the bundle and its capabilities. Remember, the body does not need the bundle to function."

Lyle took it from there. "The question now is this: if bundles are not formed in the brain . . ."

Betty interrupted, "Sorry, Lyle, but there was something I forgot to say. No one knows precisely when the bundle enters the brain. For all we know, it could have been introduced in the male's sperm or in the female's egg. But that's not too important. The key is the vibration — the true spark of consciousness. That comes to life, as I said before, in the beginning of the eighth month of pregnancy. We're certain that some chemical and/or electrical process within the brain activates the bundle's signature vibration. Until the vibration is initiated, all bundles are exactly alike. They lie dormant, waiting to begin a human journey that could possibly be eternal."

"Well put," Lyle said to Betty. "Jump in whenever you see fit."

Lyle continued. "Where was I . . . ? Oh, yeah, bundles have to be created outside the brain. That much is for certain. The question is, how and where?"

I had to interrupt. "Lyle, aren't you forgetting something? Shouldn't the question really be 'how, where, and . . . why?'"

"You really know how to open a can of worms, don't you?" Lyle responded. "This might take some time to explain. As I've told you, it takes extremely high energies, and special conditions, to fuse a particle bundle together and, presumably, make it vibration, or consciousness, ready. It's likely, particle bundles are the most complex structures in nature.

Our physicists speculate that there are several entities in the known universe where these high energy conditions exist. Bundles could be formed during the creation of stars when swirling dust, gasses, plasmas and particles are wrenched together under enormous heat and pressure. When stars and/or massive suns die and begin to collapse into neutron stars, the heat, pressure and gravities could also create bundles, and spew them out into space."

"No shit," was my galactically brilliant response.

"There are two more theories worth mentioning," said Betty, just as Lyle was about to continue.

"Of these two theories, the first I'll mention only has fringe support."

"Fringe?" I asked.

"The technical term is 'nut cases,'" she said with a wink.

"People who are one fin short of a rocket ship," added Lyle.

Betty got serious. "They're thinking alien intervention. You know, transpermia. But sane individuals don't think we're an experiment or anything remotely like that. Aliens did not create particle bundles. If they did, I'll be the first to congratulate them."

She continued. "The theory du jour, and the most plausible yet, is as follows. Particle bundles were created at the same moment the universe, most elementary particles, and physical laws were created — at the instant of the big bang. The conditions couldn't have more ideal. And it answers many metaphysical and theological questions."

I was puzzled. "How can that account for all the particles needed today, tomorrow . . . forever?"

Lyle slid in. "According to our scientists, an incalculably massive amount of particle bundles were fused in that first instant. Supposedly, enough for . . . forever.

"Where are they?" I asked. "In a bundle bank somewhere?"

"They're everywhere at every moment," answered Betty.

"Where is everywhere?" I asked in confusion.

Betty continued, "No matter where you are — here, on Jupiter, or on some planet too far to even imagine — particle bundles are constantly drifting through everything."

"I find that type of thing almost impossible to swallow," I admitted.

"Well, open your mouth wide," exclaimed Lyle. "Here's a similar, but far more extreme example. Have you heard of neutrinos?"

"Yes, I answered, but I haven't really read too much about them."

Lyle looked down at his shoes and shook his head. "You know, John, when I tell you about things right here in my dimension, you're amazed. But there are just as many amazing things to be learned in your own world, waiting for you to discover them. Why don't you just pick up a few fucking books once in a while and read. When you learned about quantum theory, you weren't here. It wasn't something amazing that *I* was explaining to you. All it took was a little walk to your Borders fucking bookstore. Open your eyes. Open your mind. Live while you're alive."

I was staring at Lyle, amazed at his tiny tantrum. He was staring at me, amazed at my lack of exposure. We both understood each other.

"Sorry," said Lyle. "Please try to understand my frustration. Too many people never really know how wonderful and amazing life is until it's over. Don't let that happen to you."

Betty had to get involved. "John, Lyle is upset because he sees some of himself in you. Obviously, he enjoyed life tremendously. But he didn't seek out and learn many of the secrets that life holds for the curious. Try not to take it too personally."

"No offense taken," I said with all honesty. "And I understand the point. I'll find more time to sniff around the Internet or bookstores."

Lyle gave me a smile of approval.

"Now . . . about those neutrinos . . ." I whispered.

"You were wondering about the theoretical swarm of particle bundles that were all over the universe. To make this a little easier to believe, I wanted to briefly tell you about neutrinos, particles which are very well known in your neck of the woods, so to speak.

Neutrinos, part of the 3F group (Fast, Fickle Fuckers), are infinitely small elementary particles. In fact, the word, itself, means 'small neutral one.' They're constantly on the move, always traveling at close to the speed of light. Created by radioactive decay, or plain old nuclear reactions, they pass through matter completely undisturbed. Most of them you'll encounter come from the sun, and, get this, more than 50 trillion of them pass through your body every second."

"That's one hell of an uncomfortable thought." I said. "Maybe I'd be better off not knowing about these 'small neutral fuckers.' These teensy-tiny no-see-ums. And please don't tell me that I'm also being pulverized by trillions of bundles. Please."

"You're not," answered Betty, seemingly unfazed by my 'colorful' language by the Sea of Galilee.

She continued, "First of all, neutrinos can't hurt people. They hit absolutely nothing when they travel through you."

"Come on, how's that possible?" I asked. "You're just saying that to make me feel better."

Betty laughed very hard. "Would it make you feel any better if I told you that's there's virtually nothing to hit? You, and everything you see, are nothing but an illusion — empty space."

"What the . . . ?" I gasped.

"Let's not go there now. That's a 'later' revelation," advised Lyle.

Betty continued. "All I was going to say is that there are nowhere near as many particle bundles in the universe. And since they have more mass than neutrinos, they don't travel as fast. In fact, it's been theorized that they're very often motionless. They know when to come to a standstill."

"I understand what you're saying, but I don't understand what you're saying. Do you understand what I'm saying?" I asked, going cross-eyed.

"Of course," said Lyle, taking a deep breath.

"I've got a quick question, completely out of context. Why do you breathe, Lyle?"

"Memory," he answered. "That's why I eat, drink, scratch my head, blink my eyes, and fart."

"Slob," blurted Betty.

Trying to regain his composure as Betty sneered at him, Lyle added, "A few scientists up here have even suggested that particle bundles could potentially be the hidden mass in the universe. It's one of today's hottest, contested topics in both dimensions."

"Wait. Wait. I know this one. It's called 'dark matter,'" I proudly said.

"Amazing," said Lyle. "I didn't know they wrote about things like that in car magazines and World War 2 books."

"Getting back to dark matter, I said, it's hard to believe that anything could be hidden these days, especially particle bundles. If your scientists can find them, why can't my scientists — you know, live ones?"

"Before I answer that, I want to remind you that you're going to wake up extremely soon. When we reconvene tomorrow, I'd like to stay in the same location because it's so easy to talk here."

"Hey, fine by me," I said. "But do you think we'll be able to do one of those memory experiences soon? You had mentioned an alternative to the Cobra: something disgusting, if I may recall."

"Absolutely," he answered.

Betty pouted. "If it's what I think it is, you can leave me out when the time comes."

"Getting back to your 'invisibility' question, John, my scientists have the luxury of being bundles, so they know how they appear, how to look for them, and where to find them. Your scientists don't have the slightest idea that they even exist. They're also impossible to detect."

"Impossible?" I asked.

'Impossible,' I said to myself, that a sheet can get so fucking tangled around your leg.

Sheet? Leg? Tangled?

I was awake.

Lyle was right.

I had left them together in the Holy land, wondering if they spent their day in dream/memory time versus real time. Yawning deeply, it hit me that I was very glad that there were no angels, harps, halos and all that Biblical stuff. It was nothing more than traditional life in a whole new light. But my acceptance didn't mean I had turned off my bullshit meter. I was still a devout skeptic.

After a large latte and a raisin bagel, I headed over to Borders book store. Today, I was going to be a detective and check out some of the info that was being fed to me. I decided to focus first on the Holy land.

To make a very long story short, I found an area map of the sea in a travel guide, and, by God, I located the Church of the Primacy of Peter and the Mount of Beatitudes exactly where Betty said they were. Upon closer examination, I was able to pinpoint the area where we were talking. Gave me a chill up my spine. Here I was, sitting in Borders, examining a map of a place I had just visited in another dimension with two charming ghosts.

Next, I decided to get some information about neutrinos. Of course, I had heard of them, but I really knew zilch about them. Sure enough, Lyle's info had been right on the money. I found everything he said, except for his '3F' reference.

A few hours later, I crawled out of Borders and had a sensible dinner. After an invigorating shower, I jumped into bed very interested in continuing my conversation with my favorite spooks.

Returneth, I did. With ease.

There I was, back by the Sea of Galilee, back with a very content Betty and Lyle. They seemed glad to see me, and I, in turn, was glad to see them. Yes, glad to see an apparition and a figment of its imagination in my room, in the middle of the night. No matter who or what they were, I felt lucky to have them as friends. I was enjoying every moment with them, and didn't want the whole crazy thing to end . . . which I knew it would, sooner or later.

"So, what were you guys doing while I was in the land of the living?" I asked.

Betty stretched her legs and whisked some hair from her face. "The day went by very quickly because we spent most of it in real time, visiting the other me at the hospital."

"How's the other you doing?" I asked, genuinely concerned.

Lyle took it from there. "Some slight improvement. She came out of her coma, but was completely disoriented."

Then he abruptly changed the subject. "John, I know you were left way up in the air after our last get together."

"So far," I said, "most of the things you've told me are based, somewhat, in reality. But this whole particle bundle thing has my head spinning."

"That's how I felt when I first heard about it," agreed Lyle. "And I was here for well over forty years before the theory was developed, so I had a good start on believing the impossible. You're trying to absorb all this in just a few days."

"Well, I've got a bundle of questions. And in no order of priority."

"And we've got a bundle of answers. But I can't promise that any of them will make too much sense. And since our scientists are always changing their minds, some of our 'answers' could be dead wrong," Betty advised me.

"Let me begin with this," I said, addressing no one in particular. "When particle bundles vanish after 150 years, where do they go? You've led me to believe they're indestructible."

Lyle took the lead. "First of all, they aren't indestructible. According to those in the know, if a bundle were to get trapped in a black hole's event horizon and sucked in, it would probably be history. It would also be a bad thing if a bundle became trapped too close to an exploding star.

One of the biggest mysteries we encounter is that quite a few people have ventured out past our solar system . . . never to return. These people, who happened to be very responsible types, were well aware of all the harmful objects and would avoid them. There's definitely something out there that can, and has, killed us. One highly unlikely hypothesis is that an impact with some powerful, exotic particle may be responsible. Or it could be that some gravitational characteristic of dark matter captures us. No one knows."

Betty chimed in. "You can't blame it on evil aliens, although some of the fringies are pointing fingers."

Lyle continued. "Right here on earth, there are two possibilities for destruction. If a bundle got caught in an enormously powerful bolt of lightning, it could theoretically get demolished or the vibration could be drastically altered. It's never happened, by the way. As I mentioned in an early discussion, if one of us were stupid enough to enter a particle collider, especially the new LHC (Large Hadron Collider), that could be suicide."

"What about a nuclear explosion?" I asked.

The Afterlife is to Die For

"Heaven forbid." Exclaimed Betty. "A blast large enough to destroy the planet could kill us, as well. But the universe won't allow that to happen."

I was very confused by her last statement. "What do mean by 'won't allow?' You lost me on that one."

Lyle interrupted. "We'll answer that one later. Now is not the time."

"Later?" I asked. "Why?"

"Lyle's right," said Betty. "I jumped the gun. That's a whole other topic that'll distract from your bundle questions. Trust me."

"Ok," I said. "But I sure as hell can't wait to hear about that. Getting back to nukes, didn't Hiroshima, Nagasaki, and even some of the A bomb testing, waste some bundles?"

"Not as far as we can tell," answered Betty. "Thousands upon thousands of victims, even those who were vaporized at ground zero, are here with some viciously horrible memories. Those 'nukes' weren't powerful enough to unbundle a bundle."

"Now let me answer the other part of your question that dealt with the fate of bundles after their 150 year life here," said Lyle.

"The most logical conclusion, as you surmised earlier, would be reincarnation. Given all the 'impossibilities' here, that wouldn't be out of the question. Unfortunately, it's not the answer. There are just too many plausible factors against it."

"Sorry to interrupt," I said, "But there have been many documented cases of people who can, all of a sudden, speak a language they've never even heard before. And some can remember vivid experiences that they've never come close to living."

"There's an explanation for all of that. I'll get into it later." Said Lyle, leaving no room for discussion. As I was going to say about the big, *150* year question, it's been vigorously debated since the beginning of time, just as people on your side have been debating the question of life after death since day one."

"Major topic." I agreed.

Betty took it from there. "When leading thinkers from all religions get here, they're shocked by what they learn. 'Shocked' is putting it mildly."

"Oh, I can well imagine." I exclaimed, giggling.

Betty continued. "No matter what they learn about the new reality, many of them continue to believe that when they leave here, they enter the traditional heaven and hell."

"You mean harps, halos, salvation, angels, St. Peter, Pearly Gates, Satan, brimstone and all that fun stuff?" I asked.

"Yes," said Betty, hunching her shoulders. "And can you blame them? It's what they believed all their lives. No matter what they experience here, they revert back to their old God fearin' ways. And you know what? Maybe they're right. Are their beliefs any crazier or more impossible than anything else here? Anything that you, yourself, have experienced?"

"I have a confession to make," I said. (long pause) "The answer is no."

"But what about your general population? And your scientific community? What do they think?" I added.

Lyle raised his hand like a kid in school. "It's all very fragmented. Lots of people from all backgrounds believe in a traditional, 'answer for your sins' life after death. Many of them are in those religious affinity groups I mentioned a few days ago. And they feed off each other's beliefs. It's human nature, plain and simple."

Betty was eager to cut in. "It's interesting to follow the thinking of people who were atheists when they got here. Some, of course, simply feel that this place is one more step before nothingness. But others, after experiencing the 'miracle' of life after death, are convinced that there's more. Some even adopt the views of holy rollers. Scientists, who are just people beneath their genius and pretentions, fall into all categories of belief, especially the one I'm going to tell you about next."

"Many of us," she continued, "including me and Lyle, strongly believe that there's at least one more level to life after we complete our 150 years here. We don't necessarily believe in a classical God . . . you know, a humanoid individual with a beard, a white robe and a booming voice. However, since we don't believe that the miracle of life, as well as the universe, was an accident or a coincidence, we believe there was a fully conscious creator. And this creator wouldn't just allow his precious, conscious creations to cease all forms of existence."

"Heavy," I said. "Please don't ask me for any remarks or opinions until I've had some time to mull this over. I'll need maybe ten years or so. But I've got the simplest of all questions. What happens after 150 years?"

Lyle gave Betty one of those 'go ahead' motions with his hand.

"I hope you don't expect a definitive answer," she said, raising her eyebrows and throwing up her arms.

I laughed, "Of course not. But just give me one theory that *YOU* would like to believe — something that could fulfill your dreams."

"That's a ridiculously tough question, because I have to fulfill one dream before I can fill the other."

"I think I know what you're going to say, and I'm sorry if I put you in an awkward position. I really am," I said.

Lyle turned to Betty. "You've just got to assume that you'll live on as yourself within Betty after she dies. Now, tell John about your other dream."

Trying to compose herself, Betty said, "There's one theory that's captured the imagination of millions, including me and Lyle. After experiencing life from the perspective of two lifetimes, we would take all we've learned, including the memories of all the ages, and enter a third dimension. This would be another flesh and blood dimension, where we could apply all we've learned about ourselves, others and the pleasures of nature. We would have a brain, but it wouldn't restrict our particle bundles."

"Question," I said. "What do you mean by the brain 'restricting' the particle bundles?"

Lyle answered, "John, I want to have a separate discussion on brain and body function, and how they affect our bundles. So let's save your question for then."

"Fine," I said. "Better later than never."

I could tell that Lyle had something important, but delicate, to address. "John, I couldn't help notice that smirk on your face when Betty mentioned a 'creator.' I've got to straighten this out before we proceed. The concept is key to a lot of what we're going to discuss."

"Please respect the fact," I said, "that this 'creator' stuff really goes against my belief system."

"Excuse me, John, but it doesn't completely contradict your beliefs," said Betty. "You don't believe in *God*, which is a different thing. We've found that a 'creator' is good middle ground for both atheists and holy rollers from all faiths."

"I'll do my best to keep an open mind," I promised.

"Let me begin with a question," said Lyle, pensively. "Do you believe in evolution?"

"Of course," I answered quickly.

"Perfect," he answered. "Now we're well on our way. Think carefully about particle bundles. They're infinitely small, yet highly complex systems, that have been prevalent in the universe since the beginning. They exist in the micro world, not in the macro world where you, microbes, molecules, and mountains exist.

When objects evolve, they move along a path from simple to complex, except for us ghosts. We evolved from very complex into just simply complex."

"Where's this going?" I asked.

"Shhhhhh," said Betty.

Lyle continued. "Particle bundles did not evolve. There was no survival of the fittest, and punctuated equilibrium wouldn't apply."

Betty interrupted. "Lyle, saying things like 'punctuated equilibrium' will only confuse John even more."

Lyle thought for a second. "Punctuated equilibrium is a spurt in development along an evolutionary path. It has been theorized, that this event helped people and all other life forms evolve into what we really are. But it wouldn't apply to bundles."

"Why not?" I asked.

"Bundles are perfectly symmetrical units, based on an even number. They would probably be out of synch, or phase, if there were three particles, and it would make no sense for two particles to bond in such a way. Besides, what could they have evolved from? There was nothing for them to improve upon. They're probably the most perfect objects in the universe."

"But couldn't they have been fused together by accident? The raw materials were there, and, as you said, the conditions were ideal."

"The odds against that happening are way beyond calculation," asserted Lyle. "Sure, particles were created. And so were some very simple atoms, all of which went on to form everything in the infant universe. But there would have been no reason for bundles. I shouldn't put it quite that way, because there was a reason."

Lyle continued, "Now where was I before I so rudely interrupted myself? Just like the hydrogen and helium atoms that helped ignite the stars, bundles definitely had a purpose. But that purpose wasn't put into effect for billions upon billions of years. That was no accident, at least on this planet, that is. Only a conscious entity can plan. Only a creator with vision and intent could think that far ahead.

I'm forgetting probably the most important reason of all why bundles were no stupid accident. They're the foundation for consciousness. They develop their own vibration that creates even the most elementary thought functions. They are magnificent, functioning devices. Not some random accident or coincidence."

While I was attempting to pick my tongue up from the ground, Betty took the lead.

"It's very obvious to us that particle bundles were created on purpose . . . for a reason. Therefore, there had to be a creator, some overall intelligence, a universal consciousness. For all intents and purposes, we live in a universe that's driven by consciousness — that's even here thanks to consciousness."

What disturbed me the most was that Betty and Lyle were actually making sense. This was beyond thrilling. Now I understood. I was becoming a believer.

Betty opened the floor to Lyle. "Absolutely nothing happened by accident. From a trillionth of a trillionth of a trillionth of a nano second after the Bang, the universe was being constructed to support our form of life, or something that would finally exploit the capabilities of particle bundles.

Everything had to be just right. When added together, everything is a miracle. We believe that the conscious universe was waiting for us to evolve so we could observe it . . . and acknowledge its presence. Some people also believe that the universe has always been in some state of quantum superposition, and our observance made it real."

"But what would have happened if a comet or asteroid had destroyed the earth before there were people?" I asked.

"Never would have happened." Said Betty. "The universe has always protected us. There have been close calls, and huge meteors have struck the earth. But, in those cases, we feel there was a purpose."

"Huh?" I snorted.

Betty continued. "Think about this. Dinosaurs were the dominant species here for hundreds of millions of years. Then they met their demise thanks to a combination of climate change, and a comet or asteroid strike. With these carnivorous monsters out of the way, mammals were permitted to evolve. And we eventually arose from the mists. That was the creator's handiwork. And there were many more seemingly accidental acts of nature that paved the way for us."

"So, do you believe this creator is some benevolent, all mighty form of life?" I asked.

"Not at all," exclaimed Betty. "It's most likely a highly intelligent, fully conscious form of energy with a single goal. All that matters is that we acknowledge it's existence, as well as our own. It doesn't give a damn about us on a personal level. But it has instilled in us the qualities of love, kindness, friendship, honesty, loyalty and everything else that helps us exist and lets life go its merry way.

Now this is going to blow you away: if the creator *was* a benevolent entity, and cared about us on an individual basis, we'd probably be on the brink of extinction by now. It cares that the collective 'we' are here. And it cares that either we or another conscious, self-aware creature will remain here. 'Here,' by the way, means anywhere in the universe."

"Ok, ok, my brain is about to ooze from my ears," I sadly admitted.

"This was a lot to absorb and understand," said Lyle.

"You're forgetting the word, 'believe," I whispered.

"The first thing I want either one of you to explain," I continued, "is how benevolence, on the part of the creator, could screw up the world."

"Expected you to ask that," said Betty.

"Umm, before you begin, I've got to use the little boy's room, so I'm going to stroll over behind those rocks for a second," I gently announced.

Lyle shook his head. "Don't even think about doing that here."

"Hey, I gotta go. I don't mean to desecrate this place, but . . ."

Lyle interrupted. "If you go, you'll really go. You'll end up waking in a soaking wet bed."

"So what am I supposed to do?" I nervously asked.

"You're going to wake up, and drag yourself into your bathroom. Sorry to say, but that's all you can do." Lyle said.

"Damn. This was really interesting," I blurted.

"I think you've got quite a lot to digest, so the timing isn't really that bad," said Lyle. "And when we see you tomorrow, we'll be in a new location, one that will inspire lots of thinking and discussion."

The last thing I saw was Betty waving and saying, "Goodbyeeeeee."

Chapter 13
Mysteries in an Emerald Twilight

That was a swift transition. From Betty's 'goodbye' to my dash to the bathroom. If I hadn't gotten back right away, I would have been very pissed, quite literally. That'll teach me not to drink a whole bottle of Snapple before I go to sleep.

It was only around 3:30 in the morning, and I was still tired enough to crash back to sleep. Didn't even have to meditate, just shut my eyes, and the zzzzzzzzzzzs came naturally.

My annoying Casio woke me with a start, bright and early.

So . . . I was wide awake, refreshed, and ready to face another day wondering about everything I had learned during the previous evening's sojourn in the Holy land.

And it was a lot to wonder about.

I was both pleased and relieved to hear Betty and Lyle's description of the 'Creator,' and the reasons for their belief. I had been afraid that this entity was going to be some man (or woman) in a white robe sitting on a cloud.

Instead, their definition could be well tolerated by most believers and non-believers, alike. Even if the particle bundle concept was a steaming heap of shit, their other reasons for the existence of a creator made sense. And for me to say that anything up there 'makes sense' is a quantum leap of faith.

The more I thought about the creator, however, one thing really bothered me. If we, in my dimension, were solely conceived to acknowledge and observe it, other dimensions weren't necessary. Lyle and Betty's dimension, along with a proposed additional one, didn't make sense. I couldn't wait to hear their answer to this one.

Taking a radically different approach to the Creator concept, I strongly felt that a traditional God could exist instead. Why not? Anything was possible in this land of impossibility. A kindly lady or gentleman in a white robe could have created the bundles and everything else. This also wouldn't rule out a conscious universe.

It would also add plausibility to the existence of Lyle and Betty's dimension, as well as anything beyond. If they were in some sort of purgatory, for example, the next level could potentially be a heaven or hell. Or maybe just another flesh and blood opportunity to change one's ways. Who knows.

It's also more comforting to think of the Creator as humanoid rather than being a mass of energy — a consciousness without a conscience. But then there was something else my two friendly ghosts said that might refute the idea of a benevolent Creator. Unless I got it all wrong, I recall them saying that benevolence could lead to our extinction.

Got to ask them about that one.

That night, I was so tired that anything would have worked as a meditation image: pumpkins, kumquats, raisins, cauliflower, even asparagus.

Glad to be back again.

Glad to open my dream eyes and marvel at our latest location. As usual, Lyle had displayed his brilliance as a travel agent. I didn't have the foggiest idea what country we were in. But any moron could tell we were in a tropical rainforest. Gigantic, exotic trees towered above us, forming a canopy that let in only sporadic rays of light. What little illumination that managed to penetrate, produced a mysterious emerald twilight. It was eerily enchanting.

Only a very slight breeze rustled the leaves, and caused processions of hanging vines to gently sway. High up in the branches, you could see what appeared to be small monkeys bounding from branch to branch. I couldn't see any of the birds, but you could hear their exotic calls.

The three of us were standing on top of the only hill in the area. Or maybe it was a small, isolated mountain because it seemed to be all stone. I would guess that it rose up to a height of about 300 or so feet. The one and only thing that detracted from this beautiful place was the extreme humidity. I was soaked clear through my clothing.

"Well, do you approve?" Lyle asked me.

"What do you think? It's incredible."

"The place is timeless," added Betty.

I took in more of the delightful scenery, and finally asked Lyle where the hell we were.

Lyle smiled. "We're in the Amazon rainforest, but I can't be any more specific than that."

I couldn't figure out why, but Betty was stamping her feet, pointing at the ground.

"Oh, so you really don't know where we are, Mr. Explorer," I said.

"He knows exactly where we are," declared Betty. "But he won't tell you. Don't even bother trying to find out."

"I don't understand what you're getting at," I admitted.

Then Betty reminded me about something Lyle had told me long before I had met her. There were certain things he *couldn't* disclose — things we, as live humans, had to discover for ourselves that would enrich us with special memories.

"Take a very careful look at what you're standing on," said Lyle.

"It's a tiny mountain," I said, in resignation.

"Look again. Do you see there are four sides? Kind of odd for a mountain, wouldn't you say? And the sides are not just equal, but stepped from the top to the bottom. Odd again."

I walked all around the flat top, taking a more careful look. Then it hit me like ten tons of cinder blocks.

"Shit. This freakin' thing is man made," I wildly exclaimed.

"You got it," said Lyle. "This 'thing' is an ancient, yet to be discovered, Mayan tomb that dates back many thousands of years."

"So how do you know about it?" I asked incredulously.

"First of all," said Lyle, "we, as in us ghosts, are born again explorers. Remember, being quantum-sized particles, we can travel through anything and see everything. We've found everything there is to find. And I mean everything."

"But . . . that's not how we know about this," he continued, spreading his arms wide. "There are hundreds of detailed memories that have been passed down from the original builders."

"I really hate to say it, but that makes sense," I said.

Betty was eager to speak. "It's not a pretty memory, John. It took thousands of slaves to construct this over a, roughly, ten year period. Many of these tortured souls died from exhaustion, disease, harsh treatment, malnutrition — everything you can think of. And when the tomb was completed, the survivors had their throats slit so they couldn't reveal the location."

"Ten years?" I asked.

"Just think about it," said Lyle. "The slaves had to carry hundreds of thousands of tons of shaped stones through hundreds of miles of the most foreboding jungle. All you see here is the tip of the iceberg. The tomb is filled with separate chambers that branch out in all directions beneath the ground. All of it was built to last forever."

"Why would they wait ten years to bury the big shot this tomb was most likely intended for?" I asked.

Betty said, "It was built in anticipation of his death. He was a very, very big shot, as you would say."

"Maybe he's the clown who came up with that 2012 prophesy junk," I said, chuckling.

Lyle asked, "What makes you so sure it's 'junk?'"

"Lyle, are you inferring there's some truth to that stuff?" I asked, startled.

"Remind me about that later. It's a long story," said Lyle.

I continued walking around, looking down the sides. Then another thing hit me like ten tons of gold.

"Lyle . . . Betty, what's this tomb filled with?" I asked, with a shit load of anticipation.

"Treasure." They both exclaimed, at exactly the same instant.

"Everything a greedy king would need for an afterlife of sheer luxury and unbridled pleasure," Lyle added.

"My legs are getting weak just thinking about what's beneath my feet," I said, with a shit-eating grin.

"When this is discovered," said Betty, "it will be one of the richest finds in all of history. There's much more gold here than Fort Knox. There are diamonds, rubies, emeralds and other gems by the ton. Most of the gold is in the form of magnificent objects, like massive figures, busts, jewelry, ceremonial masks, ceremonial weapons, helmets, shields, plates, urns . . . you name it. Many of the pieces are encrusted with jewels."

Lyle jumped in. "There's a perfectly preserved wooden ship, with its entire crew, sacrificed and embalmed. Gracing the bow is an enormous, anatomically correct bust of some gorgeous maiden. It's made of solid gold, with huge emeralds as eyes and flowing hair defined by strands of embedded rubies."

"Jesus," I remarked. "That ought to be worth a few bucks."

"It would be impossible to estimate its value," said Lyle.

"I'm beginning to realize how difficult it must have been to transport all these fragile artifacts through the jungle." I said.

"Most of the artistry was done right here, on site," said Betty. "They brought their own artists, sculptors and smelters out here to create their special miracles with precious metals and gems. A few miles to the north, they discovered a massive gold mine that provided more than they needed."

"Lyle added, "That mine has not been rediscovered, and still has veins of pure gold as thick as your arm. There are also millions of dollars worth of gold dust and scraps, scattered throughout the soil where the art shop was located. They could afford to be careless."

"How has all of this remained a secret? By now, you'd think it would have been discovered," I remarked.

"This place is nearly impossible to find," said Lyle. "Unlike a lost city that would be easier to spot, this is just a single, well camouflaged installation hidden in the shadows beneath a solid, perpetual canopy of leaves and branches. What's more, there's no legend that would attract explorers. Mayans weren't even supposed to be here. No one's even looking for this."

"But . . . now I know about it," I exclaimed.

"So what," said Lyle, laughing. "What are you going to do, tell someone that two ghosts in another dimension took you to an immensely valuable Mayan tomb hidden somewhere in the Amazon, while you were dreaming? Good luck."

"Maybe you've got a point there," I said.

"Someday, this fabulous place will be discovered by someone who stumbles upon it, just like all the other treasures waiting to be found.

"Honestly, Lyle," I said, "I really love this place, but it's just too uncomfortable to talk here. Maybe you and Betty aren't bothered by the heat and humidity, but it's killing me."

Lyle looked over at Betty, shrugged his shoulders, and said, "How's this?"

At that moment, the humidity lifted, and the temperature dropped to a very tolerable 75 degrees. That didn't even amaze me because I now took all this shit for granted.

"We wanted to give you almost the real Amazon experience. Lyle had planned on changing the temp all along," said a relieved Betty.

I asked, "What's this 'almost' thing?"

"Betty insisted that I avoid all the terrible memories of the rain forest," Lyle said.

"You mean like cannibals?" I asked.

"Worse," cried Betty, shivering. "Insects."

Lyle elaborated. "Right now, there would be swarms of horrible flies and mosquitoes crawling all over your sweating body — in your hair, your ears, your mouth, and your clothing. And they'd be constantly biting. Even worse, huge, poisonous spiders would be dropping from the trees."

"Sounds lovely, Lyle," I said, as I instinctively itched myself all over. Betty was doing the same thing.

"Anything else before we get started?" asked Lyle.

"Two things," I answered. "My pipe and something comfortable to sit on."

With my pipe in hand, I looked down and saw the big, fat cushions Lyle had thought up. They were a shade of green that complemented the forest. Now we were ready for what I hoped would be a long stay.

"If I remember correctly," said Lyle, "we were talking about the Creator, and if he were benevolent, it could screw up the world. Is that where we were?"

"Yeah," I said. "That's very puzzling. Makes no sense to me."

Betty spoke up. "You'll understand in a minute. Would a benevolent creator have prevented all the centuries of warfare and genocide?"

"Of course," I answered.

Then Betty asked, "Would that creator have prevented starvation and the many horrible diseases that kill millions every year?"

"I would think so," I answered again.

"And you'd probably think that benevolent creator would also have prevented common, everyday murder."

"Yes. Where's all this going?" I wondered aloud.

Betty continued, "Over the years, a benevolent creator would have saved the lives of many trillions of people. There's no way our earth could support the resulting population. By constantly killing off hundreds of thousands every year, people have and will survive, and will evolve into better, more responsible beings."

"Look at it this way," added Lyle, "Warfare, starvation, and disease are responsible for the majority of the earth's scientific and economic developments. These 'industries' nurture and support millions of people. War, alone, has been responsible for incredible inventions that benefit our lives every single day."

"One more thing," said Betty, "You've also got to take a close look at all the germs, flues, viruses and cancers . . . etc. Many of them are absolutely brilliant, and have displayed their own unique survival tactics. I'm not convinced that all this is 'accidental' or 'coincidental.' These enemies have evolved along with us for a single deadly purpose."

"Enough. Enough. I'm convinced," I said. "The creator ain't exactly Santa Claus for some very logical reasons."

Lyle stood up and stretched. Betty followed suit. I was very comfortable on my large, green, fluffy cushion.

Lyle yawned broadly and said, "Now that we've got that settled, let's do something more interesting."

Betty agreed.

I didn't.

That even surprised me.

"I'd love to," I said, "But . . that would leave me swinging on a hook. Believe me, I find everything we talk about just too damn interesting. Why don't we do this, let me ask you all one more thing that was bothering me about the creator/destroyer. Then I'll be ready for a break."

"Fair enough," said Lyle. "I'm very glad to see you're taking such an interest."

"Let me see how to word this," I said. "If we are here to consciously acknowledge the presence of the creator, question our own awareness, and observe the universe, then how do you account for a second, and possibly even a third, life? Wouldn't the first life generation accomplish it all?"

"As they say, the Lord works in strange ways," asserted Betty.

"Finally," I exclaimed, "A question you can't answer."

Just when I was feeling as smug as could be, Lyle stood up, put his hands in his pockets, and swaggered around. With confidence, he answered my question in a way that opened the door to even more mysteries.

"Great question, John. Well conceived. And the answer I'm going to give you is... uh... questionable. First of all, your assumption that only one human dimension would be enough to satisfy the Creator makes perfect sense. But if that were the case, why were particle bundles created with capabilities that are nowhere near fully utilized by flesh and blood brains and bodies? Once a particle bundle tunnels into my dimension, its massive powers are fully realized. And only God knows, if you'll pardon that expression, what a bundle could achieve in a third dimension. So... with that in mind, it appears as though the Creator has its own mysterious answers that are yet to be revealed."

"In other words," Betty sighed, "we can't fully answer your question because the creator works in strange ways."

"Fair enough," I shrugged. "But, Lyle, you mentioned something that I didn't understand."

"Just 'something?'" he asked with a smirk.

"You said that our flesh and blood brains and bodies didn't take advantage of particle bundles. What's that all about?"

"I jumped the gun when I said that," admitted Lyle. "I haven't had a chance to tell you about the relationship between your brain and bundle. It's a whole other discussion."

"You mean it's a 'later,' don't you?" I asked.

"Let me talk to Bet about this for a second," said Lyle.

While waiting for them to finish their discussion, I rolled over on my back and gazed up at the mesmerizing rain forest canopy. As the leaves rustled way, way above, little rays of bright sun light twinkled on and off like a disco ball, briefly illuminating small parts of the seemingly endless forest.

Lyle broke my reverie by clapping his hands once and saying, "Ok. You seem to be a sponge for information, John, and that's commendable. I had mentioned before that it would be good to take a break and go on another memory adventure, but you'd probably wake up right in the middle of it."

Betty broke in. "There are many things you'd be interested in learning, especially the brain/body/bundle relationship. But there's something else we wanted to explain to you that you'll need to understand in case a certain situation develops."

That struck an ominous chord in me. I really didn't like the implications. "What's this 'need to understand for a developing situation?'" I said to the both of them.

"Nothing to be nervous about," Betty assured me. "Remember a while ago I said you were the 'observer?'"

"I do. And it confused me."

Betty continued. "It's hard to . . ."

Lyle interrupted. "I don't want to mention *that* yet. I want to explain bundle alignment first, so everything will make more sense later."

"I'm beginning to feel as though there's another agenda here — something that's going on behind my back."

"John, let's start this over," said Lyle, sheepishly. "I'm probably not going to handle this well, and I may arouse your suspicions even more."

Betty repeated, "There's absolutely nothing to worry about."

"Then why are the two of you so tense and nervous?" I asked.

"Your presence here," affirmed Lyle, "*is* an accident and a wish come true. When I first sensed your presence during my Iwo Jima memory trip with Shorty, I seized the opportunity to make contact with you. You're actually a dream come true."

"Excuse my French, Betty, but what in the God damn fucking hell are you talking about, Lyle?" I asked in exasperation.

Betty laughed. "You're fucking excused."

"Just listen. Please don't interrupt. I'm going to attempt to explain away your confusion and nervousness," Lyle tried to assure me.

Betty laughed again. "Good luck, Lyle."

"You are not making this any easier," he answered her.

"I'd like to hear this before I wake up. Don't want to go another day with this shit splattered all over my brain," I argued.

"Sorry," said Lyle. "Here goes. For many years, I've been worried about what was going to become of Betty when the original Betty finally died and arrived here. I was explaining all this to a friend of mine, with an emphasis on this Betty's unique vibration, and what it meant in terms of eternity." Lyle put one of his arms around her shoulders.

He continued, "After a few months had passed, my friend told me that he'd been doing a lot of thinking about this, and wanted to offer a potential solution that he referred to as 'absurdly ridiculous.' Of course, I was ready to listen to anything.

My friend backtracked a bit to where his 'revelation' took root. As I knew, his big interest in life, or should I say 'death,' is Quantum Field Theory. What I didn't know is that he had openly discussed my dilemma at one of his quantum think tanks. He said that there must have been at least fifty people there, including a few world-class theoretical physicists.

Of course, they were thrilled to ponder the situation, especially when they heard it involved Betty, that famous thought construct with the phantom vibration. They understood how difficult it would be for two 'people' with practically identical memories and physical characteristics to share . . . uh . . . me. They also realized that my constructed Betty had many years of unique, personal memories unknown to the original Betty. What a mess."

WARNING

The next few pages might seriously confuse and disorient you. This is where the science gets very heavy. I have included this for those of you who want to know how spectral theoretical physicists proposed to solve the dual
Betty dilemma. It's very difficult to understand and nearly impossible to believe. Good luck.

Lyle continued. "So . . . these Quantaholics, as I affectionately call them, decided that there was only one way to solve this monumental challenge: Both of the Betty's vibrations had to be merged together through some sort of resonance convergence that I found entirely perplexing."

"Jesus Christ, Lyle," I exclaimed.

"It gets worse," he continued. "There's a particle bundle theory that defines the vibration, itself, in terms of particle/wave duality."

"You completely lost me with that duality thingy," I muttered.

Betty, who was intently, let alone nervously, listening to all this, gave out a subdued laugh and said, "Explain that, my dear."

"To clearly explain particle/wave duality is well beyond my expertise. But I'll give it my best shot. All particles, which make up all the physical things we see, also act as waves. And waves are, well, wavy — they can stretch out and occupy many points at once. Now this is where it gets hairy. Particles are in their waveform until they are observed by human consciousness. At that point, the waveform is collapsed into a particle, thus creating reality."

"I remember reading a little about this in one of the quantum books I breezed through," I said. "It made less than no sense to me then, and I assumed it was just some impossible concept."

"No," said Lyle very assertively. "It's one of the foundation concepts in the quantum world, and has been proven, time and again, in labs all over the world. It's very strange. And very real."

"If you say so, Lyle. But what does any of this have to do with Betty? And how, in God's name, does it involve me?" I questioned.

"As I've been attempting to tell you, I really don't completely understand myself, but it's all harmless, and all worth a try." Said Lyle.

"What's going to be 'tried?'" I had to know.

When I spoke, I sensed a sort of hollowness in my ears. Actually, it had begun just a second ago when I was listening to Lyle. It was very annoying. Then I felt a slight pressure on the side of my face, and when I tried to raise my arm, it felt sluggish. Lyle and Betty were looking directly at me, which made me feel awkward.

Betty spoke in hushed tones. "Good morning, John. See you later."

So that's what it was all about.

I was waking up.

I should have immediately realized what was going on.

But . . . waking was always a little different.

I had to remember to ask them if I started to fade out when I began to wake. I wondered if I got all hazy and diaphanous . . . like a ghost.

Oh, well, there was obviously nothing I could do about it. And, obviously, I was left in a terrible position — right in the middle of an important thought. No, it wasn't just important, it may have defined the reason all this was happening to me.

So . . . this wasn't some freak accident. My visit to specterville had a purpose behind it. And the purpose was somehow related to Betty and quantum mechanics. And particle/wave duality.

But what if this was all for real? I had learned enough to realize that anything was possible, no matter how impossible it sounded. By this time, I had a very secure feeling that I could trust Lyle and Betty.

My initial fears had subsided, and I was confident that nothing was going to harm me.

Contrary to what I initially expected, my day zipped by, and for some odd reason, I was able to block most of this shit out of my mind. But I couldn't wait to go to sleep — couldn't wait to be back in that unearthly rain forest, my favorite location now for serious discussion.

That was the last thought that slipped by my acorn when I meditated myself back to the land of perpetual weirdness.

When I opened my eyes in my dream and saw that green paradise, I new my wish had been fulfilled. Now all I wished was to learn the truth . . . and possibly understand it.

"Hey guys, glad to be back," I said, as I stretched. I realized that waking up in dreams felt like . . . uh . . . waking up for real. Strange.

"Glad to have you back," they said in unison.

"Let's return to that cliffhanger you left me tottering on," I asserted.

"Ok," agreed Lyle. "You were wondering about how the quantum world involved you and Betty."

"As usual, I'm way beyond confusion," I admitted. "All this stuff about particles, waves, collapsing, vibrations and, Lord knows, what else has me . . . well . . . you know."

Betty was being uncharacteristically quiet and aloof. I could also detect some hesitancy on Lyle's part, which was also understandable. His life, or should I say death, was going to be radically changed, as well, and he didn't really fathom the esoteric science that could potentially provide the solution. So, I decided it would be best if I just accepted everything he was going to tell me, and didn't pressure him for detailed answers — answers I'd never understand to begin with.

Lyle fidgeted, calmed himself, and explained, "As I've told you, particle bundles are composed of four elementary particles that are held together by some infinitely powerful force. They are streaming all over the universe like all the other particles, but unlike any of them, they can remain stationery in one place. Sorry I'm repeating things you've already heard."

"Don't worry about that at all," I reassured him. "It's a good thing you're handling it this way, because it'll be easier to grasp what you're really trying to say."

"Take your time," said a slightly perkier Betty.

Lyle continued, "It's unclear how and when bundles enter our brain. They could be introduced in the sperm or egg. They could be captured within the womb anytime after conception, but before the eighth month of pregnancy. The latest theory is that when the brain ends its seventh month of development in the womb, a bundle is attracted to the brain by some electrical or chemical signal. The signal is declaring 'we're ready for you.' So far so good?"

"You're doing fine," Betty whispered.

Lyle continued, "The real miracle occurs at the beginning of the eighth month when the signature vibration literally springs to life. This is most likely due to chemical or electrical stimulation, or even the mother's conscious observance."

"Sorry to interrupt you," I said, "but, at some point later, I'd like to know how you all 'up here' explain bundles in terms of biological evolution."

Lyle rolled his eyes and answered, "Yeah, much later. Back to what I was saying . . . the real miracle is the vibration: That's what turns us into conscious, thinking human beings. The vibration emanates from the bundle — either from the four particles, the binding force, or both together. No one's certain about that."

"How far does the vibration extend?" I asked.

"It's infinite," Lyle said excitedly. "It's how we all know, instantly, where everyone else is in both dimensions, and what they're thinking. It's how I'm always aware of the sick Betty's condition, because it also communicates health. That's also how we know when a friend or loved one is about to die."

"Makes sense," I said.

"Now we're going to get to the sketchy part of all this," Lyle sighed.

"Oh, you mean everything so far has been clear and straight forward?" I asked.

Lyle shrugged his shoulders, half smiled, and continued. "The vibration is the key. My sick Betty has a normal bundle with a typical vibration. My Betty, right here, has no bundle at all, but she has a perfectly normal vibration. The theoretical physicists are certain that both of their vibrations have to be merged in order to end up with a single being with both identities. Since both Bettys are virtually the same, the result wouldn't be someone with a split personality. It would be a linear transition."

I just sat on my big fat cushion cradling my head in my hands. That was the most ridiculous thing I had ever heard. But I assumed that it was no more preposterous than quantum entanglement and particle/wave duality.

"Well, that sounds pretty straight forward to me," I lied.

"But wait," said Lyle, "It gets much much stranger. Theorists claim that if the source of both Betty's vibrations were to come into very close proximity, human observation might be able to collapse the resonance characteristics of both vibrations together, that is, if they're acting like some unique wave function."

"Honestly, you're making it relatively easy to understand, although it all sounds like science fiction to me. I'm warning you right now, I'm going to have some tough questions," I said with sincerity.

"I can well imagine," sighed Lyle.

"Before you continue, I've got one nagging question that needs to be answered right now." I said with impatience.

"Lyle and I both know exactly what your question is," surmised Betty. "You want to know what role we need you to play."

"That's right," I answered. "And . . . could 'my role' endanger me in any way?"

Lyle did his hands-in-pockets, walking around thing. "I'll answer your questions in reverse. As far as any danger is concerned, you've got absolutely nothing to worry about. Absolutely nothing."

Then, Betty added, "The only one facing anything dangerous is me. That's why I'm so nervous and upset. This special vibration of mine is both a blessing and a curse."

"I'm sorry," I said with deep sincerity. "I understand the problem."

"Thanks for your understanding," said Betty, "but you don't know the full extent of what can happen to me."

I could see that Lyle was also very upset. He never realized that all these wonderful years in this dimension with Betty could come to such a disastrous end. None of this was his fault, but he, none-the-less, felt responsible for her special vibration — the 'blessing and a curse,' as she so aptly put it.

"Please let me continue," said Lyle. "To clearly explain your participation, I've got to back up a little. Forgive me if I repeat some things you already know. Let's go back to that simple concept of particle/wave duality. When a particle is in its waveform function, it can be collapsed back into a particle if it is observed by human consciousness. Stay with me, John.

Our scientists think that all human vibrations, in both dimensions, are, possibly, related to waveforms. If this is true, they can be collapsed or altered by human observation. If, and this is a mighty big 'if,' both Betty's vibrations are closely aligned, the signature resonances may be able to be collapsed into one. With your observation."

"But . . . ," I tried to speak.

Lyle interrupted. "While I'm on a roll, let me finish. I'll probably answer whatever question you wanted to ask. For some completely unknown reason, live human observation has a far better collapsing effect than our naked particle bundles. Otherwise, *I* would do it myself.

For the last couple of 'human' years, I've been wondering how in the hell I could find a flesh and blood presence, like you, to perform this simple, possibly life saving, act. And then, by some miraculous accident, your unencumbered vibration, set free through meditation, became consciously aligned with mine.

If you hadn't meditated with Iwo Jima on your mind, and I hadn't been involved with Shorty on a memory trip to Iwo, this would never have happened. We wouldn't have been precisely aligned. Since that first moment I sensed your presence, I've been solidly locked into your vibration. That's why you can always occupy this dimension in a meditative dream state."

"So, this is really all about Betty," I stated.

"Yes and no," she suddenly added, in a calming voice.

Lyle took it from there. "John, it started off that way. We viewed you as a means to an end. But . . . I quickly got to know you, and actually enjoyed your company. Creating interesting experiences for you, and teaching you all about my dimension created unique memories for me that I could share with others. This was all an incredible opportunity for me, and I felt that you viewed it that way too."

"We definitely enjoy your company," exclaimed Betty. "It's been fun and gratifying watching you slowly understand and accept what you call 'spookville.' And your humor has really managed to take the edge off lots of sticky situations. As far as all the science goes, never forget that Lyle and I understand it only a little better than you do."

"Thank you both very much," I said, wondering if I was blushing in my dream.

Lyle broke a very thick silence. "There are three things left to discuss. The first is the danger that Betty faces. The second is bundle alignment, one of our key abilities that I've been meaning to tell you about. This will, by the way, knock your socks off. The third is our plan for your observance."

I could see that this was all coming to a head. And I was very happy about it. What a fucking relief. I had a feeling that I was going to gain new insights into this way of life that would answer many of my questions . . . or . . . create many more.

"John, are you ok?" asked Betty.

"Never better," I answered. "Just lost in thought."

"Don't think too hard," said Lyle. "There are several possible dangers that Betty faces. First of all, if the observance concept has no effect, both Betties will have to coexist as independent entities with nearly identical memories, thoughts, feelings, hopes, desires, and physical characteristics. And they'll both be vying for my love and companionship."

"Can I give you my opinion?" I asked.

"Of course," he said. "We welcome it."

"What you just described, doesn't sound 'dangerous' to me. Sure, it would be awkward, tense, aggravating . . . and all that kind of stuff. But 'dangerous?' — no. What's more, this Betty would be eternal and would, theoretically, survive forever with a thought construct of yourself. If there's any possible danger, it's to your original Betty's sanity."

"But," added Betty, "there is the danger that all of our feelings could be seriously compromised. I mean, all three of us have a lot to lose — me, the other Betty, and Lyle."

"I can see where Betty #1 could be very hurt and jealous," I said. "After all, you and Lyle have spent over 65 years together."

Lyle commented, "My original Betty would understand. She's all heart — just like my little Betty, here."

She continued. "You're making assumptions about the Betty you used to know. She's not the same person at all. She's lived her whole life apart from you, including having a husband and her own two kids. When she dies, she'll have to endure the shock of life after death, let alone the fact that you have duplicated her. She will be painfully aware that you belong to me — not to her. Betty and I are not identical. You have to accept that."

Wow. Was I hearing what I thought I was hearing? I think Betty had just released feelings that had been building up deep inside her for years. She was a lot stronger than I had ever imagined, and a lot more human than I had given her credit for.

"Look, you two, I'm sorry . . ."

Betty interrupted. "There's nothing to be sorry about. This was all bound to surface sooner or later. We have you to thank for helping us get down to the real truth. Getting all this out is the healthiest thing to do."

"What's the 'real' truth?" I asked. "If it's none of my business, I'll completely respect that. If you want me to vanish, that's fine with me."

A somewhat stunned Lyle broke his silence. "John, you're the observer, so you may as well observe everything. True, this is extremely personal, but I'll, or I should say, 'we'll,' respect your opinion. I'll admit that my head has been in the sand for some time, and I'm afraid I know what Betty means by the 'real' truth."

Betty stepped up to bat. "The person who's in most danger isn't me. And it's not the other me either. It's Lyle. His sanity, loyalty, self-integrity, and overall security could be put to the test. If the wave function, observation thing doesn't work, and I maintain my independence, Lyle will have to make the most difficult decision of his life and death. He'll have to choose between the two of us."

"He'll have to choose you," I exclaimed, without even thinking, without even acknowledging Lyle's presence.

"I would hope so," she quickly answered. "For all intents and purposes, I'm the real Betty. I'm the one who shares most of his most intimate and loving memories. But . . . somehow, he feels responsible for her, feels that he owes so much to her."

"If it wasn't for her," interrupted Lyle, "there would be no you. I owe her that much. I'll easily admit that you and only you are my life. But I've also spent a part of every day of my life (death) watching her grow old, waiting for the day when she could see me looking into her eyes and feel me holding her hand."

Betty threw her arms up in exasperation. "Let me ask you this?" she motioned to Lyle, "If Betty had known about life after death in this dimension and all it entailed, would she have lived out her life waiting for you? Would she have shunned relationships? And marriage? And children?"

"I doubt it," sighed Lyle.

Betty continued, "If she had had a good marriage and a husband she loved, wouldn't she expect to be with him when they were both here?"

"Of course," sighed Lyle.

Betty addressed me directly. "What Lyle doesn't realize is that Betty would gladly accept any decision he made. She would understand and respect his thoughts, feelings, and desires — just as he would do the same for her."

I just gave her an affirmative nod, and tried to get more comfortable on my pillow.

"Well, then, is there anything more to discuss?" she asked.

I scratched my head. "You had mentioned that there were 'several' dangers to Betty because of this collapsing wavy thing. Want to elaborate on any other problems she's facing?"

Lyle developed a perplexed look on his face, and lit a Camel. Thinking, in a cloud of smoke, he fumbled for the right words.

"This isn't easy to explain," were his words of wisdom.

"What else is new?" I retorted, as I adjusted my pillow.

Just thinking about my pillow did it.

I felt my real one under my head and woke up.

But it was the middle of the night. And I was wide awake.

So . . . I decided to watch a movie on my laptop: "Saving Private Ryan," an epic World War Two drama and one of my favorites. That did it. After about an hour, I couldn't keep my eyes open any longer. The zzzzzzzzs hit me like a ton of bricks.

I was so relaxed and refreshed when I woke up in the morning that I wasn't even pissed off at my Casio. I was almost compelled to apologize to the fucking thing for all the lousy stuff I had been saying about it.

There was still that nagging, rational, completely sane part of me that kept warning me not to believe any of this shit. It was my last vestige of self-preservation. I knew that, deep within my heart, I didn't believe what was happening to me, didn't believe that I was really part of some preposterous melodrama involving ghosts in some strange, afterlife dimension.

Every night before I went to sleep, a caring, considerate, and nurturing voice would tell me not to meditate. As I knew for certain, meditation was the key to this profound fantasyland. Or . . . the key to an authentic paranormal experience, some anomalous link or portal to an afterlife dimension that actually exists. I kept telling my inner skeptic that I had real proof that something otherworldly was occurring. The word, 'impossible,' didn't apply any more, not since I had read about quantum theory. What's more, everything I was experiencing went far beyond my level of imagination.

As far as I can tell, my rational and irrational sides got together behind my back and arrived at a compromise. On one hand, the normal skeptic in me was allowed to lurk in the background and occasionally punch me in the nose when I got too far out of line. On the other hand, the meditating, ghost-befriender in me was given free reign. I simply had to respect my brain's decision to establish a checks and balances system.

Trying hard to banish all this from my mind, my day kind of meandered along. It turned into a blur of thinking, almond croissants, double espressos, and then . . . my trusty acorn. How I loved that acorn. How that lingering skeptic in me wanted to give it to a squirrel.

CHAPTER 14
DANGERS ON OMAHA BEACH

I was back.

And just about ready to open my dream eyes to that enchanting, green panorama. But something wasn't right. Something felt wrong. Something smelled wrong. Something sounded wrong. I knew he had changed our location. But I also knew Lyle meant well, and always came through with an interesting place to visit.

When I opened my eyes, it was late at night, and we were on a seriously lousy beach. The mildly crashing waves made a soothing sound, but everything else was for shit.

The sand was course and rocky. The area was hilly. The moonlight revealed what I thought were some jagged cliffs. And the air smelled way too briny. The only signs of humanity came from some distant lights in what appeared to be garden variety beach houses.

I was just about to make some choice remarks when I noticed that Lyle and Betty were sitting very quietly, apparently lost in thought. Then they both looked over, and motioned for me to join them.

Lyle was his usual perceptive self. "Do you miss your monkeys and parrots?"

"Of course," I answered, very matter of factly.

"I'd love to watch those graceful monkeys again, and photograph them. Why don't you just give me the precise location, so I can return with my camera?" I asked, knowing the answer I was going to get.

"Nice try," Lyle said, with a pleasant laugh. He appeared to be coming out of his doldrums.

Betty stretched and yawned. "Maybe we'll get back there. I'd also love to return to the Sea of Galilee. That would be the perfect place to tell you all about Jesus."

"Jesus? What are you going to do? Show me where He walked on water?" I asked with a smirk.

"Yeah, if you'd like," she answered seriously.

"John," said Lyle, "I wouldn't even begin to expect you to figure out where we are now, but here's a clue. Betty was born here."

That baffled the shit out of me. Betty? Born here? I'm not a geography expert, but I made what I thought was an educated guess. "Excuse my ignorance, but if Wisconsin is on one of the Great Lakes, that's probably where we are."

"Way, way off," remarked Betty. "Lyle was talking about me, not the other Betty."

"I'm always confused about which one of you we're speaking about. Can't we just say 'Sick Betty' and Spooky Betty?'"

Lyle and Betty ignored that remark, although I felt it made perfect sense.

"There's no sense going around in circles," Lyle affirmed. "Betty was born in the exact spot where I died."

I let that sink in for a few seconds before responding. "That would mean, I guess, that we're in the Normandy section of France on the infamous Omaha Beach."

Lyle and Betty both nodded "yes."

I wondered why they really wanted to visit here. Other than Betty's surprise creation, the place was filled with horrible memories for Lyle.

"John," said Lyle, "you can't possibly imagine how hellish this place was when I died here. I'm sure you've read all about it in countless books, but words never captured the brutality and suffering."

"Do you believe in extreme coincidences?" I asked.

"Very much so," he quickly answered.

"Well, it's almost impossible to believe this," I said, "but last night, when I couldn't fall back to sleep, I watched the first part of the movie, "Saving Private Ryan," where Omaha Beach was stormed on D-Day."

"By the way," he added, "that's an excellent movie. It's as close as you can get to the terrifying realities of Omaha."

"How did you see it?"

"I see just about every movie that comes out," he answered. "And I attend concerts. And I read loads of books, magazines, and newspapers. And I watch TV. But now is not the time to talk about this."

"Later," I moaned.

"Later," he mimicked.

"Now," Betty said, "Let's talk about my waveform dangers so we can get out of this place."

Lyle began, "Yesterday, you helped us realize that 'danger' is too strong a word to describe Betty's situation if the particle/wave collapse doesn't work. There will be two Betties, but we'll all manage."

Betty gently clapped her hands.

"Hopefully," added Lyle, "If your observation manages to collapse or merge both of the Betty's resonances into one, then we'll have a single, complete identity. When the sick Betty dies and tunnels into this dimension, the other Betty will vanish."

"Let me ask a question, and then do some thinking," I said. "What if the sick Betty were to lose her vibration to this Betty?" I pointed to her.

"Impossible," answered Lyle. "Sick Betty is the one with the particle bundle, and vibrations cannot be removed except by some cataclysmic event."

"When we do this," I said, "how are you going to coordinate it? I mean, how do you know she's going to pass away during the few seconds I'm here each day?"

"We would have to do it before she dies," he informed me.

Betty added, "It could be five minutes before or five months before. But it can't be done the moment she dies or once she's here."

"We've been told that it can only work when she's in a coma," emphasized Lyle. "That's when her bundle and vibration will be the most receptive and vulnerable to outside stimulation. Once her bundle has been freed by her brain, it will achieve full power, which will be far too late for us."

Now I had to ask the one question I was afraid to ask. "How am I going to do the observing?"

"That's a two part answer," said Lyle. "And both parts take a fair amount of explanation. Why don't we take a break, do something enjoyable, and then get back to all the science. We could all stand to clear our heads. What do you think?"

"Good idea," I sighed. "All these theories have my head spinning."

"What a relief," spurted Betty. "Now I can get away from the science . . . and from the two of you."

I looked at her quizzically.

She laughed. "I think I know where Lyle's taking you, and I want no part of it at all."

"Now this is beginning to sound interesting," I said with glee.

Lyle had a sly look on his face. "We're going to share a very old memory cluster that most guys find . . . uh . . . repulsively exciting. It goes back around a thousand years."

"Before you tell me what it's all about, tell me why Betty's not joining us."

"I'll answer that with a few descriptive words," snickered Lyle. "Vile, disgusting, gory, revolting, chauvinistic, filthy, and nauseously bawdy."

"Sounds delightfully intriguing," I cheered.

" Nearly everyone experiences this at one time or another," said Lyle. "It's a classic memory. I think you have a strong enough stomach to endure this."

"For Christ's sake," I exploded, "tell me what it's all about."

Lyle continued, "It's a Viking victory banquet. They had just won some vicious battle, probably after plundering a small village. Their celebration combines every element of animalistic behavior. You'll never forget this as long as you live . . . in both lives. In fact, you'll never again criticize anyone's table manners, personal hygiene, health, or sexual preferences."

"Is this for real? Or some kind of a joke?" I asked.

"The worst thing about it is that it is absolutely real," claimed Lyle. "It's a perfectly accurate memory compilation from all the Vikings at the banquet. It must have been a very special celebration. As I've told you, everything in life is memory. And everything we all remember is photographic in all senses."

"So, when are we going?" I eagerly asked.

"Let me explain something before I answer that," said Lyle. "There are two ways to access the memories. It's your choice. We could experience the banquet as an overall memory compilation. That means we could roam around, and observe everything from any viewpoint. The other way would be to observe it from a single, personal memory, which would lock you into one of their minds. The advantage here is that you'd be able to accurately feel and taste everything exactly as it was. And you'd know that person's thoughts."

"What do you recommend?"

"I'd go the memory compilation route," advised Lyle. "That way, you'll have access to just about everything. If you're not completely disgusted, we could always switch to personal memory."

"Don't try the 'personal' way," urged Betty. "Some memories are better left ignored."

"But this is very educational," Lyle reminded her. "It provides valuable historical insights into human behavior."

"Lyle . . . when are we going?" I was getting impatient.

"You'll need some time for this experience," Lyle advised me. "So, we'll do it tomorrow. Get yourself very tired, and lay off the espressos. When you wake up here tomorrow night, we'll be back in the Amazon, and we'll leave from there."

"But I'm not ready to end this dream now," I told him.

Lyle lit another Camel, inhaled deeply, and let a long plume of smoke drift from his nose. He was in one of his pensive modes.

"For a split second, I'm going to take us back to D-Day," he announced with a grin.

All of a sudden, a big fat Kraut appeared out of thin air, with his submachine gun blazing at us. As a line of bullets sent small geysers of sand exploding all around me, I instinctively ran and dove behind the closest dune.

That was scary. My heart was pounding. I tried to flatten myself out on the sand. The sand felt coarse and damp. Then it turned soft and dry. It felt like my sheets. My sheets? Of course, I had woken up.

Chapter 15
Banquet of Horrors

I stretched, rolled over to find a more comfortable spot, and instantly fell back to sleep. That was the quickest transition yet. When I woke up to that familiar buzzing sound, I was in such a good mood that I didn't even curse at my Casio. All I did was gently pat the snooze button instead of slamming the shit out of it..

While I was showering, the previous night's events began to creep back into my mind. I had promised myself that I wouldn't begin to reminisce until I had at least a few sips of coffee.

One thing that really surprised me was how ugly Omaha Beach appeared to be. Maybe it was nicer with the sun shining, but I doubted it. While I was still motoring down memory lane, I realized how excited I was about my upcoming trip to the Viking banquet. Now that sounded really incredible, and was probably why I was in such a great mood.

Lyle had advised me to get extremely tired and to avoid the caffeine so I'd have sufficient Viking time. After walking God knows how many blocks, I was almost too tired to eat dinner. But I managed. When I finally climbed into bed, my book beckoned me. After a few pages, I couldn't focus anymore, and turned to the peaceful vision of my acorn.

Before I opened my dream eyes, I just laid quietly on my big cushion, listening to the rain forest. The breeze rustling the leaves, the ubiquitous monkeys chattering, and the peculiar birdcalls performed a symphony I'd never forget. Then I caught a whiff of Lyle's cigarette and came back to reality.

"Are you ready to go to Scandinavia?" he excitedly asked.

He stomped out his Camel, rubbed his gangly hands together, and broadly grinned. "In a second from now, we'll be right outside the front door to the banquet hall. Get ready for a wonderfully wretched experience."

• • •

Then, just like an abrupt scene change in a movie, I was standing in front of a large, roughly hewn wooden cabin fronted by a muddy country road. In the distance, I could see some vegetation — mostly evergreens, as far as I could tell. But my immediate vicinity was colorless and barren. And a dark gray, threatening sky didn't help the overall ambience.

The cabin, itself, was purely utilitarian. From my perspective, it appeared to be made of a combination if huge boards and logs, joined by thick metal strips. The closer I looked, the more I realized that real carpentry skills were involved. Especially with the construction of the door and its spectacular hinges. Strange, there were no windows to be seen, at least not on the side where we stood.

It was also eerily quiet. The only sounds I detected were from some distant animals and children. Just bleating, squealing, and giggling. It was so quiet by the door that I found it hard to believe there was a rip-roaring Viking banquet in progress right behind it. I attributed that to precise weather proofing skills.

"Before we go inside," he said, "I want to mention a few important things to you."

"What's on your mind?" I asked.

"I want to get you prepared for the experience lurking behind that door," he answered. "The first thing that's going to overwhelm you is the smell, and you won't be able to escape it. Never forget that it's just a sensory memory. You are not really smelling it. Don't let your mind play tricks on you. Nothing can touch or hurt you, although it will appear as real as real can be. Think of it all as a wide surround, high definition, holographic movie."

"Jeez, Lyle, I've never seen you so worried."

"I just don't want to see you get sick and/or frightened," he assured me. "Compared to this, Iwo Jima is a ride at Disney World."

"Thanks for the concern, but I'll be fine."

"In a second," he laughed, "we're going to pass right through this door just likes ghosts in a movie."

"I'm ready," I bravely assured him.

•••

I was wrong. Dead wrong. There was no way anyone could be ready for that smell. It was putrid times a million. Overwhelming. Lyle was simply too right. In the steamy, clammy, slimy atmosphere of this place, the pervasive stink seemed to invade every pore of my body and every thread of my clothing. It was, without a doubt, thick enough to ooze.

Honestly, it was a combination of sweat, abysmal personal hygiene, shit, urine, terminal halitosis, fermenting vomit, decomposition, blood, farting, and God knows what else. Any food smells, good or bad, were camouflaged by this thick wall of stench.

I turned to Lyle and complained. "This is horrible. It's too much for me to take. I can't go a step further."

"Get over it." he responded. "It's just memory. It's not real. Keep telling yourself that. We'll wait here by the door until you can handle it, but, if you can't, we'll leave."

"I'll try," I said, with increasing nausea.

Deep down, I knew that I had to overcome this one barrier. Although it was all memory, knowing it was real made it so much worse. I tried to hold my dream nose or breathe through my dream mouth, but neither worked. All these horrors were sensed by my mind, and I hadn't even scratched the surface. My whole being was crippled by the smell.

The only solution was to rationalize away the initial shock, and concentrate on all the visual treasures waiting to be discovered.

Without stepping away from the security of the door, I let my eyes and ears begin to wander.

The cabin, which turned out to be a large banquet hall, was filled with long wooden tables for communal style dining. (Once I witnessed how they ate, the word 'dining' no longer applied.) The wooden chairs appeared as though they were slapped together, the garbage, excrement, and vomit-strewn floor was earth, and the walls were void of any ornamentation other than large sconces with equally large candles.

In the center of the room stood an enormous, smoke belching, black iron oven beside a flaming roasting pit; there was a large hole in the ceiling directly above the cooking area for ventilation. Like everything else, the ceiling was all wood, with no ornamentation.

Taking my lead, and not yet closely investigating the lively crowd, Lyle and I began to walk around the perimeter. Boy, was this place huge, far more spacious than I had originally suspected. After passing many tables, I noticed a much smaller adjoining room way in the back. The closer we got to this area, the more I began to sense something bad.

Upon much closer inspection, 'bad' turned to unfathomable horror.

Lyle stepped in front of me, blocking my view. "Now that I think of it, it might not be a good idea for you to see this," he urged.

"Hey," I said, "If I managed to get past the smell, I can handle anything."

"This is worse than the smell," he warned. "It's human suffering — really bad human suffering. And it's not part of the banquet, which is what we really came to see. I never thought we'd walk all the way to this end of the hall."

"I guess you've been in this room before."

"Unfortunately, I have," he said out of the corner of his mouth.

"If you can take it, *I* can take it." I was adamant.

Lyle moved out of my way and said, "We'll see about that."

I hate to admit it, but I should have taken his advice. What awaited me in that room made me realize how little life was worth to these cruel, miserable heathens. I could have done without this, but it was too late for me to turn around. My morbid curiosity had been piqued.

What I saw when I approached that room will be firmly embedded in the deepest recesses of my mind for however many lives I live. The room was occupied by roughly fifty to sixty people — all women from about twelve to fifty years old, all bound by ropes and chains. These poor souls were all stark naked, covered in blood, and writhing in misery on the filthy floor. Quite a few of them were, obviously, very dead.

I was transfixed. I was horrified. I was in utter disbelief.

Upon closer examination, I noticed that many of them, dead and alive, were terribly wounded. Some had missing arms and legs that had apparently been torn or hacked off. Some had broken wooden shafts protruding from their abdomens and chests: arrows I presumed. From my viewpoint, two of them were even decapitated. The dead ones were the lucky ones.

I had seen enough. And I had only seen the ones closest to where I stood. When I tried to move, I felt paralyzed. This is not real, I told myself, this couldn't have happened. This was a scene from hell.

Thankfully, Lyle broke the silence. "Let's get away from here."

"And go back to the rain forest?" I asked.

"I mean let's leave this room." he answered. "As long as you've come this far, you may as well see the rest. Nothing will come close to being as terrible as what you've just witnessed."

"What the hell did I just see?" I asked, wiping a tear from my eye. "What was that all about?" I was still completely stunned and nearly sick to my stomach. If I hadn't been continuously reminding myself that this was a memory, I would have puked all over the place.

I was glad to see that Lyle was also deeply affected, and at a loss for words. He was very human, not cold and heartless.

He finally pulled himself together. "You've heard the expression 'To the victors go the spoils?' Those women are all that's left of a ransacked village. They're being used as sex toys, even the dead ones, and the few who survive will become slaves. As you can imagine, the men and boys were killed on the spot. By the way, the other 'spoils' are being consumed at this moment. The main reason for the raid was to steal food."

We both stood outside that nefarious room, shuffling our feet, staring at the floor, deep in thought. That was one fucking hell of a mood breaker. I had been looking forward to an interesting experience observing authentic Vikings in their original habitat.

Sure, I knew they were courageous raiders, maybe even a bit vicious, but I never knew they were so inhuman. Was I being naive? That's a big yes. I did my best to snap out of it. I wanted to see as much as I could before I woke up, because I'd never return, at least not in this life. And probably not in the next one either.

While I was thinking, I became aware of the cacophony of sounds coming from all over the place. Between the shock of the smells and those zombiesque women, I hadn't yet focused on the grating noises.

It was a mixture of roaring laughter, high-pitched conversation, hacking coughs, banging dishes, sneezing, spitting, explosive vomiting, farting, and other incomprehensible sounds. Just what you'd expect from animals like these.

"I guess your opinion of Vikings is... uh... somewhat changed," he said, lighting a cigarette.

"Yeah. 'somewhat' would be accurate," I mused. "I can't believe you brought Betty here."

"She came with me the first time I went, myself. But she only got as far as one of the tables. The stink really overcame her, and then she got a close look at one of the Vikings eating, and that did it. It was bye bye Betty. I stayed a while longer."

We slowly walked over to the nearest table, and I got my first close look at these vermin eating. I'll begin with some descriptions that are easy to stomach. The Vikings were a motley crew. Most were large, heavy-set men in a wide range of ages. It was difficult to tell how young or old most of them were, because they all had long, scraggly facial hair, including heavy beards and bushy moustaches. Most had ruddy complexions, other than the sick and direly wounded ones, which I'll get into later.

Their skin and hair were beyond filthy; they were smeared with dirt, blood, and foods of all description. I had expected to see them wearing colorful clothing, pieces of armor, and metal hats adorned with horns. Not the case. There were some metal breastplates, but most wore plain, brownish tunics made from a heavy, burlap type of material. Many wore brimless hats made from the same material. Their clothing was torn and also thickly caked with blood and food.

The first gentleman I observed was ripping very rare meat off a bone with his hands, and shoving gobs of it into his mouth. Pieces of it were stuck in his beard; dangling off one side of his moustache was a vein. His nose was very badly broken, with blood running down his cheeks, through his hair, and all over everything he ate. Delightful.

The guy next to him was shirtless. He had a long, open, oozing wound that went from his collarbone to beneath one of his breasts. It was obviously infected. He was eating a large chunk of coarse, dark bread, constantly dunking it in a wooden bowl, generously filled with a thick, amber colored liquid. Lyle told me it was honey. The honey was dripping over every inch of him and into the wound. He was constantly laughing, spitting slimy chunks of bread and honey on everything, including other people's food. No one seemed to care. Delightful.

I noticed that there were several bowls of this honey on every table, and the diners were dunking everything in it: all types of meat, fowl, fish, breads, vegetables, and even cheese. They were all a sticky mess, as were the tables, floor... eccch. I also noticed that their dishes were made of battered, heavily split wood.

Many of these gourmands weren't using plates. They simply ate directly from large serving platters. Most of them ate with their hands, but a few wielded daggers that they used to stab foods from the trays, and cut it while chunks were hanging out of their mouths. One thing they all had were drinking vessels shaped like a horn or a traditional mug. According to Lyle, they were sloshing down mead, buttermilk, and beer. Some of it actually found its way into their mouths; the rest was added to everything else spilled on their hair and clothing.

The next raider I watched was more pathetic than most. He had no use of his arms, undoubtedly the result of some spinal injury. His cohorts had put his food directly on the table in front of him so he could bend his head over and slobber it up. When he looked up, his face and hair were completely caked with food. He yelled something to the guy beside him who proceeded to pour honey all over his food strewn on the table. The guy stuck his head back down and resumed slurping.

Lyle and I walked over to a different table and had to step around a dead guy lying on the floor in a congealing pool of vomit. His demise must have been recent because his face was adorned with food and honey. I figured that if they ran out of meat, they'd probably roast him. He was already well basted. There were no more critically wounded at this table — just a herd of drooling, sticky slobs, one of whom was loudly belching.

The more we walked around, the more I realized how fanatically the ransacked village must have defended itself. Many of the Vikings had wounds that ranged from minor to obviously mortal. I saw one guy with a dangling eye, another with torn off lips, many with huge gashes, a compound fractured arm with the bone protruding through the skin, and several more dead and/or close to dead on the floor and slumped at the tables.

"I think I've seen enough," I firmly told Lyle. He looked at me, and issued a little nervous laughter.

"Are you sure you don't want to switch from memory compilation to single memory, and taste the food and drink?" he asked.

"You must be out of your fucking mind," I exploded. ". . . and actually sit at a table with those demons?" Right after I gently voiced my opinion, I heard boisterous, roaring laughter and cheering from a table about five rows down from me. I had to investigate before we left. I asked myself, 'How could anything be as bad as anything I've already seen?'

It wasn't as bad. It was worse. The table was surrounded by guys, sitting and standing. Lying on top of the food was a live, naked girl; her feet and hands were pierced with large nails that secured her to the table. She was drenched in honey, and these sadistic assholes were dipping their food on her body.

That was it. I couldn't take any more. And neither could Lyle. The next thing I knew, I was standing on the Mayan tomb in the lush beauty of the tropical rain forest. The transition was miraculous. Lyle began to mention something or other about the Vikings, and I abruptly cut him off.

"I don't want to hear anything about those demons ever again. It was just too horrible, but, I have to admit, it was a valuable learning experience."

"Not another word about it," he said in earnest.

"Lyle," I said, "It still amazes me that we can go places, and it feels exactly like I'm really there. I can feel the solid ground beneath my feet, but I can't touch things with my hands."

"It's all memory," he answered, "And everything is subject to special conditions. You always walk with your feet on something solid, because that's how the memory took place. Everything is also combined with your own memories and common sense. Have you ever walked on anything that didn't support your feet?"

"No."

"The best example of a multi-faceted memory compilation was your Cobra experience. You drove an imaginary car on an imaginary road, and heard and felt an imaginary engine. It was a combination of your own driving memories, reading road tests, watching Cobras in movies, plus the memories of tons of other drivers. That's how Iwo worked. And the bomber. And Hawaii. And everything else we've done."

I pondered all that, and then asked what I thought was a good question. "I hate to mention the Viking thing, but what if I had wanted to stand on my head and jump up and down? What if no one whose memory I accessed had ever done that?"

"Have you ever stood on your head? Have you ever jumped up and down?" Lyle asked.

"I see. I'd adapt my own personal memory. But . . . what if I had wanted to fly over the banquet hall, land on a two headed horse, and fight a fire-breathing dragon? That ain't in my memory or anyone else's."

"Can you imagine doing that?" he answered very matter of factly.

"Well . . . sort of," I pensively responded.

"Then you can do it, and your mind will fill in the missing pieces," he assured me.

"One last question," I said.

"Ask all you like," he responded.

"When we went to East End Avenue during that snow storm, I put out my hand and the snow passed through."

"That was a very different type of situation," he exclaimed. "We were in dream time in real time. Memories still work, but you're more at the mercy of reality."

"I couldn't touch the snow, but my feet didn't sink into the ground."

"Your memory told you what walking was like, so you thought you were walking on the street. In real time, you have no effect over objects. You couldn't pick up a stone, but you could imagine picking one up. You could also imagine making a snowball, but you couldn't touch the real snow."

"One more question." I sighed.

"Like I just said, ask all you want," he responded.

"I can now understand how we do mind trips by way of pure memory when I'm sleeping in my bed. But . . . how did I get from my bed to East End Avenue, and see something that I didn't imagine, and wasn't in anyone else's memory?"

"This is also pretty simple," he assured me. "As you know, from your point of view, I'm dead. That means my particle bundle is free to go absolutely anywhere in real or dream time, and experience anything. Your bundle, on the other hand, is locked in your brain. However, you have a signature vibration that I can communicate with when you're in a meditative state. So . . . I went to East End Avenue, and your boundless vibration accompanied me. Remember, your vibration is your bundle's link to all your senses."

"I thought you told me that you ghosts can sense everyone's vibration at all times." I was confused.

"Of course we can. Sensing, and reading, any live person's vibration is normal. Communicating with it is nearly impossible," he explained. "But . . . your vibration was released when you meditated, and interacted with my vibration during my Iwo Jima memory trip. That was nearly a miracle. From the moment our vibrations first connected, I've been able to reconnect every time you meditate. Now do you realize how extraordinary this situation is?"

"Let me put it this way," I answered, "I'm less confused, and driving carefully on the road to understanding. But I may get a few more flat tires."

"When that happens, I'll try to fix them," he said with sincerity.

"Lyle, where's Betty?" I asked, changing the subject.

"She's with a bunch of her friends," he answered. "It's a book group. They read all kinds of books and discuss them. Just like live people do."

I thought about that for a moment and asked, "Not to sound too stupid, Lyle, but how does she read these books?"

"Several ways," he said, as he sat down. "Obviously, she can't pick up a book. That's of no concern, because once anyone has read a book it's in their memory photographically."

"But . . ." I tried to ask.

"Please let me continue," he interrupted. "Everything you have ever read, whether it was a novel, a comic book, or a matchbook cover, is in your permanent memory — every last word. All Betty and her friends have to do to read any book is to access the memory from someone's particle bundle. And that applies to people in both dimensions."

"Hold it a second," I urged him. "I just read "The Monster of Florence." Does that mean I'm broadcasting that novel via my vibration?"

"Yes," he answered in a very animated way.

"Look, I remember the story, but not word for word."

"Yes you do," he quickly answered. "You remember every word and even the page number on which it appeared. Your brain is keeping it a secret from you."

"Huh?" I grunted.

"That's one of those things I wanted to tell you about — how your brain restricts your particle bundle's most amazing capabilities. Another thing I have to explain is the other way Betty and her friends read books. You'll learn all about that when Betty and I discuss your observance with you — you know, the wave collapse thing."

"How could I ever forget that? What's it got to do with reading books?" I was confused, as usual.

"It has to do with accessing information. Let's leave it at that for now," Lyle requested.

"Later," I said, nodding.

"Just one more thing," added Lyle, "What Betty and I are going to tell you will mark an important transition point for you here. You're going to learn about a very basic ability of ours that's going to turn your head inside out."

"Shit, Lyle, I hate when you do that. Can't you just tell me what it's all about now?"

Lyle laughed, obviously enjoying my annoyance. He told me to calm down and be patient. "You're going to wake up shortly," he reminded me. "That would really leave you hanging. Want to go a whole day with, maybe, half an idea in your head?"

"Ok, Ok, you convinced me."

Turning on my side, with my head resting on my arm, I peered into the distance at the endless tangle of green. Without warning, the fleeting glimpses of sky that shone through the canopy became abruptly darker. Instant gloom. As the breeze increased in intensity, a bolt of lightning caused the emerald ceiling to explode in a patchwork of vivid illumination. A split second later, a muffled clap of thunder formally announced a flash rainforest storm. The breeze became even more pronounced, and all animal sounds ceased, as if on cue.

Being a storm lover, I was enjoying every moment of this. I got myself into a more comfortable position, closed my eyes, and relished the security of my sheets, as I pulled them all the way up to my chin. As I awaited the soothing sound of pouring rain, I heard a dog barking, followed by a piercing car horn.

That was the smoothest transition from dream to reality since my adventures had begun. It was virtually seamless. I kept my eyes closed, and tried to imagine the glorious storm I had just missed. At least I was warm and dry . . . and fast asleep again in an instant.

Chapter 16
Mind Surfing

Well . . . that was certainly a learning experience. Sure, it was a lousy memory, but I was no longer shaken up. One thing I had on my mind after the Scandinavian debacle was whether I'd be able to eat again without a gagging lump in my throat. Devouring a large order of pancakes for breakfast put an end to that notion.

My mind shifted to what Lyle had said about Betty's book club. I began to wonder . . . was I a public fucking lending library? Were literary ghosts freeloading on my reading memories? The thought was very disconcerting. Thinking about these R.I.P. book clubs led me to an obvious conclusion. They, up there, probably have movie clubs, as well. I mean, why not? It makes perfect sense. If us humans have photographic memories, our vibrations would also be broadcasting 100% accurate movie memories. Shit, they'd even be enjoying any popcorn I had overpaid for. Gotta remember to ask Lyle if I'm right.

Fast-forward through the rest of an uneventful day, and I was tucked into bed, avidly reading the latest L.L. Bean catalog. A thriller. A real page-turner. A smorgasbord of plaids, fleece, and Gore-Tex. I was so completely bored that I nearly fell asleep before meditating. That would have been a real bummer.

* * *

I was back.

Once again, we had left the Amazon. We were on another beach. Not Omaha. Or Utah. Maybe Hawaii? I didn't have a fucking clue. But . . . it was beautiful. Not elegant or serene. I would have to describe it as powerful. We were on a small grassy plane, surrounded by large, jagged rocks, directly below a high, jagged cliff. The most intrusive feature was the water. Huge waves were pounding the narrow beach, one after another, their crests rapidly falling forward, exploding in the surf. The sounds were amazing: roaring, hissing, thundering. This was Mother Nature strutting her stuff.

I found it almost impossible to believe that there were actually people in the surf — brave surfers riding the monstrous waves, all dressed in glimmering black wet suits, crouching, standing and twisting on colorful boards.

"Northern California?" I yelled to Lyle.

"Not even close," he answered.

"You'll never guess," said a very animated Betty.

"Hawaii? South America?" I was fishing.

"Australia," yelled Betty, throwing her arms up, jumping in the air.

"That's nice," I said, "But why are we here?"

"Great place for a conversation," said Lyle. "Thought you'd enjoy it."

"Lyle," I said, "Let's get down to business. It's about time you revealed your plan for this observation I'm supposed to perform. This new lesson in weirdness I'm about to receive is going to take forever."

With her arms stretched out as though to balance herself, Betty pretended to surf over to me. "Don't worry, if Lyle wanders or gets too wordy, I'll jump right in," she insisted.

Betty continued to stand there... on her board. Then she jumped off, made a splashing sound, and lied on the grass beside Lyle. He was quiet, in his usual pre-lecture, pensive state, then he broke the ice.

"Here's how it's going to work when you observe. All three of us are going to go to Betty's hospital in dreamtime, but it will be real time there. We're going to go into her room, revert to real time, ourselves, and the three of us are going to align with her particle bundle."

"How," I asked, confused, as usual.

"I want to explain what we're going to do first. That's the most important thing," answered Lyle. "The 'how' part is a separate discussion that will explain one of the fundamental abilities of ours I have yet to reveal to you. I've been saving that one for last."

"Your show," I agreed.

Lyle continued. "My particle bundle will align with hers in her brain, and both your and spooky Betty's vibrations will be with me in as full a strength as possible. John, at that instant, you'll have to repeat your meditation process, and focus your thoughts on collapsing the two Betty's vibrations together. You'll be able to meditate in this dimension, as well as in your own."

"But what am I really supposed to think about? I guess I won't be using an acorn."

"Imaging seeing two small, almost vaporous wavy masses, each with the word, 'Betty' on it," he answered. "We're really guessing here. It's never been done. In your mind, you might also attempt to theoretically measure these imaginary masses. Measuring is the same as observing in the quantum world."

"I've got a simple, basic idea," I offered. "Since we want to collapse the waves together, maybe I should just merge both Betty vibes into one. So . . . in addition to thinking them together, I'll see them together. That will be my acorn."

"Perfect," exclaimed Lyle.

Betty nodded a very affirmative 'yes.'

"How long should this take?" was my next question.

"For as long as you can hold your concentration," said Lyle. "Whatever happens will probably be instantaneous, but it can't hurt to be sure. Your thinking will most likely go in a variety of directions while you're meditating, and any nuance could also perform the task. Honestly, this is a crap shoot."

"Not to complicate things, Lyle," I said, "but here's a crazy question. What would happen if your vibration collapsed into either one of, or Both the Betties? And . . . could my own vibration get collapsed into theirs? I don't want to wake up in the morning with a high voice and a midwestern accent."

"To answer your first question," said Lyle, "I don't think that could happen because all your thinking will concentrate on the Betties, not me. As far as you being effected? Can't happen. You are the observer."

"Effects don't usually jump between dimensions," added Betty.

"All well and fine," I answered. "But that's not entirely the case here. Good old hospitalized Betty is right here in my dimension."

"But, if the collapse does work, it most likely won't affect her until after she dies," offered Betty.

"That didn't accurately answer my question, but screw it," I said in a daze.

"Nothing bad's going to happen to you," promised Betty. "If any harm could possibly come your way, we'd never do this."

"Never thought I'd say this to a ghost, but, I believe you."

"One last little thing," I continued. "Betty, you mentioned just before that 'effects don't usually jump between dimensions.' Please explain the don't usually part."

"That's up to Lyle," she said. "It's all part of his alignment lecture."

"I have a superb idea," I beamed. "I'm tired of this place. Let's go somewhere else for the rest of the discussion, somewhere very green with monkeys."

"Let's finish this discussion here without any interruptions," said Lyle. "It'll be better that way."

"Lyle, you've got the floor," I said, with a wave of my hand.

There was a moment of silence, broken by a thundering wave.

Lyle continued, "John, as you know by now, you are what you remember. And most memory comes from experience. In this dimension, we after lifers share and compare memories with each other, and keep building our own memory banks. Since all memories are passed down, they will remain part of the human record hopefully forever. Remember, the Viking and Amazon memories, for example, have been passed down for around a thousand years. They're as vivid as they were the day they were recorded."

"But you also gain memories from live people in *my* dimension, right?" I asked.

"Yes," he continued. "We don't have to wait until someone dies to experience their memories. All of our vibrations are memory conduits. That's how Betty's book club works. To read a current bestseller, we don't have to wait for someone who read it to die."

"I was thinking the other day that there must be movie clubs that operate the same way," I added.

"You're right," he responded. "The same goes for concerts, operas, TV, ballets, sports events, the theater, museums — everything that can be sensed. But, with these types of things, there are two far more exciting way to access them. Since our particle bundles are free to go wherever we want, we can actually experience all these things first hand."

"Are you saying that you can attend movies? Car races? Museum openings?" I asked.

"Yes. Everything," he proudly said. "Look at it this way, any time you go to a movie, there are thousands of 'ghosts' enjoying it with you. It's like real life . . . in real time. When we watch a movie memory, it's done in what you call dream time. Like making a digital copy in a studio at lightning speed. Yeah, it's enjoyable, but nowhere near as much fun as being with a live audience. Just think about it."

Betty interrupted. "Books are different. So is anything that has to be read. Reading requires hands that can turn pages. That's why most books, magazines, newspapers and so on are usually read by memory instantaneously."

I was letting this sink in. By now I had become so immune to virtually anything amazing that I simply took all this for granted. 'Of course they can do all that stuff. They're ghosts,' I kept telling myself. Why even question any of it? But I knew they were ready to drop a new bombshell on me. Something was missing. With that thought, Lyle opened up.

"There's one more way to acquire memories and first-hand experience," he exclaimed. "It's actually the most fascinating and stimulating way of all to participate in the authentic human experience."

"Building that good old suspense, aren't you?" interjected Betty.

"He's just making it more colorful," I responded to her.

Lyle continued. "Please, just listen carefully. We have the innate ability to go into anyone's brain and align our particle bundle with theirs. This allows us to experience absolutely everything they're experiencing, along with their related thoughts and feelings. We can live moments, days, or years of anyone's life right along with them. It's our birthright, or deathright, as you would say."

I instinctively raised my hand to ask a question. Lyle gave me a 'but-make-it-quick' look and nodded.

"Doesn't this have an effect on the person you've... uh... invaded?"

"Knew you were going to ask that," he admitted. "Usually, there's no effect at all. The person, or host, is never consciously aware if one of us, or even ten thousand of us, is in alignment."

"Ten thousand?" I asked in amazement.

"Let me answer this one," said a suddenly alert Betty. "Let's say that Bruce Springsteen is going to be performing. Any number of us can align with his bundle, and become an experiential part of his nervous system. We see, hear, feel, taste, and smell everything he does, because we're part of his sensory system. We become him. That means we're singing, playing the guitar, jumping around, watching the audience, feeling the same rush he does."

"Betty," I exclaimed. "It sounds like you've been Bruce, yourself. Or maybe even Madonna."

Betty looked forlorn. "I've only heard people raving about their own alignment exploits. I can't do it. No bundle. At least my vibration lets me access memories, and experience live events. I can go to the movies, but I can't experience one through a live person in the audience.

"I've got just one question before Lyle, here, continues his Alignment 101 lecture. Does it get any stranger than this? Is there anything even more unbelievable?" I asked half seriously.

Lyle answered through a cloud of smoke. "Yes there is."

"But, it's a later thing. Right?" Why did I even bother asking?

Lyle cleared his throat, stretched, and continued as though I hadn't asked that question. "Think hard about that perfect example Betty just gave you. You can become anyone you want, any time, any place, any where."

"I get the picture," I said, nonchalantly. "I can be a race car driver, a skier, a sports hero, a serial killer, a hot shot lawyer, a porn star, even the President. Anyone I want."

"The possibilities are endless," he emphasized. "Here's another example that's more down to earth, possibly the best way to live again. Just select someone at random, and join their life for a week or so. How about this: Go into an incredible restaurant, choose a host you'd like to become, and align with him. Everything he eats, you'll eat. Everything he thinks and says, you'll think and say. Now it gets better: You can go home with him, and if he has sex with his wife, girlfriend, or mistress, you will too. It will all be as real as real can be."

"So . . . ," I said, "that means I could walk around, find some drop dead sexy girl, follow her until she meets up with some guy, align my bundle with his, and bingo. This certainly is heaven for stalkers, let alone voyeurs."

"Is that what it all boils down to?" asked a miffed Betty. "Of all the magnificent experiences to be had, you cheapen the whole thing by chasing skirts?"

As expected, Lyle was hysterically laughing.

I said to Betty, "Come on. When you get your own bundle, you'll choose some hot movie or rock star and do the alignment thing with his main squeeze."

"You're a pig. No, you're a fucking pig," she responded.

"I'm truly sorry," I said as sincerely as possible. "You know I was just kidding around. No harm was meant. I was just responding to what you said. And my response was in very bad taste."

Her anger seemed to subside. She withdrew her fangs, and even cracked the beginning of a smile.

"Apology accepted," she begrudgingly muttered. "I just hate the idea that you could spread the word in your dimension that this is 'heaven' for perverts. Of all the wonders you can talk about, alignment *sex* would be the only one remembered. Men would be jumping off cliffs like lemmings to get here. So . . . I take it back. You're not a fucking pig. You're just a pig."

"That, I can live with," I said.

"If you two are through," said Lyle, "Can we continue?"

I jumped right in with a question I'd been dying to ask.

"One of you, maybe both of you, had mentioned that this alignment trick usually has no effect on the victim. What's with the 'usually?'"

"First of all," began Lyle, "it's not a 'trick,' and no one is a 'victim.' Alignment is as much a part of life as eating and drinking. It's the natural way of things — an incredible capability that's almost like getting a second chance at life."

"Getting back to your question, John," continued Lyle, "let's start over. We can not purposely have an effect on anyone while we're aligned. But, since our powerful sensory source is aligned with theirs, information leakage can, and does, occur. The effect can be very minor. For example, out of nowhere, the host could detect a strange taste or smell that might last a second. Or they could feel chilly or too warm. Or they could impulsively order something on a menu that they weren't thinking about."

"No big deal," was my response.

Lyle continued. "It can get a bit more extreme. Take déjà vu, for instance. That's usually caused by an implanted memory that surfaces and causes someone to think they've been somewhere before. And there are lots of cases of people who either dream of what they think are past lives, or reveal unknown information during hypnosis. Some also discover that they can suddenly speak a foreign language."

"Jesus, Lyle," I exclaimed. "That's why so many people believe in reincarnation. They're just remembering other peoples' memories."

"Now you see," he answered. "Here's another example: Someone's doing a crossword puzzle, and they can't think of a word. Then, zingo, it pops into their mind. This can happen naturally . . . or . . . it could be thanks to one of us. I could go on and on and on with examples of info leakage. It's usually meaningless or beneficial, but never harmful, as far as I know."

"I'm going to have to give this a lot of thought," I said. "Plenty of strange things have happened to me and to people I know. Now, maybe I can put them into perspective."

"No one can get into your head and control you," he assured me. "But there are live people, referred to as 'sensitives', who know when we are aligned with them. It's very rare."

"Let me guess," I said. "These are the ones who go into a meditative trance, and speak the words of dead people."

"Yup. You could put it that way," agreed Lyle.

"I always thought that stuff was idiotic crap."

"It usually is," he said. "Most of the time, these 'psychics, clairvoyants, palm readers, and crystal ball readers' are frauds — cheap parlor acts that pray on gullible people. But . . . some are very real, and able to do incredible things. You'll learn more about this when we have our 'brain' discussion. I promise it's going to amaze you."

"Tell me now," I pleaded.

"Now's not the time," he asserted. "We have to finish what we came here for."

I agreed with him. It made sense. We had to complete the discussion about observing, collapsing, and alignment.

Betty broke her silence. "We've gotten a lot accomplished. There's not too much more to talk about."

"I've still got a few more questions," I said.

"You do?" intoned Betty. "Can't say I'm surprised."

I aimed my first question at her. "How and when are you going to know if my observance worked?"

"I was hoping you weren't going to ask that, but it was inevitable," said Betty, scrunching up her shoulders. "The answer is, we don't actually know. I'm guessing that, if my vibration disappears, something has worked."

"Something?" I asked.

She continued. "It could mean that your observance worked, and my vibration was merged with Betty's."

"Or?" I asked again.

"Or . . . it could mean that if my vibration and particle bundle are together as a wave form, the whole unit could have collapsed."

Lyle was getting extremely fidgety. I could tell that he wanted to handle this topic, because it was beginning to go badly.

"Can I please take it from here?" he asked.

"If you must," Betty answered reluctantly.

Lyle attempted to relax. "More than likely, nothing will happen. We came to that conclusion earlier. It's also a real long shot that Betty's vibration will simply vanish. Getting back to your original question, John, Betty's answer was correct. We won't know it worked for certain until sick Betty dies."

"But . . ." I said.

"Please let me continue," interrupted Lyle. "My physicist friend told me that the observance could leave both Betty's vibrations in an indeterminate state. Nothing would happen until Betty's bundle is released from her brain and tunnels into this dimension. During that immeasurably brief moment, when she is both here and there, the full collapse could occur. Remember, those are the unique conditions under which spooky Betty, as you refer to her, was created."

"Well . . . I'm glad you got all that cleared up," I exclaimed. "Unfortunately, it makes less than no fucking sense."

"I agree, and I'll say the same for Betty," admitted Lyle. "It's all theoretical, and all we have to go on."

"Lyle, there's something you forgot to mention," advised Betty.

"I know what you're thinking," said Lyle, with a Camel precariously dangling from his lip. "I was just about to get to that. There's a chance that, right after your observance, I might detect a subtle change in either one of or both Betty's vibrations. This could also mean that it worked, but won't be finalized until spooky Betty dies."

I looked up in the air and stated, "I'll simply have to take your word for everything you said, because I'm still completely confused, and I mean completely."

"I hate to ask," said Betty, "but do you have any more questions?"

"You've got to be kidding me. Do I have more questions? I could be asking you things until doomsday. But I'll keep it very simple. If my observance causes your vibration to disappear, what will happen to you?"

"Nothing at first," she answered. "I'll just become a very complex thought construct. You won't know the difference. But when sick Betty dies, I will re-emerge within her as a true human, and the thought construct will be . . . uh . . . deconstructed."

"A tiny bit less confusing," I assured her.

"Less confusing?" she asked with a laugh. "You're not a very good liar."

Lyle uttered a nervous little chuckle and said, "I can't believe what I got you into."

"We got you into," corrected Betty.

Lyle continued. "All you did was read about Iwo Jima, meditate, and fall asleep. Then we came along, proved that there's life after death, filled your head with all sorts of impossibilities, involved you in our anomalous, personal problems and now I, I mean we, have proceeded to take you beyond the point of utter confusion."

"Bet you never imagined that ghosts could be this scary," added Betty.

"Let me ask you this: when this... uh... revolutionary observance has been completed, which will probably be soon, will my time be up here?"

"First of all, your trip to the hospital will be soon," said Lyle. "Betty is deeply in a coma, but her life signs are stable. We can't afford to wait until it's too late."

"I would think that you'd want to do it immediately. A blood clot can kill someone instantly," I added.

Lyle continued. "I can tell what her body is doing from her vibration. Trust me on this. And trust me when I tell you that your time here will not be up right after your observance. We've got lots more to tell you, and more for you to experience."

"Great," I exclaimed. "I was afraid that . . ."

"Lyle interrupted. "However . . . your time with us will have to end in the near future. As you know only too well, this is seriously interfering with your life — more so than Betty and I expected. In fact, this is your life now — these few seconds every day have taken over most of your existence."

"That's bad, very unhealthy," added Betty.

"I can't argue with that," I reluctantly admitted. "I'll just enjoy it while I can.

"On a more positive note," Betty said very slyly, "you'll be with us full time before you know it."

"You call that 'positive?'" I laughed.

"You never ever believed in life after death," she exclaimed. "Now you've got plenty to look forward to. Just imagine this: You can be a devout pervert for 150 years."

"If you're gonna put it that way, I'll go along with the 'positive' angle."

With that morbid thought slowly sinking in, I felt myself beginning to drift. What a strange feeling. Of course, I knew what was happening; I was making the transition between dimensions—from fast asleep to peacefully awake.

Chapter 17
Preparing for the Preposterous

I glanced at my Casio and fell back to sleep. When it finally jangled me back to reality, I wondered if I could observe the buzz and collapse it into another dimension. Wishful thinking.

Everything after that was a complete blur until I had a few sips of coffee. I was human again. My morning vanished, and after a late lunch I spent the rest of the day walking and thinking about how far I had progressed since that first night on Iwo Jima. If everything to date was true, then I was part of some ridiculously impossible afterlife experiment that warped the imagination. That alone was almost too much to think about.

But, as usual, I pulled myself together, and completed yet another day. My last thought before I meditated into oblivion was whether I was going to open my dream eyes on the tomb, or find myself in some startling new place.

No more beach. No more complaints. Lyle had read my mind. Before I even began to open my eyes, I knew where I was. The distinctive scent of exotic foliage on the gentle breeze, the distinctive calls of mysterious birds, the wild chatter of frisky monkeys, the comfort of generously stuffed cushions, the untouchable treasures waiting below . . . all my senses screamed 'tropical rain forest.'

After a bone crunching stretch accompanied by a serious yawn, I glanced over at Lyle.

"So, Lyle, my friend, when do you think this observance is going to happen?"

"Soon," he answered, "but I can't be precise. She's in a deep coma, but her vital signs are strong. That Betty's a real fighter."

"Whenever you see her, I assume you align with her bundle."

"Of course," he responded.

"Then you must be aware of all her thoughts."

"I am. And they're all over the place. Being in a coma, heavily medicated, and separated from reality, she has no concise or focused thoughts. Just a jumble of memories. But . . . uh . . . well, nothing."

"But what?" I stressed.

"I'm certain she knows I'm there. And . . . she's trying to communicate with me."

"You mean she's talking to you?" I asked.

"No, not really. Between the coma and all the drugs, she's not thinking in a normal way. Her brain is only focused on life preservation. You know, involuntary things like breathing, blood flow . . . etc."

"As usual, you've got me a bit confused," I said, rolling my eyes.

"I wasn't finished," Lyle responded. Between her random, completely jumbled thoughts, I feel she's trying to communicate with me through some poetry she must have read at some time. Or . . . I could just be reading into things."

"Wishful thinking," I sighed.

"Exactly," he answered, lighting a Camel.

To break a rather uneasy silence that developed, I decided to mention something to that had been puzzling me.

"Lyle. I can't understand why you waited so long to tell me about your particle alignment abilities. You made such a big thing of it. So much drama and suspense."

"When you're right, you're right," he answered directly and sincerely. "At first I thought you'd find it beyond impossible. Then I thought you'd perceive it as a terrible, even frightening, invasion of privacy."

"Well, the thought of having people in my head, experiencing what I'm experiencing, definitely creeps me out." I admitted.

Lyle blew a long plume of smoke directly into the air, and answered me. "It's just life. Nothing more or less. This ability is as natural as your ability to read, or tell the difference between chocolate or vanilla ice cream."

"I'm going to want to try it with you, if that's ok."

"I was hoping you'd want to," he said. "Give some thought to what you'd like to experience."

"I'm starting to think about it right now. I'm also thinking... where's Betty? She seems to like this place as much as I do."

"What is it you find so intriguing about the rain forest? We could be anywhere in the world, including Purchase, Mohonk, and Mt. Lemmon. But you seem to prefer being here."

Before I answered him, I thought about that for a few moments. It was a question that I had also been asking myself. Why here instead of a location that would be oozing with great memories from the best times in my life? I knew why.

"Lyle, when I'm here with you and Betty in this dimension, I'm immersed in the incredible and the impossible. In order for me to actually believe any of it, I have to focus and concentrate. Just as all this mind blowing information is completely foreign to me, so is the Amazon. Of course, it's absolutely gorgeous, but it's a strange environment that I can't identify with. It stimulates no memories. In Purchase, Tucson, or any other place I could even remotely identify with, I'd be snapped back to reality, which would be counter productive."

Lyle was deep in thought, coiling his hair with a finger.

I added, "Did I make any sense?"

"Perfect sense," he quickly answered. "We'll leave those special places for your own personal memory adventures. I may throw you a curve once in a while, but we can always return here."

"Lyle, getting back to our most vital topic, what I don't understand is why we're waiting until the very last minute to do the observance. I'm hardly ever here, and it's not like you can call me on my cell, and tell me to get my ass over to the hospital. If she were to suddenly pass away, it would be all too easy to miss the opportunity."

"I'm well aware of that," he admitted, "and, believe me, I'm very nervous about it. The reason I'm waiting until the last minute is because my scientific friend advised me to. He said that the weaker she gets, the more the collapse is possible. And with my ability to read and interpret her vibration, I'll know when the end is near. But I'm not going to take any chances."

"Assuming this is going to happen momentarily, please take me through the observance steps once again. Now I'm getting nervous."

Lyle walked around, shuffling his feet, with his hands in his pockets. He was deep in thought.

"Get very very tired tomorrow," he urged. "When you open your dream eyes, you'll be in the hospital. The three of us will be there in our own dream time, but, it'll be real time there. Following me?"

"Just like on East End Avenue," I answered. "Any people we see will be in ultra slow motion."

"That's right," he immediately responded. "With all three of us standing by her bed, I'll switch us from dream time to real time. Then, I'll align with her bundle and access Betty's and your vibrations. At that moment, everything will go black, because you'll be in her head. Got it?"

"When you go from dream time to real time, I'll be entering the reality of my own world. That means I'll only have a few seconds to accomplish everything before I wake up. Can't this be done in dream time?" I asked.

"No," he flatly stated. "Sick Betty is in real time, so we all have to be. Our vibrations have to be precisely synchronized . . . so I was told."

I nodded.

Lyle continued, "Once we're in her head, try to lose all sense of yourself, and concentrate, through meditation, on both Betty's vibrations. You can envision these vibrations in any way you find comfortable. After you've observed the vibrations, try to merge them together in your mind. I was just advised that the simple power of suggestion could be as effective as collapsing the wave functions together. Alternate pure observance and merger until you wake up."

"It all sounds very straight forward," I assured him, trying my hardest not to laugh. The whole thing sounded completely convoluted and insane, but I was determined to go along with it and give it my best try.

"Tomorrow," Lyle continued again, "develop a vibration image early in the day, and concentrate on it every once in a while. You should be perfectly familiar with it before our alignment. As we discussed a day or so ago, when you meditate tomorrow night before you fall asleep, use the vibration images instead of your acorn, if possible."

"I'm not going to wait until tomorrow to develop an image," I announced. "I'll do it right now. The vibrations will be envisioned as small, vibrating rods. That will be easy for me to remember and manipulate."

"Sounds fine to me," he agreed.

Lyle stood up, and walked around the top perimeter of the tomb, puffing away, as usual.

"You feeling ok?" I asked him as he walked towards me.

"Fine. Just thinking about everything."

"There's a lot to think about," I added.

"Too much," he declared. "I wish Betty were here, right now."

"Since she's not here, I've got a question for you: a guy to guy thing."

"Hope I can answer it," he said.

"Just between you and me . . . do you really believe there's a creator behind all this?"

Lyle sat down and got comfortable on his cushion. For the first time since I had known him, he took off his decrepit shoes, and scratched his feet.

"Before you answer that question, I've got another much simpler one. Why do you scratch your feet? I mean . . . you don't really have any feet."

"But I do have feet," he answered with a smile. "In my head, or I should say, my mind, I'm just as human and alive as you are. Through old habits and memories, my feet really itch. That's also why I smoke. I have many memories of enjoying cigarettes; they calmed me and . . . uh . . . tasted great. I'm not hooked on nicotine, but I've still got the habit. You enjoy smoking your pipe up here, don't you?"

"Of course," I answered, knowing what he was going to say.

"While you're puffing on that imaginary pipe down here in the Amazon, you're really fast asleep in your bed in New York City."

All of a sudden, my pipe appeared in my hand. Of course, I started smoking it.

Lyle had a sly little glint in his eyes. "You never inhale that pipe, do you?"

"Never," I truthfully answered.

"Well, just for the hell of it, inhale some imaginary smoke."

I followed his advice, and began to cough terribly.

"See that," he said. "You're choking out of habit . . . out of memory. Now, I want you to imagine what would happen if I let the memories of all the vicious bugs that are really here creep and crawl into your dream."

I gave that a little thought, and instinctively began to itch over every inch of my body.

"Ok, ok, ok. I get your point," I declared, as he giggled away.

"Between your photographic memory, the immediate memories of others, and the endless field of knowledge, anything is possible. And if you need a non-existent memory to justify or support a situation, your mind will invent one."

I just sat there like some fucking moron, itching and coughing my ass off. And good old Lyle was enjoying every minute of it.

"Now I have a question for you, John. When you think about all these impossible wonders, all the miraculous things in both of our dimensions, do you think it's all one big accident? Or can you dig deep into your soul, and consider the possibility of a creator or, at least, some level of intelligent design?"

"That's been on my mind since we first discussed the subject. To accept either of those two 'possibilities' would smash my entire belief system to pieces. I don't think I even have the ability to accept it. I know I came close to being a believer before, but, the more I think about it, the more I gravitate to accepting nothing beyond chance and evolution."

"Everyone with half a brain believes in evolution," exclaimed Lyle. "Between the fossil record, DNA studies, and carbon 14 dating, all the proof is there. But there are just too many things that evolution doesn't account for. A prime example is the human race and consciousness. We couldn't have evolved to where we are in such a short period of time."

"About four or so million years?" I asked

"Roughly," he agreed. "But we've been barely civilized humans for only about twenty thousand years. By comparison, dinosaurs evolved for close to three hundred fifty million years."

"Yes, I know that," I answered, yawning.

"And then there's this small matter of the afterlife," Lyle continued. "What does that have to do with evolution? Wait a minute, I forgot to mention particle bundles. They're all over the universe. Where did they come from and why? They're amazingly detailed structures that enable all life and all consciousness in both dimensions. Intelligent design is written all over them."

"You make some excellent points," I admitted. "But 'points,' no matter how profound they may be, don't have the power to topple a belief system that's always made perfect sense to me."

"Forget about evolution," advised Lyle. "Let's go back to the beginning, and think about the big bang."

"A purely random event," I declared. "It's probably happened over and over again a trillion trillion times. But this time it got it right, and we went from amoebas to rocket scientists."

Lyle continued, "Maybe, but highly highly unlikely. The odds against that are incalculable — way beyond anyone's imagination. Let me give you an interesting comparison I once heard. Now, I know you're very interested in wrist watches."

"Very," I answered, without hesitation.

"Picture a highly complicated watch with many hands, multiple functions, and hundreds of minute parts — levers, gears, springs, jewels, pins, screws, bearings — that fit together with incredible accuracy. If you took all those individual parts and dropped them from an airplane flying at sixty thousand feet, what would be the odds against those pieces joining themselves together in the air, and precisely reassembling the watch before it reached the ground?"

"Totally impossible," I exclaimed.

"The odds are far better for that to happen than for the creation of this universe and life," answered Lyle, with a crafty little smile.

"Where the fuck did you hear that one," I asked in disbelief. "At a metaphysical barbecue?"

Lyle laughed, knowing full well that I was going to have that kind of a reaction.

"My science friend mentioned it to me. Said it's been verified by some of the top minds in physics."

While Lyle was talking, I was swatting at an imaginary fly or mosquito that was buzzing around my head. It was a 'no-see-um,' and very annoying. When I hit it, I came to a very scary realization: my hand was on my Casio.

Chapter 18
The Observance

Well, that was that. Another evening vanished into thin air. Right in the middle of an interesting conversation. Poof. Not a fly. Nor a mosquito. Just my pesky Casio. I had absolutely no idea I was waking up. And I don't think Lyle did either.

It took me all of a second to realize that this was not going to be a good day. I knew precisely where I was going to be the next time I opened my dream eyes. We were going to be at the hospital — the one dream experience I wasn't looking forward to.

Now I had to somehow endure all the hours until I could jump back into bed, meditate, and get my observance thing out of the way. Everything had been building to this moment; it was the reason why I was invited into this strange dimension, so I was told. But who knew for certain? Maybe it was a test. Maybe it was all just my imagination.

No. I couldn't honestly accept that. I had come too far, learned too many things, felt too many new emotions. This was very real, and I was part of it. In fact, I was part of something that could become an historical scientific event . . . up there, of course.

It was obvious that this was going to be a long, long day . . . an unproductive one, to say the least. I was certain that the coming evening's observance would be the only thing on my mind. How could I think of anything else?

The solution was obvious: I'd go to Borders, find an interesting book and spend the day reading. So that's precisely what I did. Of course, my thoughts always drifted to my coming quantum conundrum. When this happened, I concentrated on what I was supposed to meditate on during my observance. I'd see two little vibrating rods right next to each other, and merge them into one. Over and over again I did this. At one point, I decided to draw the scene I was trying to visualize. What an inspiration.

Using a pencil, I drew two lines about half an inch long and an eighth of an inch apart. As I stared at them, attempting to picture them vibrating, I took my thumb, and rubbed in all directions over the pencil lines. This smudged the lines, and joined them within a cloud of diaphanous graphite. Perfect. The vibrations appeared to merge through an optical illusion. Now I had an image that I could repeat over and over in my mind. It was a great acorn substitute.

After finishing my dinner, I walked around a bit, pensively puffing on my pipe, freezing my ass off. When I finally got home, I was thoroughly tired from all the reading, thinking and worrying.

As I washed up for bed, the thought occurred to me that this night's dream was going to be extremely short, maybe only a couple of minutes. Then, I'd have another day to go through before finding out if there were any tangible results from my observance.

My meditation on the cloudy, converging lines went perfectly. In record time, I passed out cold.

Before opening my dream eyes, my first recollection after meditating was the cocktail of smells: Alcohol. Disinfectant. Cleaning fluids. Musty old magazines. Wilting flowers. Sickly sweet air fresheners.

Then my ears perked up to the symphony of lonely sounds: Muffled voices. The soft whimper of some crying. The intermittent squeaking of wheels. The beeping, whooping, and hissing of machinery. Distant moaning. Shuffling footsteps. An unanswered telephone. A hawker on a late night infomercial.

I didn't even have to open my dream eyes to know exactly where I was. As planned, as feared, and as anticipated, I was in the hospital. I was in a tiny area whose borders were defined by an all-around draw curtain. There was a bed, a small night table with a lamp, flowers, box of Kleenex, and a few personal effects. Hanging on the pale yellow wall was a bevy of blinking electric monitoring equipment.

Beside the bed was a tall, thin metal stand holding two transparent bags with drip solutions. Plastic tubes from the bags, and wires from the electronics, all converged at one destination: the shriveled, little old lady lying perfectly still on the bed. It was Betty.

She looked so peaceful lying there in a coma. All that moved were her nostrils, gently flaring with each labored breath. I had expected her to have a waxen, death-like complexion, but, surprisingly, her pink cheeks made her appear quite healthy. The closer I looked at her, the more I realized that she bore no resemblance to the young, lively, spooky Betty I had gotten to know so well.

I was so completely focused on her that I hardly noticed Lyle and Betty standing close beside me. Sheer determination was written all over Lyle's face. Apprehension was written all over Betty's. My face was probably a combination of both.

Lyle tapped me on the shoulder, and motioned his head towards sick Betty. "We have to align with her right now. I brought us here in real time, because I thought the jump from dreamtime could have possibly woken you up. You ready?"

"Very," I answered with no hesitation.

Instantly, everything went black, the blackest black I had ever experienced. And all the sounds abruptly vanished. Maybe it was just my imagination, but I could have sworn I heard the faint beat of a heart. But I didn't have time to dwell on it.

Without a moment's thought, I began to meditate, switching back and forth between just observing the vibrations and merging them together . . . just as I had done so many times the day before. Knowing that I was going to wake up shortly, I concentrated harder than I had ever tried before, using will power as much as visualization. That's most likely what kept me asleep far longer than any of us expected. I was mesmerized, probably close to being in a fucking trance.

After what seemed like a long time, the intense black slowly dissolved to tinges of gray. Then it grew a tiny bit brighter, revealing the late night landscape of my room. I had woken up with my eyes wide open. What a totally weird sensation, but not unexpected, considering where I had been and what I had been doing.

I glanced at my clock, and squinted to read the time. Only 1:40 AM? God, it was early. I rolled over into a far more comfortable position, closed my eyes, and realized that I was in a very happy, peaceful mood, confident I had performed my observance beyond expectations.

What a load had been taken off my mind. Lying there, I first realized how tense I had been. My nervousness and apprehension had been growing exponentially ever since those earlier days when I had initially learned of my . . . uh . . . responsibility in this . . . uh . . . impossible dimension. I even remembered being frightened. But now I could relax; it was all history — the whole fucking thing.

My next thought was an obvious one. Was my observance successful? I realized that it was ridiculous to think, let alone worry, about it. I'd get my answer to this soon enough — that is if they even had an answer, which I doubted they did. Unless I was wrong, which was a distinct possibility, neither Lyle nor Betty would know for certain until sick Betty died. And who the fuck knew when that that would happen? Today? Tomorrow? In five years? The suspense was going to be murder, especially for Betty.

Slowly but surely, I managed to get all those thoughts out of my mind and fall back to sleep. The next thing I remember was my Casio buzzing me back into consciousness, and the thought of a steaming hot café con leche that was patiently awaiting me at Juan Valdez.

Finally, with caffeine sailing through my system, I felt like a human being again. Inevitably, I began thinking again about my spectral friends and that cute little old lady. I mean, how could I avoid it? This had become the dominant thing in my life. There was no escaping it. The rest of my day was uneventful and just zipped by. Luckily, it wasn't cold enough to prevent a nice long walk, which I thoroughly enjoyed. All things considered, I was in a great mood by the time I got under my covers and began my nightly meditation. Just for the hell of it, instead of concentrating on my trusty old acorn, I used the merging vibrations again. That worked wonderzzzzzz.

...

I sensed a tapestry of twinkling bright light dancing on my eyelids. I heard some hysterical chattering and squealing, and a long, high-pitched squawk. I felt a very slight breeze, and the sticky lick of humidity. I smelled the pungent perfume of rotting vegetation. I imagined rows of golden figurines sleeping in hidden vaults. I knew precisely where I was.

And I was glad to be back.

When I opened my dream eyes, I saw Betty sitting on the edge of the tomb with her back to me, her blond hair gently moving in the wind. Without even slightly turning, she began to speak.

"Good morning, John. Oh ... I guess I should say 'good evening.'"

"Hi, Betty," I exclaimed with exuberance. "It's been a very long day."

She just sat there, staring off into the distance, still facing the other way, not moving a muscle. And I began to worry. Was something wrong? Did yesterday's efforts fail? Had she been disfigured by some quirk of fate? Had the fire gone out of her effervescent eyes? And where the fuck was Lyle? This was a piss poor time for him to be absent. Shit.

"There's nothing to report," she declared, startling me.

"You mean we don't know if it worked?" I asked, with trepidation.

"Too early to tell," she said with resignation.

She was still facing the opposite direction, so I remarked, "Gee, Betty, it's nice talking to the back of your head."

That did the trick . . . inspired her to turn around immediately. And it was the same old Betty: warm smile, sparkling eyes, expressive eyebrows. I was relieved. Nothing to worry about . . . well . . . almost nothing.

"Sorry," she sighed. "I've got a lot on my mind, if I even have a mind. Lyle and I have no idea how long it's going to take to find out if our adventure last night worked. We may have to wait until Betty dies."

"Do you feel or sense anything different?" I asked.

"No. But it's easy to imagine things if you think hard enough about it." She flicked her hair off he face, and proceeded to stare at her feet.

"I wish there was something I could say or do, but . . ."

Betty interrupted. "You've done more than your fair share. You performed your observance, and surprised Lyle and I by how long you were able to concentrate. That was, by far, your longest dream."

"I managed to get myself extremely tired." I said.

"How'd you do it?" she asked.

"I read voraciously all day," I answered.

"You should do that every day," she advised. "You'd always have plenty of dream time."

"That would be kind of unhealthy. I've got to do some walking."

She scratched her head, looked right at me, and said with a laugh, "Then read books about hiking."

"Well, at least I didn't collapse your sense of humor," I said with a grin. "By the way, where's your significant other? I figured he'd be here to discuss last night's experience."

"Believe me, he wanted to be here," she readily admitted. "But . . . he thought it would be more important to remain in the hospital with Betty."

"I guess that makes sense," I said.

"He's trying to find out if any of my unique, personal memories were duplicated within her bundle or vibration. These would be memories that only I share with Lyle."

"Wouldn't that be a simple thing for him to access if he aligned with her?" I asked.

"Normally, yes," she answered. "But thanks to her coma and medication, her mind is somehow all jumbled. It's got Lyle very frustrated . . . and upset."

"Sorry to hear that," I said, with gobs of sincerity.

"Lyle's going to take a break pretty soon," she said. "There's nothing more he can do."

"Could you have picked up any of sick Betty's personal memories?" I asked, thinking that was a reasonable question.

"No," she firmly answered. "I already have all her memories. Lyle has always kept me up to date. I'm supposed to be her duplicate, you know."

"Oh," I uttered, completely at a loss for words.

"John, would you mind if I changed the subject?" she nearly pleaded. "This is all just too much for me now. If Lyle detects anything, he'll let both of us know."

"I completely understand, and I'm sorry I was pushing you for answers."

Betty smiled. She just sat there, closed her eyes, and rubbed her temples. Abruptly changing the subject, she asked, "The last thing you were discussing with Lyle was whether or not he really believed in a creator or intelligent design. Is that right?"

"Yup," I answered. "He had just given me his wrist watch analogy. If you dropped a completely disassembled watch, hundreds of tiny pieces, from an airplane, the odds against the watch reassembling itself while falling are not as great as the formation of the universe and life."

"I've heard him talk about that," said Betty. "It's a startling comparison. The odds against us and the universe being here are just too enormous to ignore."

"I agree that it's impossible to ignore, but that's no justification for a creator. It still could have been by chance. The universe may have come and gone more times than the human mind or any computer could ever calculate."

"That's a possibility," she agreed. "But a remote one. Using forever as a benchmark still doesn't account for all this to have happened by chance. Any one thing, or any ten things, that have made life possible could have been by chance. But certainly not everything. This universe was definitely created for conscious life."

"Look, I absolutely respect your beliefs, and your facts and observations are very compelling," I assured her. "But I am just too well set in my own belief system."

"We're at an impasse. But I like the challenge," she hissed.

"Let me ask you this," I said, licking my lips. "If there's a creator, then who created him . . . or her?"

"A single intelligent entity could have been created by chance," she proclaimed, "Or, a life force could have always existed within an eternal primordial vacuum."

"Bull shit," I exclaimed. "What a freakin' cop out."

Both of us were distracted by hysterical squealing and loud squawking. It appeared as though a monkey had seriously pissed off a couple of birds, then grabbed a handy vine and swung away . . . business as usual in the deep jungle. The lull in our conversation was very welcomed, since it was venturing into profound disagreement. We were both rock solid in our beliefs. I wished Lyle had been there to intervene. Betty walked around a bit, then sat down again in front of me.

"Some beliefs originate in your heart," she said, looking deep into my eyes. "I believe, as does Lyle, that our universe is the product of intelligent design, for the sole purpose of creating conscious, self aware life forms."

"But, I . . ."

"Shhhhhhh," she interrupted. "Everything points in that direction. Just shut down the left side of your brain for a couple of minutes, and listen to me. Please."

"Fair enough," I acquiesced, even though this was left brain territory.

"About a trillionth of a second after the big bang explosion, everything fell into place for the eventual creation of conscious life. If anything had gone even slightly differently, from the temperature fluctuations to the formation of elementary particles to the first spark of gravity, there wouldn't even be a universe. At this point, the odds against any of this happening are one in a zillion zillion."

"Zillion?" I asked.

"Shhhhhhh," She interrupted again. "After hundreds of millions of years of more impossible odds, our galaxy formed out of nothing more than swirling dust and gasses. Fast forward to the galaxy you now recognize. If our sun wasn't precisely as it is — size, composition, temperature . . . etc. — life could not have formed, let alone evolved. If the earth was not the exact distance it is from the sun, or wasn't in its precise orbit . . . no life. If the other planets were not in their precise orbits in relationship to the earth . . . no life. What if all these things I just said worked out perfectly, but the earth didn't develop an atmosphere, let alone a precise mixture of gasses?"

"No life," I answered. "I get it."

"I don't think you do," she continued. "Without intelligent design, how do you account for three possible dimensions for life, particle bundles, signature vibrations, quantum entanglement, and 427 Cobras!"

"Well, if you put it that way, a very benevolent God did have a hand in creating the Cobra. As far as everything else goes . . ."

Betty stood up, put her hands on her hips, and aggressively loomed over me. "Seriously, there are just too many, as you would say, fucking miracles, for all this to have been created by chance."

"I've read that astronomers predict that there are many more planets just like earth in the universe. How do you account for that?" I asked.

Betty sat back down, laughing. In fact, she found it difficult to stop. Once she calmed down to a mere giggle, she asserted, "Thank you. Thank you sooooo much for proving my point. How could chance be responsible for that? Impossible."

"What I . . ."

"Shhhhhhhhhhhh. Let me continue," she hissed. "There's no way dumb old chance could have been responsible for potentially hundreds or maybe even thousands of earth-like planets; some probably with life, possibly even conscious life."

"So you believe in aliens? Little green men?" I asked, with a wink.

"Chances are, there's intelligent life throughout the universe," she said with conviction. "Some may be green. Some purple. Some may breathe methane. Some may be twenty feet tall. Who knows?"

"Assuming you all know everything, then you must know whether the earth has ever been visited," I asserted.

"There's no conclusive proof," she assured me.

"Conclusive? That means . . ."

"Shhhhhh," She continued, "Thousands of people claim to have seen flying saucers and aliens, and many claim to have been abducted."

I had to interrupt. "Ok . . . well, since you're dealing with people's photographic memories, wouldn't it be 'conclusive' one way or the other?"

"Not necessarily," she answered. "Hallucinations, drugs, hypnosis, and the collective conscious can trick the mind, producing false, unnaturally induced memories that seem perfectly real. That's an unfortunate problem when it comes to studying any kind of phenomena."

"Well that's for freakin' sure," I shouted. "Which means you can't prove shit."

"That's an astute way of putting it," she stated.

"Let me ask you a theoretical question. If there's a creator, why bother with life other than ours?"

"Because the creator may not have known which life form was going to evolve into conscious, self aware beings, so he or she seeded the potential for life across the whole universe. Remember, particle bundles are everywhere."

"Let me chew on that for a second," I sighed.

"Your second is up," she said in an instant. "Don't think of the creator as a mythical God. That will lead you down the wrong path. Think of a conscious life force that exists all over the universe — one that created everything in order to produce and sustain life. This force wouldn't give a God damn what the life was like; it would only care about its potential."

"Now that we've evolved, do you think this 'life force' is satisfied? Its goal has been accomplished."

"Impossible to answer," she declared. "Maybe there are other creatures who've made better use of particle bundles. Maybe there are other types of particle bundles that can only be utilized by non-carbon based life forms. It's the big mystery, and the possibilities are endless."

"One final question. Could there be more than one creator or life force?"

She gave me a completely cockeyed look and said, "You don't even believe in one, so why ask about more?"

"I was just . . ."

"Just nothing," she interrupted. "Could be one, or could be a hundred. Doesn't matter. You're missing the point. Can you at least understand why Lyle and I believe in intelligent design rather than plain old dumb chance? This is all I'm asking you to consider."

"Please . . . respect the fact that I have to mull this over," I said. "You've said a whole bunch of convincing things that might, just might, make me sort of change my mind."

"There's one more interesting piece of information that we have to tell you about before you can make a sound decision," she revealed.

"Oh no, 'interesting?' Sounds very mysterious," I remarked.

"Interesting . . . and . . . mysterious," she assured me.

"I'm ready. Let's hear it," I exclaimed.

"Wait a second, I said 'we' have to tell you," she reminded me.

"What?"

Betty continued, "Lyle has to be here when we talk about this. He wants to judge your reaction."

I thought about this for a couple of seconds. "I know that he's hooked into my vibration right now. Won't he know all my reactions, and everything I think and say?"

"Yes," she answered. "But it's not the same as being with you in person. He's going to want to talk to you about it too."

"Ok. I guess there's no point in arguing with you."

Betty had a little smirk on her face, and said, "None."

"At least answer this," I said, "Is this piece of vital information going to blow my mind? Scare the shit out of me? Alter my life? Make me carry a sign saying 'The Creator Is Coming?'"

Betty rolled her eyes and shook her head. "For all I know, it might do all of that to you," she said, looking me right in the eye.

"One last question: Is this something I could find in a science book?"

"You don't quit, do you?" she remarked. "The answer is 'no.' It's something that only we know."

"Just you and Lyle?"

"As usual, I'm being left in suspense. Lyle had built up all kinds of drama before he revealed particle alignment to me. Then, when I didn't fall on the floor from amazement, he realized that, by this time, I wouldn't be blown away."

"What we're going to reveal to you is not at all scientific, and has nothing to do with our special abilities. It's a matter of history," she assured me.

Somehow, I felt a sense of relief. "That I can wait to learn about."

Betty seemed relieved that I was finally off her back. We were right in the middle of one of those awkward lulls in conversation. While I was searching the canopy for my favorite monkeys, Betty broke the thickening ice.

"I wanted to ask you about . . . what's wrong? You look strange," she observed.

"I'm fine. But didn't you hear that terrible noise? And I could swear that I hear people yelling. Is that possible? Could it be part of this memory?"

Betty laughed, waved her hand and said, "Bye. See you tomorrow."

CHAPTER 19
FLYING BACK IN TIME.

Wham. "What? Betty? What's going on?" She was no longer there. Neither was I. A car accident in front of my building. People screaming and cursing at each other. "You fucking moron." "Hey, get a cop." I heard it all. No wonder I had woken up.

It was around 2:00 am, and I couldn't fall back to sleep. So, I turned on the light, picked up my book, and began to read. All it took was half an hour of reading a terrifically boring book to do the trick. Lousy books definitely come in handy. Fast asleep again.

My day was a typical one. Lots of thinking. Lots of worrying. But at least it flew by. After a healthy dinner of hummus and pita, and a long, invigorating walk, I nose dived into bed. To make my journey to dreamland a swift endeavor, I returned to that piece-of-shit book I was reading. It worked better than sleeping pills. I turned off the light, meditated on a shimmering, translucent acorn, and . . .

I was asleep and awake . . . somewhere?

I wanted to attempt to guess where Lyle had taken me this time. The surface I was sitting on was hard and flat, so, I wasn't on the tomb, or a beach, or a lawn: it was a floor. In an enclosed space. But where? I sensed nothing familiar, except . . . wait a second . . . the air. There was something about the air. Something familiar about the scent.

As I slowly opened my eyes, chills of joy ran up and down my spine. 'Thank you, Lyle,' I said under my breath. He had brought me back to my childhood home, and I was sitting on the floor in my old room, right beside my cherished old model airplanes. I didn't know what to look at first.

Rotating gradually, I gazed at everything in that wonderful room, overflowing with memories. Directly to the right of the airplanes were my bookshelves, stacked high with all sorts of memorabilia from my childhood.

Next, I studied my large, red, Formica desk that was piled high: school books; a mess of papers; assorted, chewed-up pencils; a ragged notebook covered with doodles; a swivel neck lamp; bottles of model paint; brushes; glue; x-acto knives; and what looked like two small airplanes under construction.

Coming full circle, I was gazing, once again, at my airplanes, and enjoying the scent of diesel fuel. That was the first familiar smell I had detected. Earlier, when I had shifted slightly, I had also picked up the mingling scents of paint and glue coming from my desk. I was *really* there. In my room. With all my old stuff. I had traveled back into time.

As I picked up what I dearly remembered as my favorite plane, I was blown away by the reality of everything. I was fast asleep. But, I was wide awake in my old room, holding objects I hadn't seen in close to fifty years. The idea of a full sensory photographic memory was beginning to make sense to me.

So . . . as I had always done when I handled one of my planes, I began flipping the prop on the beautiful little engine, listening to the sucking, popping sounds of air being compressed and released by the tiny piston. What a precise piece of miniature equipment. It was an .051 cu. Inch E.D. Bee, a diesel engine made in England in 1960. The model it was attached to was a Guillows Trainer, a rugged airplane with a wingspan of roughly 20 inches. And it was a graceful flyer.

Instinctively, I reached for my flying kit that was on the floor, between this and another plane. It was a small box with a can of diesel fuel, a fuel pump, a spare propeller, a screw driver, pliers, a spinner wrench, repair tape, an x-acto knife, and my trusty Jim Walker U-Reely.

This device was a handle that contained twin rolls of very thin wire that you could reel in and out. These control lines attached to the plane, allowing you to make the plane go up and down with the gentle flick of the wrist. The plane would fly in a circle around you, firmly held in orbit by the control lines.

With the plane in one hand and the flying kit in the other, I stood up and headed for the door. It was a beautiful day, and I was going to fly the plane in my old back yard.

Making a right turn, I walked down a fairly long hallway. When I came to the circular staircase to go down, I stopped to study an old, framed photograph that had been hanging on the wall for as long as I could remember. I had always enjoyed this shot of an ancient truck, with its huge, all-metal tires. The driver always seemed to smile at me.

When I reached the bottom of the staircase, I walked through the dining area and out the side door of my long gone home. The day was bright and clear; the temperature, mild; and I was tingling over every inch of my body.

As I walked towards the back yard, I passed the jungle gym where I had met with Lyle for what seemed like ages ago. Then I passed our garden, almost grabbing a handful of cherry tomatoes. Although my mouth was watering, I decided to indulge later. 'Got to get this fucking plane in the air.' I murmured to myself.

Once in the yard, I put everything on the ground, attached the metal leads from my U-Reely to the plane, and pressed down on a lever to unlock the control lines. Holding the handle, I walked out fifty feet of the twin lines, flipped the lock back in place, and placed the handle on the ground. Now, all I had to do was return to the plane, and get the engine started.

Sitting back down, I squirted a tiny amount of fuel into the cylinder and flipped the prop. Between the high pitched screeching of the engine, the strong smell of diesel exhaust, and the heavy vibrations running through my arm, I was in heaven. I can't even begin to describe how many memories were released. I was twelve years old again. Incredible.

By this time, I had expected Lyle to appear, because it required two people to fly a control line plane: one to release it, while the other held the handle, and flew the plane. All of a sudden, he was sitting beside me with one of his shit-eating grins.

He chuckled mildly, and began examining the plane. Holding it very carefully, he flipped the prop as though he knew what he was doing. From his delighted expression, it occurred to me that he may have had experience with flying models. Turned out I was right.

"Nice plane, John," he exclaimed. "And the engine is very interesting. It's a diesel, isn't it?"

"Yup," I answered. "It's from England . . . an .051 E.D. Bee."

"I once had a model plane. So did most of my friends back then. But the only small engines available where I grew up were spark ignition. It was a very popular hobby."

"These days, it's really a grown up hobby," I informed him. "Kids are too busy with their computer games. Everything's changed."

"Believe me, I know," he said. "Once in a while, I go to model plane meets, and watch the action. I can't believe how the planes, engines, and control systems have changed. It all seems so complicated."

"Computer technology has invaded the hobby," I added. "And thanks to air and noise pollution restrictions, many people can only use electric engines. And you know what that means."

"Yeah." He said, shaking his head. "No gas, no great smelling exhaust being belched out from twin pipes, and none of those loud, bone rattling sounds."

"A travesty." I declared.

"Glad we've got this in common," he said, handing the plane back to me. "Now, let's get this thing into the air."

So . . . I filled the tank, squirted some fuel directly into the cylinder, and flipped the prop. Vroooooooommmmmm. Then I handed the plane to Lyle, ran out to the control handle, got into position, and motioned him to launch. And what a perfect launch it was. He tossed the plane into the air evenly and precisely level. His experience was immediately evident. As soon as the plane began tugging on my arm as it arced around me, I was flooded with even more memories. At first, I kept the plane low and even with the ground, trying to re-familiarize myself with the art of control line flying. Luckily, it came back to me right away.

With a long, misty plume of exhaust smoke trailing my roaring little airplane, I put it through all its paces for a few minutes until it ran out of fuel. Then I had to carefully glide it down so it could belly land on the grass as gently as possible. My landing was superb. After letting the engine cool down for a couple of minutes, I refilled the tank, but let Lyle re-start it and rev it up. Once again, it flew like a dream, and brought me back to a wondrous time in my life. As soon as I landed it again, Lyle excitedly shouted to me.

"John, can I fly it? Please?"

"Of course," I responded.

Within a couple of minutes, the model was back in the air, flying in a tight circle, with Lyle expertly controlling its every move. Watching him was nearly as much fun as flying it myself. Lyle was so into it that he just had to fly it again. As he landed it perfectly for the second time, I wished that Betty could have been there. She would have enjoyed every minute of it.

"Lyle," I said, "I've got another plane that we absolutely have to fly. You'll love it."

"What kind of a plane?" he excitedly asked.

"It's a Stuka dive bomber with a much larger diesel — an E.D. .015 Super Racer with twin stack exhausts, rear carburetion, and a bearing mounted drive shaft."

"Sounds fantastic," he answered. "But . . . did you say it was a Stuka?"

"That's what I said. And it's got a 40 inch wing span."

"But, John, that's a Nazi plane."

"It's just a model, Lyle, and I was young when I built it. Everyone built German fighters and bombers back then."

"Yeah, I guess so," he answered a bit sadly. "But did you put any swastikas on it?"

"No. Not so much as one," I answered proudly. He seemed relieved.

It was a beautiful, calm day, so both of us just sprawled out on the lawn with my plane resting between us. The grass smelled great, and so did the burnt diesel fuel that was smeared all over the engine and wings. Then I had an idea.

"Hey Lyle, want to taste something really delicious?"

"Always ready for that," he quickly acknowledged.

I jumped up, ran over to the garden, and picked a bunch of sun-ripened cherry tomatoes. Lyle loved them, and as we gobbled them all, I noticed a strange smirk on Lyle's face.

"What?" I asked with concern.

Lyle reached his tomato dripping hand over to me and said he wanted to shake my hand.

"What's on your mind?" I asked.

"I wanted to congratulate you," he said, as he released the iron grip he had on my hand.

"For my perfect landings?"

"No, you moron. I'm trying to get serious. It's for the great job you did observing."

"Thanks," I answered. "But Betty said there was no indication that it worked."

"That was a half lie," he admitted, with a broad grin.

"What do you mean by that?"

"Directly after your observance, I detected a change in Betty's vibration. Actually, it was a significant change. Her vibration decreased in intensity. This is a startling result."

"Why didn't she tell me?" I asked, incredulously.

"I wanted her to have a serious discussion with you before we said anything. That's why she continued the creator discussion."

"I'm missing the point," I argued.

"We wanted to see if you noticed anything different about her. Anything at all."

"As far as I'm concerned, it's the same Betty. Nothing different about her. Is that good? Or bad?" I asked with great concern.

"That much we don't know," he admitted, as he lit a Camel. "But it's far better than having nothing happen at all. When or if sick Betty comes out of her coma, I may be able to tell if she has assimilated any of 'spooky' Betty's personal memories."

"Yeah, Betty mentioned something about that to me," I recalled.

"Sick Betty's mind is a mess now," he noted. "And I'm afraid it has something to do with all the drugs they're giving her. I'm not going to hold my breath about this, but her vibration has also changed."

"With all this on your mind, I'm surprised you were able to get into this flying thing with me."

"Are you kidding me?" he asked, with his head obscured by a dense cloud of smoke. "This was great. It took my mind off everything else."

"What's the next step?" I asked.

"Got to keep an eye on both Betties. See if there are any changes. Maybe sick Betty will reveal a memory she shouldn't have."

"That would be incredible," I exclaimed.

"That's putting it mildly," he answered, through another cloud of smoke.

"Where's Betty now?" I asked.

"She went to see a movie with some friends," said Lyle. "Model airplanes are strictly for guys."

"Are you thinking what I'm thinking?" I asked, as we both stared at my plane.

"I'll fill up the tank," he declared, sitting up very quickly.

Obviously, we both wanted to fly my plane again, and lose ourselves in the innocent joys of childhood.

From the moment Lyle reached for the fuel pump, everything became a blur of fun and excitement. Not another word was spoken. We communicated through the scent of diesel exhaust, the high-pitched howl of the tiny engine, the banking and diving of the plane, and the precisely executed belly landings on the manicured lawn. As a final reward, we indulged in as many cherry tomatoes as we could strip from the vines.

"Lyle," I said, "No matter what you tell me, there definitely is a heaven."

"In this case, as in many others, I completely agree," he happily responded. "This is all one of life's wonderful miracles that transcend both of our dimensions."

"But I don't feel as though I'm asleep in another dimension," I said with certainty. "This is as real as real can be."

"Do you want to know why?" he asked.

"Why?"

"Because it is real." He assured me. "It's all a natural part of life. There's nothing amazing or strange about it."

"I disagree with you. It is amazing."

"And you still believe that this and everything else is here by chance?" he slyly asked.

"Oh, shit," I announced. "Back to the good old creator stuff."

Lyle blew a smoke ring and heartily laughed. "I'll let you off the hook. No more talk about that for now."

"Just for now?" I asked.

"Well . . . it might come up again, you narrow-minded bastard," he joked.

"Oh yeah. Of course. I'm in for another dose of this indoctrination. Now that I think of it, Betty told me that we're going to have a Jesus conversation."

"It's an interesting story," Lyle assured me. "Even you will find it uncanny and very thought provoking."

"You can't reveal it here and now?" I asked.

"Betty's got to be part of it. I promised her. She's always been much more involved in religion than me," he said apologetically.

"I understand," I professed with reluctance.

As I mulled things over, I picked up the airplane and methodically flipped the prop. Lyle was carefully watching me, with another one of those mischievous looks on his face. You could almost read him like a book, only, this time, the book turned into a fantasy I'll never forget. He gently took the plane out of my hands, and began to pump fuel into the tank.

"Again?" I asked with joy.

"I've got something . . . uh . . . interesting in mind," he answered, with a note of mystery.

After he started the engine, he asked me to throttle it up to its ultimate level of power, which I gladly did. Taking my time with the tiny controls, I brought the engine to its top rpm capability. After giving Lyle a thumbs up, he topped off the tank with one last squirt of gas. Before I knew what was happening, he handed me the plane, quickly got up, ran over to the control handle, and signaled me to launch. He wanted to fly the plane again . . . at least that's what I thought.

I tenderly tossed it into the air, watched him execute one full circle at only around five feet off the ground, and experienced an extraordinary, somewhat disorienting sensation. The next thing I knew, I was aboard the model plane. 'Holy Shit,' I cried. He had put me in the tiny cockpit, which was roughly the size of a thimble. Holy

227

Shit. A tiny version of myself was actually flying in my fucking model. It was all too real.

Peering out the left side of the cockpit, I saw the glinting metal control wires leading out fifty or so feet to the handle in Lyle's steady hand. As the plane circled, he brought it to as high as it would climb while tethered.

I was terrified.

My stomach was in my throat.

It was more exciting than anything I had ever experienced.

Then Lyle did the unimaginable.

He disconnected the control lines.

And waved goodbye.

I was on my own . . . flying by thought, memory, instinct, and imagination. My nerves were stretched to their limit.

WOW. Shit. Fuck. Damn.

Lyle didn't realize it, but the angle he released me at had me heading straight for the barn on the far end of the field.

The plane was rapidly approaching.

I froze.

"I can't control this fucking thing," I screamed into the air.

"Use your head," I urged myself.

"Don't be an asshole and crash," I moaned.

"Steer with your mind. Your mind is the control handle."

It worked. Thank God.

With only a few feet to spare, my rear flaps went up, the tail tipped down, and the plane jerked up and over the barn. Close call.

My altitude kept on increasing, which was exactly what I wanted, because my yard was framed by very tall trees. The last thing I wanted was to have to steer through branches. I wasn't ready for that . . . Yet.

When I learned how to mentally access the rudder, I steered back over my yard, and looked down at Lyle. He was jumping up and down and waving.

Once I had come to terms with my fear and gurgling stomach, I began to seriously test the sensitivity of my flaps, rudder and throttle. They were all extremely responsive. While I got myself accustomed to this new form of craziness, I kept the plane high, level, and in a broad arc.

The view was spectacular; I had never seen, or even imagined, my home from this angle, so I assumed I was accessing some pilot's memory. I have to gain altitude, I thought to myself. At that moment, my engine's exhaust port, which was right in front of me, spit a small stream of fire, and the plain streamed up at least another two to three hundred feet.

It was all so unnerving. But all so breathtaking. Knowing full well that I couldn't get hurt, I settled down, rolled the plane into a steep, banking turn, and looked straight down. Shit. I could see every angle of our property: my house; the garage; the colorful flower beds; the front, back, and side yards; the jungle gym, the vegetable garden; the barn; the driveway, with a late '50s car in it; and, of course, Lyle. He was looking straight up, shielding the sun from his eyes.

Now that I was flying with skill and confidence, I decided to leave the general area, and fly over to my old elementary school, which was only a mile down Purchase Street. Giving a moment's thought to my gas situation, I realized I could never drain the tank. Well . . . at least I hoped I couldn't.

My most direct route, as the crow flies, took me directly over Manhattanville College, one of our closest neighbors. Originally a large monastery, the college and surrounding property, was, and still is, truly magnificent: gentle rolling hills; enormous, ancient Oaks; dense forests surrounding three sides; white marble statues in many sizes; beds of flowers; and several large, stone buildings that always reminded me of castles. From my vantage point in the cockpit, few things appeared to be familiar, but I could see students and Nuns strolling from building to building.

Dropping my altitude to treetop level, I flew over the front gates that led directly to Purchase Street. As I made a wide, sweeping left, I radically lowered my altitude to roughly four feet off the ground, and roared towards the school. By flying close to the road, the sense of speed increased dramatically, which made it all the more thrilling. A car was coming directly towards me, tempting me to fly right through it. Instead, I had fun swooping up and over it at the last second. WOW.

So . . . there I was. Flying down my old neighborhood street in what was, in essence, a small toy airplane made of flimsy balsa wood. But I had proudly built it. And had chosen and mounted the miniature diesel engine that was madly howling and vibrating just a few inches in front of my face. Electrifying. And scary as all fucking hell. The ribbed, aluminum cylinder was easily twice my size. And the exhaust port was belching flames, burnt oil, and a furious white haze that passed by my face by only an inch or so. Was this what it was like to fly a vintage fighter plane? I couldn't help but wonder.

Completely lost in outrageous wonder and joy, I didn't realize how close I was coming to my old school, which was a right turn into a large oval driveway. When it dawned on me, I quickly pulled up my rear flaps, sending the plane skyward at a ridiculous angle, above and beyond the trees. Banking right, as hard as I could do, I zoomed directly over the ball field.

Still gaining altitude, I banked to the left, flipping the plane on its side. From that point, I dove to about two hundred feet from the ground, flew over the school, banked through another tight turn, dropped altitude, and sailed about ten feet over the crowded driveway. Obviously, I had gotten there just after final dismissal.

Trying to see if I could identify any of my old friends, I repeated this crazy maneuver two more times. For all I knew, I, myself, could have been in that mass pouring out the doors. My sister, too. But no one seemed familiar.

Feeling confident about my flying abilities, I kept the plane low, flew sideways through a row of trees while simultaneously banking back onto Purchase Street. Fantastic. Unbelievable. Impossible. Returning home was a snap. Approaching Manhattanville, I soared higher than ever. From that height, I could even see my house and yards.

All of a sudden, my engine began to cough and sputter, spitting more oil than ever on the wings. I knew what was happening. My fuel was spent. When the engine died completely, everything became eerily silent, save for the wind whistling over the wings and frozen prop. From the altitude I had gained, I knew I could glide the distance to my house.

With little trouble and just a few adjustments, I nosed onto my property, sailed to the right of my house, buzzed over the jungle gym, passed maybe a foot over the vegetable garden, felt my tail slice into the ground, and smoothly belly-landed about sixty feet from a broadly grinning Lyle.

Stunned, and in another world, I just sat there in the cockpit, and let everything fly through my mind. I kept asking myself, 'Did I just do what I thought I did? Did I fly my model airplane to Purchase School and back?' It was way, way beyond my imagination. My 427 Cobra experience paled by comparison. All I knew was that I now owned this memory and would cherish it forever. Even if it was some kind of an insane hallucination, my life had been changed — for good.

The next thing I realized, I was back to my normal size, sitting on the lawn in front of my plane. Resting my elbows on my legs and my hands on my face, I silently and intently stared at this dream machine. I had the chills. My eyes were tearing. I was immobilized. I was waking up from the dream of a lifetime.

Chapter 20
The Qumran Conundrum

Well, that did it.

That was the one.

The best experience to date.

Lyle will never be able to top it.

It was astounding.

Way beyond outrageous.

Even if I never got back to that mysterious dimension, I'd be satisfied knowing that I had achieved the ultimate fantasy. After I shut off the alarm, I just rolled over on my back, closed my eyes, and tried to relive every moment of my flight beyond reality. But it was real, at least it seemed that way, and that's all that counts.

No dream had ever been as spine tingling. From whizzing high over my old home to the g forces I felt from those hard, banking turns, the effect sent chilling vibrations through every molecule in my body. I could still smell the exhaust that coated my face, and I could still feel the wind whipping through the hair I once had.

When I finally landed my fat ass at my usual table at Juan Valdez, I floated back down to reality. Boring. Really boring. You know, Lyle was right. This dreaming stuff had become my life. After all, how could anything (in my dimension) possibly compete? Impossible. I didn't want it to come to an end, but I knew it definitely had too. Just not too soon, I hoped . . . not until I learned everything I wanted to know and had a few more wild experiences.

Finally, my day came to a close. When I meditated, I focused on a tiny piston traveling up and down in a tiny cylinder. Beautiful. Perfect. Sheer bliss. Solidly asleep.

Uncomfortable. That was my first response before I opened my dream eyes. Obviously, I wasn't on the Mayan tomb. It was hot, but very dry. Smelled like the ocean. Sort of. I didn't even attempt to guess where I was, and opening my eyes didn't help either. Lyle and Betty were sitting on some low, flat rocks in front of me, waiting for some kind of remark.

"Guess," uttered Lyle.

"Try," urged Betty.

"The desert," I answered.

"Well that's pretty damn close," remarked Lyle.

Taking a few minutes to look around, I realized that, wherever I was, it was desolately exotic. A desert, but more than a desert. Odd. We were in a valley surrounded by tall, heavily eroded cliffs. They were striated and rounded, almost in the shape of beehives. There was no vegetation to speak of, and the sand was extremely coarse. Somehow, I sensed that the area reeked of history.

"Any ideas?" quizzed Betty.

"I'm completely stumped," I admitted.

"We're accessing a memory that goes way back in time to about 900 AD," announced Lyle.

"We're just about half a mile north east of the Dead Sea," said Betty.

I let that sink in, then asked if there was anything special about the place, assuming we were here for a reason.

"Look very closely at those cliffs," advised Lyle. "See those dark areas?"

I squinted to where he was pointing. "Yeah. I think I see them."

Betty perked up. "Those are the Caves of Qumran."

"Huh?" I responded.

"You tell him," Lyle said to Betty.

Betty got herself comfortable on the cushions that appeared out of nowhere.

"Between 150BC and 68AD," she said, "this area was occupied by a group called the Essenes. It was these people who predicted the coming of the Jewish Messiah. Know who I mean?"

"Jesus Christ, Betty. Give me a little credit for something," I said, with a pronounced smirk.

She stared hard at me, scrunched up her nose, and cleared her throat. "These Essenes were getting all set for this blessed event through fasting, prayer and purification. Then along came the Romans, and put an end to their actions — an end that you would not call polite."

"Keep going," I said. "You've got my interest."

Lyle chimed in. "Many, many years after the Romans, the story of this very unremarkable place picked up again. In 1947, a young Bedouin shepherd had lost one of his goats up in those hills. While he was searching in the caves, he stumbled upon one of the most important discoveries in history."

"I think I . . ." I tried to speak.

"He found a long lost cave full of jars," he interrupted, "with 190 linen wrapped scrolls."

"Of course," I blurted. "The Dead Sea Scrolls."

"Right," yelled a very excited Betty. "Just think about this: If the memory we're experiencing is from 900AD, then those scrolls are hiding right up there in those cliffs at this moment. Aren't you thrilled?"

"Tickled pink," I answered.

It was pretty obvious to me why we were here. They wanted to talk about Jesus. Before getting into anything heavy, I 'slightly' altered the subject.

"Lyle, I wanted to thank you for making a real pilot out of me yesterday. It was way beyond amazing."

"I thought it would knock your socks off," he beamed. "I have to try that myself. Believe it or not, it's an experience I've never had."

"One more question before we get into the topic du jour," I was stalling. "Anything new with the Betty situation?"

"Nothing new," answered Lyle, with a sigh. "But I'm absolutely certain that she's aware of my presence, and, on some level, it's what her thoughts are focusing on. There's definitely a poem or song in her mind that's meant for me. It's got to be something she recently read or heard. It's really baffling me."

"Do you have any thoughts on this, Betty?" I asked.

"This isn't supposed to happen," she flatly said. "So I don't know what to think. But I believe Lyle. He's not imagining it. If he hadn't had this feeling before your observance, I'd say that's what caused it. We just have to wait, and see where it goes."

"Time to completely change the subject," I bluntly announced. "It's pretty obvious to me that we're here for my Jesus education. A couple of times, you've mystified me by hinting at some special secret about Him. And you ended our 'creator' conversation on this note. As they say, the ball's in your court."

Lyle cleared his throat, and paused for a moment of thought. I had a feeling Betty was going to take the lead, but she was waiting for him to speak.

"Well," he began, "you're right. But, first, we just want to find out, in a nutshell, what you know about Jesus."

"Just off the top of your head . . ." Added Betty.

"For many years, I assumed that He was a figment of everyone's imagination — someone who was invented to provide a foundation for the whole Christian religion."

Lyle and Betty gave me an understanding nod.

I continued. "But . . . after a lot of reading, thinking, and soul searching, I've come to believe that he was, in fact, a very real person. He was a highly intelligent, charismatic individual who taught and delivered sermons that emphasized love, compassion, equality, and fair treatment for *all* humanity. Of course, in those turbulent times of severe repression, that took extreme commitment and bravery. It's no wonder that he was finally denounced, tortured, and crucified. "

That certainly caught Lyle and Betty by surprise. They were very animated and obviously pleased by what I had said. No doubt, they had been nearly certain that I was going to say some detrimental things about good old J.C. Then . . . I continued . . .

"On the other hand, I absolutely don't believe that he performed any miracles whatsoever. Curing lepers by touching them? Walking on water? Turning water into wine? And I also find the beliefs in Immaculate Conception, Son of God, and Resurrection highly preposterous. These are myths created by superstitious, ignorant, impressionable people who wanted to believe them — had to believe them. That was the real beginning of true evil."

"Could you go into more detail about your last statement?" asked Betty. "Believe it or not, your thoughts and feelings are important to us. Just try to be fair and objective."

"From what I've read about Jesus," I continued, "he didn't advocate organized religion; faith, whatever direction it took, was in your heart, to be practiced in the privacy of your own home. He was also staunchly opposed to any form of exploitation."

"I know what you're getting at," injected Betty.

"Please, let me finish," I asserted. "After Jesus perished, there was no 'Christian' religion, per se. People weren't running around wearing Crosses, Crucifixes, fish or any other religious symbols. That all came much later when the Church was firmly established.

If Jesus knew what the Church did in His name, He'd roll over in His grave reciting Hail Maries. No other organization in history has been responsible for more human subjugation, brain washing, exploitation, torture, misery, mass murder, and so much more evil. The Church made up all this paranormal crap about Jesus to instill fear and loyalty. The thicker they laid it on, the more people succumbed to Christianity, and added to the ever-expanding coffers of the Church.

Of all the blasphemy in the world, nothing comes close to equaling what's been said and done in the name of Jesus. I could expound on and on about things like Evangelist thieves, pedophile Priests, the Vatican's position on abortion, and so much more. But, I'll leave the rest of my thoughts and feelings to your imagination."

"John, I can see that you're kind of neutral when it comes to the Church," mumbled Lyle.

"Yuh think so?" I commented.

"Would you be surprised if I told you that we agree with much of what you said?" asked Betty with a controlled smile.

"That's a big yes," I answered, stunned.

Betty continued. "We don't completely condemn the Church, but many of their practices have always been . . . uh . . . questionable. But we're not here to discuss the Church. Just Jesus."

"Then tell me this," I commented, "Do you believe all the miraculous things associated with Him?"

Lyle jumped in. "Honestly, we don't know what to believe. It's a very tough subject that no one can provide definitive answers for."

"Why not?" I asked in disbelief. "Didn't He leave all kinds of transparent thoughts and memories here that have been passed down through the ages? And what about all those who supposedly witnessed the miracles? Aren't their photographic memories accessible? I thought that the famous saying from the X-Files, "The Truth Is Out There," applied to this dimension."

"Ninety nine percent of the time it does," answered Lyle a bit frazzled. "But not this time."

Now I was beginning to get interested. Something was amiss. Something made no sense. I was bracing myself for yet another mind-blowing revelation.

"Here's the main problem, John," Lyle stated. "We have absolutely no memories from Jesus. None."

"That makes no sense," I exclaimed.

Betty threw Lyle a look of desperation. "Stop beating around the bush, trying to build your usual drama."

"John . . . Jesus never got to this dimension," exclaimed Lyle, raising his eyebrows.

"What do you mean?" I asked, incredulously.

"I mean that His particle bundle never tunneled here when He died," said Lyle. "And, believe me, there's no mistake about this. It's a heavily researched fact that has resulted in endless speculation since the moment He failed to get here."

Was I shocked by what I had just heard? No. Not in the least. To me, everything in this dimension was a mystery, and this was simply another. But . . . it was fascinating.

"Come on," I remarked. "There's gotta be a logical explanation. How often does this sort of thing happen?"

"Never," he answered.

"Never," Betty confirmed.

"After all I've learned from you all, never is never an acceptable answer to anything."

Betty shook her head no. "It's a fact of life, when a human's brain ceases to function, their bundle arrives in our dimension. We always know when someone is going to cross over, and there are always witnesses: friends, relatives . . . whatever."

"No exceptions to this . . . rule?" I asked, suspiciously.

"There have been rare occasions," Lyle informed me, "but they don't apply to Jesus."

"Rare occasions?" I asked.

Betty fielded this question. "During mass, unexpected, quick deaths — Pompeii and Hiroshima, for example — peoples' bundles can escape detection. But they're usually accounted for later. Extremely powerful electrocution has also been known to destroy a particle bundle on very rare occasions."

"Maybe that's what happened, I declared. "When He was on the Cross, an enormous bolt of lightning hit him."

"Nope," said Lyle. "Something like that would have been very well documented. There were many witnesses: many at the site of His crucifixion, and many, many more eagerly awaiting His arrival here. Remember, He was an exceptionally popular, heavily revered personality . . . the Messiah to many. The memory records don't report any lightning at all."

"So, he just plain vanished into thin air," I whispered.

"If you want to put it that way," intoned Betty.

"Well . . . how would you put it?" I responded.

"As you can imagine," she began, "there have been loads of explanations over the years. This is a hotly contested topic. Of all the theories, Lyle and I have it narrowed down to two that we kind of believe. Or, I should say, would like to believe."

"I'll attempt to accept what you're going to tell me," I said with complete honesty, "But . . . I hope it doesn't have to do with any of that Son of God and miracles stuff. That's avoiding any semblance of reality."

Very surprisingly, Betty laughed, and shook her finger at me.

"Don't worry, it's not what you may think."

"Thank God for that," I responded.

Lyle jumped in. "Not to intentionally create any suspense, I'll begin with our second favorite theory — a simple one that begs little discussion."

"Good idea," added Betty.

He continued. "Maybe Jesus' particle bundle never got here because it skipped this dimension, and went directly to the third . . . you know . . . where we hope we go after our 150 years here. That would give us, you included, some hope that something very special awaits us all. Don't ask me how this is possible; no one has a logical answer."

"That theory implies some sort of divine intervention, doesn't it?" I asked, with no prejudgment or hostility in my voice.

"Valid interpretation," Lyle answered, cutting off Betty as she was just about to speak.

"Could be divine or purely scientific," inferred Betty. "It all depends on what anyone wants to believe. Those who believe that Jesus is the Son of God think the third dimension is Heaven, and where we are now is purgatory. Others feel that His disappearance is an anomaly, somehow related to His specialness — His undisputed paranormal abilities. And, of course, there are those who strongly feel that it's all a load of you know what."

"So far, I'm afraid to say that last category is the one I fall into," I admitted. "And, by the way, I'd like to get a bit more info about His 'undisputed paranormal abilities.'"

"John, when we relate our favorite theory to you, that may be suitably answered," explained Lyle.

"Fair enough," I said.

Betty took the lead on this one. "Luckily, you're going to be very familiar with the central idea behind this theory. It's something that you already accept as a fact of this life.

"It would be safe to say that you've got my full attention," I stated.

Before a single word could roll off Lyle's tongue, Betty continued. "John, please let me say what I want to say without any questions or interruptions. You'll have plenty of time for that later. I'm going to be as brief and to the point as I can."

"Knock yourself out," I said, giving her a thumbs up.

"Given everything we know about Jesus, it's entirely possible that He was some form of a . . . thought construct. Think about that for a moment: a thought construct. It would explain just about all of the mysteries surrounding every moment of His glorious life, beginning with the concept of Immaculate Conception. It would account for all His miracles; they could have been carefully crafted illusions, completely real to any witness. Then there was the impossibly brutal torture He endured walking the Cross along the

Via Dolorosa. Add to that His Ascension, as well as His ghostly appearances after His death, and what have you got? A thought construct in the wrong dimension. But placed there on purpose."

"Thought provoking theory," I exclaimed. "But . . . how is this possible? Who or what constructed Him? And . . . why? That ought to keep you busy for a while, and I don't want to hear any copout answers."

"Do you think we presumed that you would blindly swallow what we just hit you with?" questioned Lyle.

I answered him with one of my are-you-shitting-me? expressions.

"Betty and I can't give you any exact answers. No one can," he very quickly admitted. "But we can give you some of the more popular explanations. You've just got to bear with us."

"Illuminate me," I replied with a tight grin.

"I'll begin with your 'how is this possible' question," exhaled Lyle. "As you already know, thought constructs are formed through a combination of personal memory, imagination, desire, emotion, and accessing the field of knowledge. And, since both of our dimensions are virtually identical, they can be present anywhere. Now . . . here's where it begins to get dicey and overwhelmingly subjective."

"Ah . . . the good part," I exclaimed.

My interruption gave Betty a chance to put in her two cents. She began with a question: "How did people in your dimension, John, see Jesus? That's a problem. People here can see thought constructs, like me, because their particle bundles are free of all sensory restrictions. And I can see a thought construct because I have a signature vibration. Following me so far?"

"So far, so good," I replied. "But could you refresh me about the 'sensory restrictions' obstacle?"

She continued. "Simple: When a person is technically alive, their brain puts all sorts of restrictions on the particle bundle, really limiting its capabilities.

Lyle interrupted. "John, that whole thing's a separate, startling conversation that we'll have later. Sorry Betty, keep going."

"There are a few explanations that are a real stretch, so you'll have to use your imagination, and be a little open-minded."

I gave a very affirmative nod. Betty seemed relaxed.

She continued. "Here goes. Jesus' thought construct may have begun as a fertilized egg that tricked Mary into a false, yet real, pregnancy. As He grew, He developed a normal frequency that would make Him visible in your dimension."

"I'm totally lost," I sorely admitted. "And, yes, stretch is the understatement of all time."

Lyle couldn't resist. "Keep an open mind — a very open mind. Please. Everything, absolutely everything, is governed by frequency and vibration: everything you hear, see, feel, taste, and smell. That's how the universe works. If Jesus' quantum being was broadcasting at a frequency acknowledged by your brain, He'd be perfectly visible. Obviously, Mary had the normal frequency, and through the phenomena of resonance, Jesus adjusted to it."

"What's this 'phenomena of resonance' you mentioned?" I asked.

"When two or more vibrating entities are brought into close proximity," he explained, "they will always self adjust themselves to a common or dominant frequency. Here's a good example: If you put two clocks side by side, their beats will slowly but surely become identical. Their balance springs will mysteriously become synchronized and rotate as one. Hey, another time, remind me to tell you how this effects identical twins."

"It's still way beyond my comprehension, but keep going," I said. "So, Jesus could have been born as a normal, biologically correct human being, but with thought construct origins," said Betty.

"You mean He changed into a real human?" I asked, thoroughly perplexed.

"Well . . . it's a theory with absolutely no proof," she reluctantly admitted.

"Then you could just as easily surmise that He had a normal particle bundle that just plain didn't tunnel to your dimension. Anything can be concocted to explain this," I said.

"True," confessed Lyle.

"Look, I think you've covered my 'how's this possible' question," I stated very matter-of-factly. "I'm just going to have to stick it all in that nothing's *im*possible category, and leave it at that. To be painfully honest with the both of you, everything you've been telling me about good old JC is definitely interesting and highly thought provoking."

"That's exactly how we wanted you to react to all this. Nothing more," gushed Betty.

Lyle nodded in agreement, exhaling an enormous cloud of smoke.

"Some of it makes sense. Even to me," I said, wincing. "All of Jesus' miracles, that I could never possibly believe, could have been illusions. A thought construct visible to, and interactive with, live humans could completely shape peoples' belief systems."

"Not to screw up your mind any more than it is right now," said Lyle, "but some think the resonance in His voice could have had a hypnotic quality. Can you . . ."

"Enough. Enough," I exclaimed, laughing. "While I've still got a little of my sanity, and I'm still asleep, let's go to my second question: who or what constructed Him?"

"I'll leave this to you," he said to Betty.

"The most prevalent explanation is, as you can well imagine, very faith based."

"Yes . . . I can imagine," I responded. " I'm sure people believe in divine intervention — that Jesus was a product of the Creator and/or intelligent design."

Betty resumed. "Yes. It's a very easy-way-out explanation. It's what people want to believe — what makes them feel good and secure."

"Then why not simply believe that He was God's Son?" I asked. "And, through one of His numerous miracles, He was able to skip your dimension? Why even bother with the thought construct angle?"

"That's the most obvious belief . . . the one you don't want to hear about," proclaimed Betty. "The thought construct theory is an explanation that we, Lyle and I, choose to believe. It's more scientifically plausible, and within the realm of human capability."

"I see," I acknowledged. "Now let me guess: both of you think that Jesus was the handiwork of the creator."

"Yes," uttered Betty.

"Me too," whispered Lyle.

"Personally, I can't give you my own opinion at this point. Maybe never," I said. "Aren't there any more explanations? I can't believe . . ."

Lyle interrupted. "Of course there are more explanations. Many of them. But only one that's not completely absurd, only one that makes any sense."

"Any sense?" I asked.

"Continuing along . . . ," breathed Lyle, ". . . some believe that Jesus was created by prophesy."

Lyle looked at me for a quick reaction.

"Now I'm totally lost," I responded.

"I knew you would be," declared Lyle, swinging his head back, with a bold laugh. "I'll attempt to explain, but it'll be as tough as swallowing a fully grown saguaro cactus."

"Ouch," I joked. "I'm ready."

Lyle got serious. "Let's begin by going way back a couple of thousand years to a time before the arrival of Jesus. For most of the human race, life was not exactly a day at the beach, if you know what I mean. Slavery, starvation, disease, torture, brain washing, subjugation, abject poverty, and more horrors than anyone can imagine ruled the day."

"I've read all about it, and I've seen most of those Spartacus kind of movies," I told him.

Lyle continued. "What people wanted more than anything was hope — something that could make their lives better, and insure a more humane future for their children. This was a dream shared by a large part of the world's population... in both dimensions. Remember, those who had already perished were observing the miserable lives of their friends, loved ones, and all the others who were still suffering."

"So far, you haven't lost me," I assured him.

"This is all pretty straight forward," he assured me. "Down the line, it will, however, require a leap of faith."

"No doubt," I agreed.

Lyle continued. "So... you've got countless people in both dimensions deeply thinking and dreaming about the same things: how to change the world and make life more bearable. They knew this would require a profound paradigm shift — a major change that could radically alter the path of history and humanity. In their minds, this meant the coming of a very special individual — one who could shape this change, and bring about a new world order."

A light went on in my head. "I know exactly what you're going to say."

Lyle opened his mouth to speak, and nothing came out. He froze in place. The light began to fade. I blinked my eyes. And woke up. Shit.

Chapter 21
Bewilderment in Bethlehem

When I woke up, I glanced at my watch and couldn't believe that I had only been asleep for about fifteen minutes. That whole conversation had taken place in such a ridiculously short period of time. Actually, I had been dreaming in deep sleep for only a few seconds. I wished these dreams would last longer, and I couldn't understand what natural mechanism cut them so damn, fucking short. It wasn't fair.

Luckily, I was able to fall right back to sleep, despite the fact that I had so much on my mind. In the morning, I went through all my rituals in a complete blur. It was only during my second cup of outrageously potent coffee that the whole Jesus thing crept back into my head.

It wasn't exactly life altering information. And . . . it was all subjective. So I really didn't have to believe so much as an ounce of it. Yes, it was nice and interesting information, but nothing that would ever have an impact on my life.

Before I knew it, my evening ritual was upon me. And, as usual, my beautiful little acorn performed its magic.

I was back. But back where? My dream eyes were still shut, resisting the temptation to discover where Lyle had taken us this time. Believe it or not, I had come to find the suspense enjoyable. My senses told me that we were no longer in Qumran, although the weather was pretty much the same: hot and dry, with a slight breeze, and we were sitting on a flat stone surface. The big difference was that I smelled vegetation.

After listening to Lyle and Betty whispering to each other for a few seconds, I finally opened my eyes to a burst of painfully bright sunlight. Squinting with all my might, I kept my head down and began to examine the ground I was sitting on — uncomfortably, by the way.

We were on a street within a courtyard — an ancient location composed of rough, flat slabs of what I thought was limestone. Once my eyes were accustomed to the glare, I looked straight ahead into a cloud of cigarette smoke. There was Lyle, Camel clenched between his teeth, holding hands with a joyful, smiling Betty.

"Sorry, John," announced Betty. "We're not in the jungle."

I looked around, trying to figure out what was so amazing. We were seated directly in front of a large, severely ancient building made of flat, irregularly shaped stones, worn almost smooth through time. The oddest feature was the small doorway, crudely made of three, equal sized, flat rectangular slabs: two vertical with one on top. It was way out of proportion, and seemed as though you'd have to duck down to enter the building.

Even stranger, the doorway was offset to the right, within a much larger, vaulted shape. And that, in turn, was within a larger square. To my left, running adjacent to this building, was a low wall directly in front of a dense row of medium height trees. I couldn't tell what type of trees they were, but they were a dark, beautiful green, and obviously well-manicured.

I shrugged my shoulders and rolled my eyes. "I give up. Where are we?"

Betty laughed, and immediately got serious. "We're in Bethlehem. And the building you're staring at? It's one of the holiest, if not the holiest, place on earth: the Church of The Nativity, the site where Jesus was born."

"Well . . . you guys don't play around, do you?" I said with a slight chuckle. "Just the right atmosphere for discussing Jesus' creation."

"But...," I continued, "can you do something about the seating arrangements? The street's as uncomfortable as all hell. Oops, I shouldn't have put it that way."

By this time, nothing should astonish me, but, within the blink of an eye, we were all sitting in relaxing director's chairs.

"Thanks for the miracle, Lyle," I responded. "Jesus would be proud."

Lyle motioned to the doorway. "I couldn't help but notice how long you were staring at that. Pretty unusual, isn't it?"

"Yes," I answered. "And pretty evident that I'm about to get a detailed explanation."

Betty spoke up. "To put it in the proper perspective, I'm going to have to give you a short history of the Church."

"I'll listen carefully," I assured her.

"It is believed and pretty well-documented that Jesus was born in a small cave right here at this site. In 326AD, Constantine built a Church over the sacred cave."

"Question. Why did they wait that long to build something, anything, over such an important location?"

"Simple," Betty retorted. "Christianity didn't become a well-established religion until long after Christ's death."

"Thanks," I said. "Go on."

"That Church lasted until 530AD when it was destroyed by Justinian who proceeded to build a much larger one on the same site. And this, John, is it."

"But what about the strange doorway?" I asked.

"I was getting to that," she asserted. "The large square area was the original door built by Justinian. It was subsequently reduced in size to form that pointed arch doorway, known as the Crusader entrance. That occurred around 1015AD give or take several years. Can you trace its shape?"

"Easily," I answered.

She continued. "The final door, that very small one, was built around 1550AD during the Ottoman period, and is known as the *Door of Humility*."

"But why did they put such a small door on such an important Church," I said in wonderment.

"Two reasons," she quickly answered. "First of all, the small size was intended to prevent looting; horses and carts couldn't be driven through. And, in order to enter the Church, you have to stoop down, which is a sign of respect . . . and . . . humility. That's it. End of lesson."

"Well done," I declared. "That wasn't too painful. And, it was interesting."

"Now, let's pick up our Jesus conversation where we left off yesterday," said Lyle.

"We were talking about the countless souls in both dimensions who dreamed of a singular person who could correct the evils of the world — someone very, very special," offered Betty.

"The Messiah," I exclaimed, raising my arms in the air. While many people were hoping for the coming of the Messiah, some were actually predicting it."

Lyle put up his finger to make a point. "Most people who were dreaming about someone who could change the world didn't necessarily think of Him as the Messiah. However . . . the people who spelled out the prophesies knew He was going to be the Messiah. That's a big difference."

"I've read that some of the prophesies were really on target."

"It's almost frightening how accurate the predictions were," Lyle assured me. "They predicted virtually every event in His life. I mean every event. It went far, far beyond coincidence."

"Not to change the point again," I sheepishly said, "but I guess that means the future is predictable."

Lyle shook his head. "Usually not. That's a subject for a whole other conversation that we'll definitely have."

"Just because the predictions were uncannily precise doesn't necessarily make a case for a creator," I added, getting back on topic.

"That wasn't the point I was trying to make," Lyle said, seriously. "I'm still on the thought construct angle."

"Got ahead of myself, I guess."

Lyle continued. "Have you heard anything about the power of the collective conscious? And the collective unconscious?"

"Of course," I quickly replied. "When many people think strongly about the same thing, there can be a powerful effect. Even when they're not actively thinking about it, if the topic is important to them, it's still working in their subconscious. What's more, the thought can transfer to other peoples' minds. That part of it I'm a little fuzzy on."

Lyle clapped his hands together. "Just think about what you just said. The power of collective minds can be extremely influential. Taking that a step further, they can have a profound effect on reality — on the material world."

"Please don't get metaphysical on me," I said with a laugh.

Betty jumped in. "This is not craziness. It's fact. History is filled with examples of collective thoughts translating into tangible effects."

"Wait a second, I think I know exactly where all this is going," I claimed. "I'll wrap this up in a second. The collective conscious and subconscious, plus all the prophecies, created the Jesus thought construct. He was the creation of countless minds in both dimensions, all working together on the same concept."

"Basically," agreed Lyle, "that's it in a nutshell."

"Have other famous people been thought constructs?" I asked in amazement.

"No," answered Betty, definitively. "There's absolutely no record of this happening at any other time. There's never been such a strong desire for a very special, world changing individual either before or after Jesus."

"Not true," I exclaimed. "How about the desire for the second coming of Christ?"

"That's nowhere near as powerful a desire," said Betty. "But . . . it is definitely possible if such a person were needed, and enough minds became entwined in the thought. Hopefully, things won't get bad enough for that to happen."

"But it could happen," I sighed. "Judgment Day."

"Of course it could," agreed Betty, with a solemn look on her face.

"Another question: Did Jesus have a signature vibration? Like Betty? I mean, wouldn't he have had to in order to accomplish everything He did?"

"Maybe," answered Lyle. "But there's not a shred of proof. Betty is the only construct with a proven vibration. It is assumed by many that Jesus definitely had a vibration. On the other hand, many, many believe that He didn't."

"Doesn't make any sense." I exhaled.

"Think about it," whispered Lyle. "If He didn't have a vibration, it would mean that He was under the control of a higher entity — either the proverbial God or an intelligent creator. It would be absolute proof that life as it is was not by chance or coincidence. No other explanation would make any sense."

"OK," I eagerly said. "He had a vibration."

"Believe what you want," said Betty. "Now you understand how the subject is so hotly contested . . . up here."

"Some things never change," I said, with resignation.

"There's no reason why they should," said Lyle. "This dimension is simply an extension of life. People don't change. They just see things from an entirely different perspective."

"I have to admit," I said, shaking my head, "that this Jesus puzzle is truly fascinating. I can't even begin to imagine how the Vatican would react if they got wind of it."

"If they knew, and they might, it would be an enormous secret," Betty added.

"I thought you all know everything there is to know."

"Not really," answered Lyle. "We know what we want to know. I've never tried to access that singular thought, and, besides, I'm not very interested in faith and religion to begin with."

"What about you, Betty?" I asked.

"I've never heard anything about this either." She assured me.

"It's still fascinating to me that Jesus could have been a real, solid, flesh and blood thought construct in my dimension," I said, rolling my eyes.

I could see that Lyle had something on his mind.

"Ok, Lyle. What is it?" I asked. "You've got that perplexed look on your face, and you just screwed up blowing a smoke ring. What's on your mind?"

"Jesus was not solid. You are not solid. I was never solid. Nothing at all is solid. Everything is an illusion."

I just sat there, and let that sink in. It immediately occurred to me that I must have misunderstood what he said. Me? An illusion? Maybe in his world, but surely not in mine.

"Could you please repeat that for me?" I asked, with a quizzical look.

Lyle shook his head and chuckled. "I had a feeling that was going to screw up your mind. As I said, everything, absolutely everything, is an illusion. It's a fact of nature, and the quantum world we all live in. Not to rub it in, but you're more of an illusion than I am."

I shot him one of my yeah, right looks, rolled my eyes back and laughed. He didn't react.

Betty shrugged her shoulders. "I've had this explained to me. Lyle's not stretching the truth or exaggerating. It is what it is. Nothing to worry about."

Then I shot him one of my *you ain't shittin' me?* looks.

"This isn't going to be easy, and I'm far from an expert on the subject," he fully admitted. "But I'll take you through the facts as they've been related to me. Thanks to some of your quantum readings, some of it will make sense to you. I hope."

"Uh . . . facts? Did you say 'facts?"

"Theories," he answered. "But they've been postulated by leading physicists."

"I'm listening," I wheezed.

"This is going to be way oversimplified. As you know, everything in the universe is made of atoms. And atoms can be broken down into smaller components, which, in turn, can be broken down into fundamental quantum particles. And probably even farther than that."

"Gotcha so far." I said with a nod.

"Now, back to the atom. Atoms are, for all intents and purposes, empty space. Yeah, there are electrons in their own haze zipping around the nucleus, but they occupy next to no space. When atoms group together to form molecules, which group together to eventually form you, for example, you get what appears to be a solid form."

"Yes. A visible form in color that has mass, weight, functioning components, and, hopefully, consciousness and intelligence," I said.

"One hundred percent true," he replied. "But . . . it's all an illusion, playing tricks on your eyes. It's mostly empty space."

I just shrugged my shoulders. "Lyle, I know all of this. It's just the way matter, light, and being work in our physical reality."

"Right again," he gladly admitted.

"So . . . what's the big deal? In itself, it's definitely amazing, but it's no revelation."

"John," he said, "did you really think that my little lesson about illusion was going to be so stupidly simple?"

"I never expected it to be. That's why I was so surprised."

"I'm thinking," he quietly said. "Trying to figure out the best way to explain this."

"Take your time," I told him.

He cleared his throat. "Everything in the world is connected — absolutely everything. Try to envision a thick, infinite mist whirling around at nearly the speed of light. This mist, made of quantum particles, is continuously flowing through you and absolutely everything else. Have I lost you yet?"

"Not yet," I responded. "I'm picturing a mist of tiny quantum particles rushing through me and everything else."

"Good." He shifted in his seat. "All of these particles were created at the same instant during the big bang, so, in a way, they all know each other. It's the most basic level of quantum entanglement."

I nodded, without so much as a hint of knowing where this was going.

Lyle continued. "All of these particles have their own spin characteristics: they're sort of like fingerprints. However, they can exchange these characteristics with each other. Lost yet?"

"Not completely. By the way, how do you know all this shit?"

"My science friend explained it," he answered, with a slight hesitation. "I'm pretty sure I remember what he said."

"Pretty sure?" I asked, with a note of doubt.

"Even if I'm off by a few points, you'll get the general idea. Now, picture that particle mist again, but, this time, focus your thoughts on just a couple of particles. We're going to travel with them."

"Ok," I replied, closing my eyes.

He proceeded. "As these particles enter your body, or anything else, for that matter, they each take the place of an existing particle, and adopt its spin. Then, another particle comes by, and the process is repeated. It's endless. The mist flows at close to the speed of light, and constantly replaces anything and everything."

"What you're saying is that nothing is ever here. But... everything is always here."

"Illusion," he said, raising his eyebrows.

"What about my brain? And flowing blood? And how about . . ."

He interrupted. "Makes no difference. It's all made of the same particles. Remember, they're simply building blocks for atoms, molecules, and so on. They form blood cells, amino acids, proteins, bones, eyes, your heart . . . everything."

"What if I'm in the middle of forming a memory? Let's say I'm in the middle of a conversation that, like everything else, requires memory. Are there memory particles?"

"Aha. Good thinking. Great question," he exclaimed. "Now here's one of the most fascinating aspects, in answer to your question. The only structures in the world that are not affected by the quantum mist are . . . particle bundles. Their binding forces are so strong that they resist replacement. Not to get off the subject, but this fact absolutely reeks of intelligent design. Just think about it: the key to self-awareness, consciousness, memory, and the afterlife defies all physical structure."

"I just want to know if this means that there's no particle mist in your dimension?" I asked.

"My dimension is your dimension . . . basically," he reminded me. "We're not effected. Not an illusion. Just the purest essence of life: memory, imagination, and knowledge."

"What about Betty?" I asked.

"She's pure memory," he responded. "Nothing physical."

"But I can see her. And touch her."

He continued. "You're accessing memory by your uncluttered bundle. Betty is no different from your 427 Cobra. Or the Thompson you fired on Iwo Jima. Pure memory and imagination. Intangible. Illusions. But very, very real."

I had a question that I was dying to ask. "If particle bundles are theoretically eternal, and all matter is constantly replaced, why do we grow old and die?"

"Another very perceptive question," he announced enthusiastically.

"Well, you've certainly got my attention," I said. "This is one of the most fascinating things we've ever talked about. It's outrageous."

Lyle continued. "As you know, everything is always in a state of flux — constant change and movement. Particles that formed anything, from a tree to a car to a dog to a bathtub now form you, then . . . woosh . . . are gone and replaced. Every new particle takes on the identical identity (position and spin) of the particle it replaced."

"Ok, I get it," I said, nodding my head.

"There's lots, lots more," he loudly proclaimed. "Listen carefully. When I said identical identity, I should have said near identical identity. You see, everything is always in a state of perpetual change. Immeasurably small changes in spin and position occur as each particle takes another's place."

"A bit confusing," I murmured.

"I agree," declared Betty . . . finally coming to life.

"Ok, I've got a good analogy," he said. "Bear with me. Now, picture an apple, a beautiful, bright red, ripe one sitting on your kitchen table."

"Just like me, it's constantly being replaced." I said with assurance.

Lyle continued. "Now you've got to use some imagination. Picture that apple after a week or so of sitting on the table. The color has dulled. It's no longer as crisp and firm. There are small brown spots. And, it has slightly shrunk. The apple is changing through perfectly natural processes."

"So, what else is new?" I remarked.

"Just hear me through," he pleaded. "The apple is being bombarded by light, sound waves, air currents, and rogue particle collisions. Gravity is pulling on it. All sorts of bacteria and parasites are attacking it. And thousands of other factors, including your own conscious observation, are altering its construction. The apple is enduring random, entropic energy loss, drastic system disorder . . .

many factors that are commonly referred to as rot, decay, or just plain old age."

"But if new particles are constantly replacing . . ."

Lyle interrupted me. "I know what you're asking. Particles that replace others are always in their original state. It's the systems they're in that always get compromised. Particles that replace minutely altered particles adopt the altered identity. The process repeats and degrades until the object disappears from existence, depending upon physical conditions. That's the case for everything . . . from mountains to freight trains to you."

"You just said that this all 'depends on physical conditions.' What do you mean by that?"

He thought about that for a second. "Let's go back to our apple. If it were colder in the room, the apple would last longer because lower temperatures slow down all processes. If you flash froze the apple, sealed it in a vacuum container and shielded it in a solid lead vessel several hundred thousand miles thick, it could last for billions of years. Conversely, the hotter it got, the quicker the apple would degrade. Of course, people have it a lot harder than apples."

"Yeah, I can imagine," I mumbled.

"People are the ultimate victims of environmental and self-destruction," he grunted. "We smoke, drink, eat terrible foods, take all sorts of drugs, play sports, get into fights, watch television, use computers and cell phones . . ."

I interrupted. "The last things you just mentioned are passive activities. How can they hurt us?"

"Radiation," he declared. "We bathe ourselves in it. And it plays pool with our particles. How many times have you stood in front of a microwave oven waiting for your food to be ready? How many times have you purposely exposed yourself to the sun?"

"I get it. I get it."

"We spend every day shortening our lives. Even supposedly healthy things like playing tennis, jogging, or even taking a nice long walk in the country are slowly killing us. Add all that to disease, flues, viruses, parasites, gravity, natural radiation, genetic disorders, birth defects, and a million other things, and what do you get? Adios, amigo. R.I.P."

"Pleasant thoughts," I exclaimed.

"That's life," he exclaimed.

"What's the sense of making such a big deal about this particle mist and endless particle replacement?" I asked very seriously. "Apples rot. And we die, no matter what your theoretical physicists dream up."

"I agree," he whispered. "But think of the future, and the impact this theory could have on life."

"Undoubtedly, you're going to elaborate," I said with a laugh.

"I thought we're here in Bethlehem to talk about Jesus?" I added. "Particle physics has rather little to do with the Church of the Nativity."

"It came naturally," admitted Lyle. "We just drifted into this discussion, and I didn't want to change the subject. Ultimately, it reinforces the fact that life, let alone the whole universe, is a miracle. That's sort of an ongoing theme here in the Holy Land."

"Amen," I said with a chuckle.

"Hopefully, scientists in your dimension will discover this theory one day," Lyle noted.

"Certainly not in my lifetime," I asserted.

All of a sudden, Lyle abruptly stopped talking, and just stared blankly into the distance. It was scary. I had never seen him act that way. Then he stood up, and pace back and forth for a few seconds. Betty stood up too, apparently very concerned about something.

"I have to leave right now," he stammered.

Poooooooofff. He disappeared. Just like that. One moment he was here, the next moment he was gone. And I had a sneaking suspicion why he vanished. Then . . . I looked at Betty.

"What?" I hesitantly asked. "It's sick Betty, isn't it? Something happened."

"You're right," she uttered. "Lyle sensed something, and had to leave. I think she's trying to say something . . . you know . . . that poetry Lyle mentioned the other day. I'm going to join him."

"Want me to come?" I asked, hoping she'd say 'no.'

"Nothing you can do, but thanks for asking," she said. "We're going to be in real time, so you wouldn't last too long anyway. You'll probably wake up before we get back. See you tomorrow."

Poooooooffff. She vanished, too.

'So, what am I going to do now?' I asked myself. I was still fast asleep, and didn't feel I was going to wake up any too soon. Then I glanced at the Door of Humility and had an idea. As long as I'm here with some time to kill, I thought, I may as well do some exploring. Be an invisible tourist. Honestly, it seemed like an interesting idea, because I had heard that this Church of the Nativity was an interesting place with many beautiful rooms.

After dragging my ass off my comfortable director's chair, I made my way over to that small door, and peered inside. It was pitch black in there. Maybe there was a small tunnel you had to walk through before anything came into view. More than likely, my eyes (dream eyes, that is) were still acclimated to the bright sun reflecting off the light colored stones. That's why it was black as coal.

Acting with the utmost humility, I stooped down, and entered the Church. After stepping around two feet into the darkness I had the most terrifying experience I've ever had in my life — something worse than any nightmare I could imagine — something that made me question the safety of these spectacular dreams.

I had fallen into what I can only describe as complete nothingness. I was in a void where most of my senses ceased to exist: my eyes and ears were gone; there was no sensation of temperature; nothing touched my body; my only sensation was weightlessness and falling either up or down. In this sheer emptiness, reality ceased to exist. It was horrible . . . as frightening as all hell.

• • •

After what seemed like an eternity, but probably just a couple of seconds, I woke up in a cold sweat. Actually, I was soaked, still shaking with fear, and my heart was beating ridiculously fast; I could feel my pulse surging through every part of my body.

Once I calmed down to a point where I could think rationally, I got pissed off at Lyle. And for good reason. This was his fault. He let this happen to me — not on purpose, but through sheer negligence.

His thoughts and awareness must have been so focused on Betty that he forgot about me, and let me slip into a realm of oblivion between our worlds. That was my only explanation for what happened. Considering how the shock of this experience made my heart palpitate, I'm absolutely certain that I could have had a heart attack.

After what felt like several hours of drifting in and out of a dizzy, semi dream state, the best thing happened; my alarm clock went off, and shook me back to the land of the living. It was wonderful to stand up, and feel the floor beneath my feet.

Still, I couldn't manage to get any of this off my mind. It haunted me relentlessly the entire day. That night, I was very nervous when I jumped into bed. I was afraid of meditating. The only solution was to skip it for a few evenings. It would certainly send a message to Lyle who, I hoped, realized what happened to me. So my acorn had a night off.

When I woke up the following morning, I felt quite refreshed, and my fears were not foremost on my mind. Thank God for that. But, throughout the rest of the day, I had very mixed feelings about my dreaming dilemma. Of course, I wanted to return to all the good stuff: the astonishing memory trips, the stimulating discussions, and the friendships I had developed. Deep down I knew my one really horrible experience was a fluke, probably just a normal nightmare. After all, maybe all of this was simply an extraordinary figment of my imagination.

Or it could have been something else that kept popping into my mind: remote viewing. I had read a lot about that phenomenon during my immersion in metaphysical (eccch) books. In a nutshell, perfectly ordinary people can go into a meditative state and clearly view things in the past as well as the future. Sounds like bullshit, but plenty of very upstanding people believe in it. Not me, though. However, it's easier to believe in remote viewing than in the experiences I was having.

It's entirely possible that my dreams were purely imagination driven. But the proof I had experienced in real time on East End Avenue could have been the result of remote viewing, which, in itself, is as paranormal as hell. It was crystal clear that, one way or the other, something very mystical had a grip on me for at least a few seconds a day. Not so terrible when you really think about it.

So, I put all my worries and crazy thoughts aside, and, that night, I jumped into bed, and let my acorn take me to who the fuck knows where.

CHAPTER 22
PERPLEXED IN PARADISE

Well, just as I had assumed, I hadn't returned to that fearsome void. Before I opened my dream eyes, I concentrated on where I might be. But when I heard the captivating cry of some astonishing bird, I knew precisely where I was. Lyle must have known what had happened to me and was probably painfully aware that it was his fault for allowing it to happen. So, he brought me back to a place I loved — a place where I felt very comfortable.

When I opened my dream eyes, I was looking directly at Lyle, and I could tell from his overall body language and facial expression that he was both embarrassed and concerned. When I glanced at Betty, I got the same feelings.

"If you've been reading my mind," I said, "then you know I was contemplating not coming back."

"John," he answered, "I can't begin to tell you how sorry I am. I did access your thoughts, as well as your whole memory of the event. It was certainly terrible."

"Terrible?" I questioned. "That doesn't nearly cover it. I was scared to death. It was probably to worst nightmare I've ever had."

"I know. I know," he said with all sincerity. "I was so locked into Betty that I didn't realize what you were doing. Then it was too late. Please believe that I am truly sorry and will never let it happen again."

"Look . . . I know it wasn't done on purpose," I said. "If I thought for one moment that it was some sick practical joke, I wouldn't be sitting here now . . . or ever again."

"You know I'd never pull any shit like that on you," he exclaimed.

"Of course not," added Betty.

"I really didn't think so," I said, rolling my eyes. "But . . . how the hell did it happen? Where was I?"

"Here's exactly what happened," said Lyle. "When you access a memory for virtually any location, there are millions of them. Some of them are very deep and detailed, while others are superficial. Unfortunately, the memory I had accessed was only of the front of the Church; the person had evidently never gone farther than the door."

"And you had no way of knowing?" I asked.

"No," he emphatically answered. "Not unless I had anticipated the problem.

"So, have you ever . . . uh . . . fallen off the edge like I did?"

"Lyle lit a Camel. "No. That would be impossible for me or anyone else in this dimension. If I began to enter a void, which has probably happened many times without my knowing it, my senses would instantaneously access another memory of the exact same place so there would be a seamless transition for me. Unfortunately, you have no access powers of your own here."

"I understand what you're saying," I admitted, shaking my head. "But, tell me, where did I go when I stepped through that lousy door?"

"You fell into a nothingness area outside of any memory domain," he admitted. "It was pure nonexistence. If nowhere is a place, that's where you were. I wish I could be more specific."

"Could it have been dangerous?" I asked.

"Not at all," he quickly answered. "Horribly frightening, but nothing more. Don't forget, you were asleep in the safety of your own bed. Look at it this way, if you drove your 427 Cobra into a tree at 160 miles per hour in this dimension, you'd either wake up right away or climb out of the wreckage laughing."

"But my heart. It was beating a mile a minute, and I was sweating profusely. Those are real physical reactions," I reminded him.

"That could be the result of any frightening dream," he countered.

"True," I replied. "But couldn't I have had a heart attack? Or maybe some sort of a seizure? The trauma was very real."

"You've got a very strong, healthy heart," he stated. If you didn't, I'd never let you have these experiences."

"How the hell do you know how healthy I really am?" I asked.

"Let's just leave it at that. I know you're healthy," he persisted.

"Ok . . . what's going on?" I asked. "I can tell when something is rotten in Denmark."

"I just didn't want to get into this health thing," he mumbled. "You wouldn't like my explanation. You wouldn't even believe it. Or respect it. And I'd probably lose lots of my credibility with you."

"Well . . . now you have no choice," I exclaimed. "You've piqued my interest way too much. Tell me, and I promise to be respectful and objective. It's probably something important that I should know."

"I just can't wait to hear this little discussion," sighed Betty.

Lyle sat back down on his cushion, trying to collect his words. Obviously, he was uncomfortable.

"Any day now," I muttered, with a grin.

"I'm just going to state it without beating around the bush," he said.

"Ok," I replied, getting ready to flinch.

"I read your aura," he said, looking away from me.

"What?" I blurted. "You've got to be kidding me. My aura? Do you expect me . . ."

"Just wait a minute," interrupted Betty. "After all the strange things you've learned from us — all the supposed impossibilities —

you shouldn't jump to conclusions so fast. Auras are real. Every living thing has one: trees, animals . . . and . . . you."

"But . . ." I attempted to put in my two cents.

"But nothing," cried Lyle. "You promised to be objective. At least listen to what we have to say."

"Ok," I relented.

"Please don't interrupt," pleaded Lyle. "I'm fully aware that metaphysical books delve into the phenomena of auras. I know how much you disrespect everything that has to do with that subject. And I know how much you detest palm readers, clairvoyants, and probably anyone who claims to read auras."

"Right you are," I snipped.

Lyle continued. "As Betty mentioned, Auras just happen to be a very natural part, of all living things. The color bands that flow around your body indicate life force. Most colors follow a normal pattern, but, if there's some sort of a physical problem, the colors change. Your chest areas show no abnormalities."

"Do I look completely healthy to you?" I asked.

"Perfectly normal heart," he replied. "But I could see several former trauma areas. There's aural discoloration in the area where you had your cancer and surgeries; I could see where you had recent surgery for a double hernia; you've got a couple of tiny kidney stones; and . . . you've got a problem area that you've got to take care of as soon as possible."

"Shit. Now you're scaring me. What's wrong with me?"

"It's nothing life threatening," he readily assured me. "Color patterns around your jaw are telling me that you've got several unattended tooth problems — some very serious cavities."

"I just can't believe this," I exclaimed.

"It's true," quipped Betty.

"I meant that I just can't believe that you actually figured all that out. Everything you said is right on the money, including your warning about my teeth. I know I've got to get some teeth fixed, but

I hate going to the dentist. I also know I've got a few tiny kidney stones. Pretty amazing."

"It's not amazing," he assured me. "It's just life as I know it . . . now."

"Does this mean that people in my world who claim to see auras aren't full of shit?" I asked, with a smirk.

Lyle winced. "I would guess that at least ninety-nine percent of them are frauds, liars, con artists, and charlatans. As you say, 'full of shit.'"

I squinted. "But . . . that means that there are some people who can actually do it."

"Yeah," he assured me. "Just like there are people who can read minds, bend silverware, levitate objects, faith heal . . . you know . . . all that metaphysical garbage. And, I hate to say it, it's all perfectly natural — as normal as breathing, belching, or taking a dump."

"How's all that possible?" I asked in utter disbelief.

"It will all be revealed to you when we have our brain versus bundle conversation," he promised me. "That's going to really warp your mind."

"I'm still pretty shocked that this aura rubbish could be true," I grumbled. "Can you tell me what an aura is, in the first place?"

"I'll try," he said as he scratched his nonexistent head. "To start, you've got to think back to that particle replacement conversation we had. Now close your eyes, and picture a mist of particles flowing around a body. Some of these particles are on their way in to replace others. And the ones that have been replaced are on their way out, but they still have all the spin characteristics they adopted. I know this is hazy, but are you with me so far?"

"I think so, but I'm not certain," I admitted. "Keep going, though."

"The frequencies and/or wave patterns that correspond to the particles that are leaving create colors at a spectrum that's invisible to the human eye. These colors indicate normalities and abnormalities for every part of the body. You look as confused as all hell."

"You got that right," I concurred. "How do you know which colors indicate healthy areas and problem areas? And how do teensy tiny particles have an effect on light and color?"

Lyle took a quick look at an annoyingly loud monkey, and continued. "There are standard aural colorations — healthy and unhealthy — for every part of the body, and it's always been that way. We learn how to read auras from others; it's info that's been passed down. Living people have learned it the same way, as well as through experimentation."

"Ok. I can buy that . . . sort of," I affirmed. "But how is this visual and in color?"

"How is anything visual? How is anything either black, white, clear, or in vivid colors?" he asked, to make a point.

"Well . . . ," I said, "everything in the universe reflects light in its own particular color spectrum — from a rainbow to a chunk of stone."

"That's an acceptable, relatively accurate answer," he replied. "And everything, including your rainbow and stone, is made of fundamental particles. These particles that are swirling around you are densely packed enough to reflect their own corresponding light and color, but at an invisible wavelength. Somehow, and don't ask me to explain, their unique spin, clustering, and interference patterns determine the colors."

"Let me see if I've got this right," I said. "You're seeing unhealthy, unnatural colors around my jaw that are indicating cavities. Do all the colors around my jaw reveal a problem?

"There are many bands of colors," he stated, "and only a very narrow section of them tell me you've got cavities. On the other hand, the colors corresponding to where you had surgery elsewhere on your body indicate recent trauma — not problems."

"You can leave it at that," I affirmed. "I've got enough of the basic idea. Without going into too much detail, how does all of this shit apply to faith healing? It just popped into my mind, and I'm mildly curious."

"For starters, don't go looking for a faith healing dentist," he said laughing.

"Why not?" I asked.

He laughed even more. "Seriously, from what I've heard, it only works with soft tissue. But don't ask me why."

"Fair enough," I uttered. "Then . . . how does it work with soft tissue?"

Lyle continued, speaking slowly. "In a nutshell, authentic faith healers, and they are extremely rare, work in two different ways. Those who actually see the aura can consciously — in a meditative, observance trance — manipulate the particle spins until the aural colors revert to normal."

"You're saying that, in a way, these healers are replacing diseased or defective particles with normal spinning ones?"

"Yes," he answered. "The healer doesn't have to know the specific problem. They just have to see the unhealthy, abnormal discoloration. There are also healers who can't see auras at all, and this is where it gets really weird."

"Really weird?" I asked. "As opposed to just mildly weird?"

Lyle shot me a 'shut up' look and continued. "All these healers have to do is move their hands over your body, just above the surface, and they can sense the problem areas by interacting with the aura which is invisible to them. Then . . . they correct them."

"Yeah . . . definitely weird," I muttered, after humming the tune from The Twilight Zone.

"One last thing, and then let's get off this subject," Lyle said. "I've heard of healers who can 'supposedly' do it from a distance — even over the phone. But I've got my own doubts about that."

"I think the cell phone service providers have a separate charge for that," I added.

"That would make sense," he agreed, chuckling.

"Question: If people can remote view, why can't they remote heal?"

Lyle looked very surprised. "I'm impressed. What do you know about remote viewing?"

"I've read about it," I answered. "And, although it seems impossible in itself, it's easier to believe than all this stuff that's been happening to me in this... uh... dimension. The more I think about it, I may be a victim of remote viewing. I'll go into this later. Now's not the time."

For a brief moment, Lyle seemed quite startled by my little revelation.

"Like so many other miracles and seeming impossibilities," he said, regaining his composure, "remote viewing is for real, but rarely works. People believe otherwise, as you'll read in numerous books on the subject, but... fanatical believers are experts at stretching the truth. They see what they set out to see. As far as remote healing goes, I've only heard of a few instances that could be proved without a doubt."

Finally... Betty joined the conversation.

"Getting back to what we were talking about before, there's another reason why all methods of faith healing can be successful, remote healing included. Even if the healer is a complete fraud, which is usually the case, the powers of suggestion and belief can do the trick. What I mean is this: if the person who needs healing believes in the faith healer, as well as in faith healing itself, they can heal themselves. The mind is a powerful thing, and has full control of the body."

"You're basically talking about the placebo effect," I observed.

"Exactly," she exclaimed. "It's possible, but very rare, for people to cure themselves of virtually any malady or disease. The best medicine is in the head."

"You're one hundred percent correct, Betty," Lyle proudly said. "But, John, don't attempt to think away your tooth problems. It ain't gonna work. That kind of thing needs a real medical professional."

"Shit," I cried. "I knew you'd say that."

Lyle asked me if I had any more questions about auras or faith healing. I told him that I was more informed than I ever hoped, or wanted, to be.

"Now that we're through with that mumbo jumbo," I said, "why don't you update me on sick Betty."

"She had a few bad minutes," reflected Lyle, "but, once again, she's stabilized. If she didn't have such a strong heart, she would have passed away a while ago."

"I hate to ask you this, but did you ever consider faith healing?" I asked with a bit of hesitancy.

"No," answered Lyle. "Maybe I should have, but it didn't even occur to me. It's too late now, though."

"Any vibration changes?" I inquired.

"Nothing new," he replied, with a peculiar expression on his face.

Betty was imploring him with her eyes to say something that he was obviously hesitant to reveal.

She hunched her shoulders, and addressed him. "Lyle, what's the big deal? Tell John. He's not going to laugh or anything. And he cares about what's going on."

Lyle nodded ok, and looked at me. "As you probably recall, I've mentioned a few times that I could swear she was trying to communicate with me. In fact, I could have sworn she was repeating a poem or something that related to her situation and my presence."

"I remember your mentioning that," I said. "I assume you've learned more?"

"Yes. Lots more," he gushed. "In her mind she said things like "I feel you all around me, your memory's so clear," and "I know you're there a breath away." I couldn't believe what I was hearing, but she repeated it a few times. She also mumbled other things I just couldn't understand. You gotta realize this is killing me."

Lyle looked away from me and changed the subject.

"I want to get back to something you said before — something that I feel is seriously bothering you. It's this remote viewing thing."

"Yeah," I said with some hesitation. "What it all boils down to is the undeniable fact that my broken glass and dog poster proof of this dimension could be due to remote viewing. I would love to get more definitive proof, something far more tangible — nothing that could be accessed through remote viewing. But I have a strong feeling that that's going to be impossible."

With a troubled look on his face, Lyle began to slowly shake his head.

"I'm at a total loss," he firmly stated.

"Doesn't surprise me," I responded.

He lit a Camel and continued. "I wish I could have you wake up with an exotic leaf, or even a gold coin, in your hand. But I can't. I can't have any kind of a physical influence or effect on you or your world. Everything we do together is all in the mind. I mean we're not really even in the Amazon now."

"So you can't think of anything at all that would do the trick," I said.

"No. Nothing that you couldn't achieve by using remote viewing," he sadly admitted. "Even if I gave you the location of Emilia Earhart's wrecked airplane, which I wouldn't do, it wouldn't be valid proof. Anything like that could be accessed through remote viewing."

"But what if I didn't attempt to actively remote view anything?" I asked, with a shred of hope.

"Wouldn't matter," he confessed. "It would be on your mind, and you could get the info subconsciously when you meditate. Nothing short of physical evidence will solve this problem."

"I have an idea that would work for me, but it's an impossibility," I said, shrugging my shoulders.

"I'm tempted to just read your mind about it, but I'll let you illuminate me instead," he muttered.

"I only wish I could talk to sick Betty about you; she's a physical link between your world and mine. That would easily solve the remote viewing problem."

"Yes, it would," he readily admitted. "But you're right about it being an impossibility. She's too sick to respond, and if she happened to come out of her coma, she could be hurt or confused. Anyway, I want to keep my personal life separate, especially when it concerns Betty."

"I guess that's why I don't know Betty's last name, or yours, for that matter. I don't even know where her hospital is located, despite the fact that I was actually there."

"Just in your head," he reminded me.

"Don't you think my observance could qualify as an involvement in your personal life?" I asked.

"You're right," he admitted with considerable reluctance. "But it was a different level of personal involvement. Anyway... it's all a moot point. I doubt if Betty will ever have another lucid conversation with anyone in your world, John."

I stretched and yawned. "Oh well, so much for concrete proof."

"Look, I hope it's not for many more years, but you will have proof." He declared. "I look forward to shaking your hand and welcoming you to this dimension when your time comes."

"Now I want to mention something else that's been rattling around my brain," I exclaimed. "It's going to surprise you, that is, if you haven't been invading my mind."

"Honestly, I don't know what you're going to say," he uttered with some hesitation.

"I've decided to write a book about my series of dreams: everything I'm learning and, experiencing."

"Not a good idea," Lyle declared immediately.

Now, I was surprised. "I thought you said that it didn't matter if I revealed everything . . . that you weren't doing anything wrong by exposing me to all this shit."

"Jesus. Will you please let me finish what I was saying?" he asked, with a touch of annoyance.

I raised my eyebrows and nodded "yes."

"I'm not the least bit worried about any of this information reaching everyone in your world," Lyle said with utter sincerity. "Hardly anyone would believe a word of it anyway. What I'm really worried about is you. If you managed to get it published, all but a handful of people would think you're either crazy or a pathological liar. Seriously . . . if you do it, don't use your real name."

"First of all, I'm not at all sure I'm going to write it," I disclosed. "But I'll certainly take your opinions and recommendation into consideration. You know what? A book could be the ultimate therapy for me."

"Hey, I've told you what I think," noted Lyle. "In the end, you've got to do what your heart tells you to do. What do you think, Betty?"

"I'm sure John will look perfectly smashing in a straight jacket," she said with some bold laughter.

"One thing's for certain," I stressed, "as long as I'm having these dreams, I'll never be able to write a book. My concentration went down the toilet right after Iwo." I spread out my arms, and motioned all around me. "This is all that's on my mind."

"But, it's all been worth it? Right?" asked Betty.

"Don't get me wrong, I've enjoyed every minute of being here — well, almost every minute. It's been one of the most fascinating experiences of my lifetime. And, I'd do it all again without hesitation."

"Really glad to hear you say that," exclaimed Lyle.

"Me too," added Betty.

"I thought it was pretty obvious that I valued these experiences," I added.

"We thought so," stated Betty.

"You know, once I got hooked on coming here, I was worried about how much longer this would continue. But now I'm thinking a little differently," I admitted. "I've had a change of mind."

"Change of mind?" Lyle asked, with a touch of nervous laughter.

"Let me explain," I said. "Coming here has changed my life positively, and . . . negatively."

"Negatively?" Lyle interrupted, raising he eyebrows.

"Bad word choice," I replied. "Since my second Iwo dream, this dimension is the only thing I've been able to think about. It has completely taken over my mind to the point where I've become completely unproductive."

"Are you saying you don't want to come back again?" asked Lyle, with extreme concern.

"No. Not at all. That's not completely accurate," I stammered. "I don't want to abruptly cut this all off. I just want to put a time limit on it. Something like another week or so of dreams. But . . . with one important condition."

"That's a relief," Lyle exhaled. "And, as I'm sure you're aware, I'm very happy that you've found your experiences so captivating, but I'm truly sorry that it's so thoroughly taken over your life. I didn't foresee that. And . . . I respect your desire to end your visits. Temporarily," he laughed.

"What's that 'one important condition' you mentioned?" asked Betty.

"You must promise me that as soon as sick Betty passes away, and you know the final results of my observance, you'll inform me. Please. You have to promise me."

"You've got my personal promise," exclaimed Lyle.

"Mine too," added Betty with absolute sincerity.

"Just keep meditating before you fall asleep," advised Lyle. "Whenever we know about Betty, I'll bring you back. It could be in two weeks from now . . . or two years. But you'll know when the time comes."

"I appreciate it," I assured the both of them.

"Let's get serious now," Lyle advised. "Before you . . . uh . . . desert us, we've got a lot left to discuss with you."

"Believe me. I'm well aware," I replied. "All the laters."

"There's not as much stuff left as you might think," Lyle guaranteed me. "And we've got a few more memory experiences to access if you want to."

"And don't forget that I've got a bunch of random questions to ask regarding many of the subjects we've already discussed," I pointed out.

"We'd be surprised if you didn't," added Betty.

"In fact, here's a question that I'd like to get out of the way before any others," I uttered, shifting my eyes between the two of them.

"Give it your best shot," asserted Lyle

"I asked this a while ago, but the answer I got was kind of vague . . . not very convincing at all," I claimed.

Lyle chuckled, rolled his eyes, and gently shook his head back and forth.

I continued. "Why am I really here? Was it specifically to be the Betty observer? Was it to add me to your memory bank? Or something else?"

"Yes and yes to your first two questions," he said.

"And yes to your last question," interjected Betty.

I knew it. Something weird was going on. As soon as Betty made that statement, Lyle slammed her with a surprised and angry look.

"Jesus, Lyle, by the look on your face, I can tell that you're wishing I'd wake up right about now," I said with an evil grin. "But no such luck."

"I'll explain everything," he conceded.

"You bet your ass you will," I concurred.

"As I told you a while ago," he stressed, "you're here by accident . . . and . . . opportunity. I had no idea you were going to fall into my life during that Iwo memory trip. Do you realize how rare of an event that was? The odds against that happening are probably a zillion to one. After I accepted this amazing happening, and discovered how easily I could get you to return, I immediately realized that you might be a wish come true."

I nodded. "You'd been thinking about the possibility, or I should say 'impossibility,' of a live human observance for your collapsing theory."

"Correct," he responded. "Then . . . many things at once began to happen. I got a kick out of talking to you about all the wonders in my dimension, and I enjoyed your reactions to all our memory events: from the B-29 to the Cobra to flying the model plane. When Betty came into the picture, she also enjoyed your company very much."

"To be one hundred percent honest with you," he continued, "I've also had a selfish interest in everything we've all said and done. Thanks to you, I've acquired some extremely rare and valuable memories — memories that are now firmly embedded in the knowledge bank."

"So . . . what's next?" I inquired. "Where do we go from here?"

Lyle snorted. "Enough of this boring conversation. I want to do something exciting. Like I said before, I've got a few more memory escapades up my sleeve."

"I could also do with some fun," chattered Betty.

"Betty," responded Lyle, "you'll approve of the memory experiences I've got in mind."

"I've got a feeling that we'll have to wait until tomorrow to do anything," I announced. "My dream time for this evening is coming to an end, and I don't want to blank out in the middle of something."

"Point well taken," said Lyle nodding. "Maybe we should start answering some of your questions while you're still here."

"Only one thing I want to know right now," I responded. "What new memory experience do you have on your warped mind?"

Lyle released a very devious, guttural laugh. "It's a secret."

"Come on," I blurted.

"It's a surprise. You'll love it. So will Betty," he whispered.

"So I guess it doesn't include Angelina," I said with sorrow.

Lyle gave a mischievous chortle.

"Pigs," yelled Betty. "You're both pigs."

There was something about the way she said that that got me laughing hysterically. She was getting angrier by the second, and I was laughing so hard that I couldn't catch my breath.

Within a few moments, I came to a very obvious realization.

I was still laughing my ass off, but it was into my pillow.

I had woken up.

After I rolled over to get more comfortable, I drifted right back to sleep.

. . . with a broad smile on my face.

Chapter 23
Boggling the Mind

When I finally woke up from what felt like a perfectly normal night's sleep, I didn't even get pissed off at my Casio when it viciously assaulted my ears. My dream had been pleasant and productive, and, as usual, I had learned some fascinating new impossibilities.

Honestly, the only thing of significance that mildly disturbed me was the annoying subject of proof. I would have to live with what I had. Would have to believe Lyle. After all this time, the skeptical part of me ept raising its ugly head. But I had to remain skeptical. And cautious. It was the sane thing to do.

After an absolutely delectable cappuccino, I decided to take a long, brisk walk. It was time to think. I had to gather my thoughts about all the additional questions I was going to ask Lyle. I was anxious to hear what he had to say about several topics.

The rest of my day breezed by; I have no idea where the time went. That night, I ripped into a fascinating new mystery/thriller. When my eyes were ready to fall out of my head, I threw the book on the floor, groped for the light switch, rolled onto my back, and meditated myself out of this world.

Then I opened my dream eyes in some God forsaken area that I couldn't even begin to identify. It reminded me of a moonscape, but we were definitely on the earth. The land was deserted, and consisted of low hills and valleys strewn with boulders, and broken with rough, stone outcroppings. If not for a few patches of brown-fringed green and some very low bushes, the area was devoid of life.

With the sun very low in the sky, everything was bathed in a soothing, yet mysterious, golden glow, which made the atmosphere all the more unearthly. There was absolutely no glare, but a few of the expansive clouds were rimmed with what looked like a vivid neon light. From our vantage point on one of the larger, jagged hills, all the topographical elements cast deep shadows that haphazardly bisected each other. The overall effect was magnificently eerie. It all made me feel calmly alert.

"I give up," I exhaled. "Where on earth are we?"

The moment I asked, three comfortable director's chairs appeared, all facing the sun.

"Go ahead, Betty, you tell him," said Lyle, lighting a butt.

"Somewhere in Wyoming," she answered, with a bright smile.

"Somewhere?" I asked.

"Somewhere special," said a very animated Lyle. "Just look around you. Look at the stark, powerful, natural beauty. This is the essence of Mother Nature. I couldn't think of a more peaceful, and at the same time stimulating, place to talk. It's as perfect as that mountain ledge we were on, but with an added surprise."

"Well, I can't argue with that," I said with conviction. "And I'd be willing to bet about the surprise. We're probably right on top of some incredible dinosaur fossils that have yet to be discovered."

"Right you are," said Lyle, laughing. "Maybe I'm becoming too predictable."

"That brings something to mind," I noted. "It's a shame dinosaurs didn't have particle bundles. We could . . ."

Lyle abruptly interrupted me. "They did. All living things with some form of a nervous system have always had particle bundles," he informed me. "But most don't have signature vibrations. Only conscious ones do."

"Let's see if I've got this right," I said. "Even amoebas have particle bundles? But no vibrations? How about trees?"

"Yes, amoebas have particle bundles with no vibration." He answered. "We think the bundles may affect basic instincts. Bundles have also been found in plants, but they may be just lodged there, and purely nonfunctional."

"What does it take for an animal to have a vibration?" I asked, even though I thought I had guessed the answer.

"It has to be an animal of a higher order, one with a sophisticated nervous system and a degree of consciousness," he said, nodding.

"You mean like apes and dolphins?" I asked.

"Exactly," he replied. "And . . . whales, dogs, cats, birds, horses and many others. You'd be surprised how smart many animals there are, even those that appear to be stupid. For all we know, dinosaurs may have had vibrations."

"Then wouldn't they be here? In this dimension?" I asked. "And what about apes, for instance? Can you experience their memories?"

"First of all, any animals with vibrations may very well be here," he stated very matter of factly. "We don't know because we can't sense them. Could be some form of simple incompatibility."

"It's a shame you can't be reunited with your pets here," I noted.

"Boy . . . are you right about that," he declared. "That would be wonderful."

"I assume you can have a pet by thought constructing one," I added.

"People have certainly done that," he replied. "But they usually construct an ideal human friend or companion, someone they can shape to their own desire."

"You know, you just answered one of the important questions I wanted to ask you," I said. "I've been wondering about animals and bundles, and whether or not they . . . uh . . . got to heaven."

"For all we know, they skip this dimension, and go directly to the next one," he said.

"Yeah. If there is another one," I replied.

"Hope so. Counting on it," he wished out loud.

"Honestly, I'm with you on that one," I proclaimed. "Now . . . are you ready for my next question? It's a good one."

"You've got my full attention!" he responded with verve.

"Something I said a tiny bit earlier reminded me that I just had to inquire about flying saucers, aliens, and related matters. Not that I expect you to reveal anything at all, but . . ."

"We've got nothing to hide from you," he confessed. "Believe it or not, we're in the dark about this as much as you are. And maybe even more."

"Come on, give me a freakin' break," I quickly responded.

"No, really. I'm not pulling your leg," he said with real sincerity. "We have absolutely no conclusive proof. Some fascinating possibilities, but no substantial proof."

"But how's that possible?" I suspiciously inquired. "You've been telling me that everyone, even complete morons, have photographic memories that you all access and analyze all the time. So, wouldn't you know everything there is to know about sightings, abductions, and especially the Roswell incident?"

"Believe me, I can see why you're confused and in disbelief," he mumbled. "Just listen to me for a minute. And keep an open mind."

"I always do," I countered.

Lyle stretched his legs, and cracked his knuckles. "You're right. Everyone has an extraordinary, photographic memory. Everything you sense, whether it's sight, sound, taste, touch and smell, goes into permanent memory. What's more, as I've told you, your memory far exceeds your basic ability to sense. Your particle bundle heightens your senses: you record light wavelengths that are invisible to you, sound frequencies you can't hear, scents you can't smell and so on."

"That's what I was getting at," I interrupted. "Vivid memories like those should give you the absolute truth about everything. Including UFO's."

Lyle continued. "Unfortunately, that's not the case."

"You've lost me. Completely."

"Gimme some time to explain," he exhaled. "Memory is memory, whether it's fake or not. The real memory bank is fooled all the time."

"Fooled?" I asked in disbelief.

"Yes. Dreams are recorded as memory. So are drug and alcohol induced hallucinations. And hypnotic suggestions, as well."

"Well . . . that must really screw things up for you," I observed.

"At times it certainly does," he continued. "As far as UFO's and aliens are concerned, we've got thousands of 'memories,' and I've accessed many of them. Eliminating all the common sightings of 'lights in the sky' and blurry images of supposed flying saucers, there are many memories of fascinating space ships, hovering and landed. Since so many of these are so different, you'd have to assume that we've been visited by God knows how many civilizations, which, in itself, is highly improbable. The same goes for alien creatures. Just too many of them to be factual."

"What about abductions?" I asked.

"Lots of them. Too many of them," he exclaimed. "Most of the memories are fuzzy without the high level of background detail associated with authentic memories. Of course, they seem real to those who have supposedly experienced them."

"I've read numerous, personal accounts of abduction victims, and they're all virtually identical. How's that possible?" I asked.

"That's all the more reason to be skeptical," he replied. "The descriptions are in the collective subconscious. It's exactly what abductees could be expected to experience."

"I guess that makes sense, but you can't be one hundred percent certain," I added.

"It's all a matter of interpretation and what you want to believe," he admitted. "But look at it this way: if a civilization were advanced enough to make the nearly impossible journey to earth, wouldn't they want to make real contact instead of just yanking bumpkins out of trailer parks and sticking probes into them?"

"I've come to that conclusion, myself, while reading about this crazy phenomenon," I said.

"I'll tell you about an interesting hypothesis I once heard," he said, lighting another Camel. "These 'aliens' are highly evolved human beings from way in the future who've traveled back in time to harvest sperm, eggs and DNA samples. Obviously, they wouldn't have any distance to travel, and they'd avoid formal contact like the plague."

"Talk about ridiculous . . ." I declared. "Yeah, it's a nice explanation, but I thought time travel was completely impossible."

"Nearly impossible," he quickly responded. "Quantum physics allows for time travel, but those scientists who seriously contemplate it, admit that the amount of power and technology required to make it happen is astronomical — way, way, way beyond our capabilities. But, you've got to admit that it's fun to think about."

"That's for sure," I said with a laugh. "Maybe these blokes from the future have been interfering all along. Maybe they helped the Egyptians build the pyramids, and other stuff like that."

"Keep dreaming." He sighed.

"One last question before I wake up, which I'm sure will be soon. What about Roswell? All bullshit?"

"I just knew you were going to bring that up," he said, exhaling a huge smoke ring that could have almost passed for a UFO. "I'll tell you absolutely everything I know . . . nothing left out," he promised. "But, to be completely honest with you, there's really . . ."

"Shit," I cried. "Lyle, I'm waking up. I can feel it. And right in the middle of . . ."

That was it. I had vanished back to reality. Back to the comfort of my own bed, with about five hours to go before I'd wake up for real. But, first, in order to fall back to sleep, I had to get Roswell off my mind. After what felt like an eternity, Roswell became Rozzzzzzzzzzzzwell.

Chapter 24
The Hoax and the Moonlight Sonata.

Woke up feeling very refreshed.

Now I had to get through a day of painful suspense in anticipation of my upcoming Roswell discussion. As I let a rather large breakfast go down, the subject of my possible book forced its way into my mind. It immediately, and a bit frighteningly, occurred to me that I could forget some key, interesting nuances if I procrastinated, without jotting down so much as a word or even a thought. But I was virtually certain that I vividly remembered every second of every dream. It also occurred to me that having my vibration massaged, so to speak, may have radically increased my memory.

The remainder of my day was the definition of monotony. That night, which I had really been looking forward to, I read for several hours before meditating myself to sleep. Instead of focusing on my traditional acorn, I opted for a tiny, spinning UFO. It worked. Perfectly.

I opened my dream eyes standing up, very precariously balanced.

Waiting for my eyes to adjust to the apparently intense sunlight, I squinted at my feet. Detecting a little movement close to my right foot, I looked closely, and saw something that made me jolt.

It was a tarantula.

A big one.

Very hairy.

Obviously some poor slob's frightening memory.

By this time, I was immune to anything like this, knowing full well that it couldn't have any effect on me. But it was momentarily startling. I guess that's why I heard Lyle laughing. When I looked up, he was intently staring at this gargantuan spider lumbering along, most likely searching for some unlucky bug to dine on. I also immediately noticed that Betty was nowhere to be seen. The spider couldn't have scared her off: that much I was certain.

"So where do you think we are?" asked Lyle, broadly grinning. Amazingly, he wasn't sucking on a Camel. Yet.

I slowly turned in a full circle, studying the garden-variety landscape. It was basically flat and featureless: lots of rocks, lots of clumps of dirt, tangles of weeds, and patches of rough, overgrown grass. Ugly. Not what you'd call a prime vacation spot or tourist trap. I was wrong about that.

"What were we talking about when you woke up yesterday?" he asked.

"Roswell," I answered without hesitation.

Then I let it sink in for a second.

"Roswell," I exclaimed. "So that's where we are."

He spread his arms out wide and said, "Yup. Beautiful, scenic, Roswell, New Mexico. We're right at the sight of the supposed crash, actually on a ranch just outside of the town."

"Doesn't look like much," I noted.

"What would you expect?" he asked. "A huge crater? Glowing rocks?"

"Those would be nice," I answered. "Maybe a few alien bodies would also add to the atmosphere. But, I've gotta admit, this is the best place to discuss this stuff."

"Not much for me to reveal, unfortunately," he said with a somewhat sad expression on his face. You may not believe me, but . . ."

"Before we get into that," I interrupted, "I've got a few questions to ask you on another subject."

"Fine," he said. "But let's not get into anything that'll steer us into some long, unrelated explanation."

"Sure. So why isn't Betty here? I've been worried about her because she hasn't been her usual self. I'm afraid that maybe my whole observance thing is changing her."

His answer made me feel better, calmed my nerves. "You're right, she hasn't been herself. But it has nothing to do with you. She hasn't changed at all; she's just been very nervous about sick Betty, wondering about her own fate when the inevitable happens."

"That's very understandable," I commented. "But where is she?"

"In the hospital, sitting on the bed, watching her namesake," he said. "It's torture for her, but that's what she wants to do."

"That leads me to my next question: How's the real Betty? Is her condition improving or getting worse? I'm sorry that I haven't asked about her in a while."

"Don't give it a moment's worry," he assured me. "You've had lots on your mind. It's hard to give you a precise answer because she varies from day to day. But she's always in that damn coma now. Luckily, as far as I can tell, she's not in any pain. So it's just a matter of time."

"What about that communication you had with her?" I asked. "Has it continued?"

"Oh, yes," he loudly remarked. "She keeps reciting lyrics from what I believe is a song. And the words are uncannily on target, considering the situation. I'm definitely on her mind, and she senses I'm with her."

"If you don't mind my asking, how's that possible?"

"Fuck if I know," he stammered. "Nothing surprises me when it comes to the mind, alignment, and extra sensory communication. Who can say what's possible and what isn't?"

After several long moments of dead silence, he asked me if I had another question. I told him I had a million more, but one foremost on my mind: the Roswell story — the truth as he knew it.

With a bit of hesitation, he began. "I started to tell you before that you may not believe what I'm going to say, and it'll probably be a let down."

"At this point, I'll believe anything," I said with resignation.

Lyle turned his head back and forth observing the area and laughed. "This whole Roswell thing, John . . . it's a hoax. As far as anyone can tell, the only thing that crashed was some government weather balloon and instrumentation. Yeah, it may have been some secret, experimental spying device, but that's it. End of story, amigo."

"But what about all the talk about strange metal with weird writing? And how about the alien bodies?"

"All bullshit," he assured me.

"But how can you be so certain?" I asked, already suspecting what he was going to say.

"We've looked closely at the memories. Lots of them. All over the place. People claim to have heard that it was a UFO and that there were bodies, but hearing ain't reality. There's nothing definitive other than that the government tried to cover up the fact that this was a pre-satellite spying probe. Remember, in 1947 we were already scared shitless of the Russians. Oh, one last thing of interest. Our government probably perpetuated the UFO cover up story so it would cover up the real story. Brilliant, if you really give it some thought."

"Want to know where the real brilliance lies?" I asked. "With Roswell, itself. They're fucking public relations geniuses. They've exploited every last angle of this idiotic event; the town is now a Holy city, a fucking Mecca, for every UFO loony in the world."

"I can't argue with that," he loudly exclaimed. "Sorry I dragged you all the way out here just to pop your Roswell bubble."

"Now you owe me an extremely intriguing experience," I said, half seriously.

"Got the perfect thing in mind," he beamed. "How much do you like music?"

"I guess I like it as much as most anyone. But I'm no expert."

"Well, you're going to find this memory experience absolutely fascinating."

"So cut the suspense . . . what's this all about?

"You'll see in a couple of minutes," he said. "But first I've got to go and check up on sick Betty, and get my other Betty to join us. She needs something to cheer her up."

"I agree, of course. But . . . does that mean you're going to leave me in this dismal, fake place all by myself?"

"Why don't I snap you over to your favorite spot," he said with a grin. "I won't be long at all."

Instantaneously, he vanished, and, at the same moment, I found myself back in my favorite place: the Amazon rain forest. It felt wonderful being back. What a pleasant change from muddy old Roswell.

While I waited, I decided to flop on my back on my big fluffy cushion, and watch all the action above. As I stared deep into the boundless canopy, a slight breeze blew the large, undulating fronds back and forth, creating a bright, twinkling effect.

My thoughts drifted to what Lyle had just said: a musical experience. I was wondering what he could possibly have in store. Maybe it was an historic concert. Elvis? Madonna? The Beach Boys? Realistically, it was probably something from his heyday. Probably Sinatra, The Andrews Sisters, or one of those famous big bands. Regardless, it would be fun.

As I pondered all the possibilities, I was so relaxed and content that I closed my eyes, and began to drift away. The next thing I knew, Lyle and Betty were standing right beside me. I was startled. But relieved that they were there.

"Gee, hope we didn't wake you, John," commented Lyle.

I just stood up, stretched, yawned and nodded.

"Hey, give me a chance to wake up," I groggily announced. "I almost fell asleep in my sleep, if that's even remotely possible."

"For you . . . anything's possible," said Betty.

"So . . . I see you couldn't resist our musical adventure, could you?" I asked. "Ready to rock 'n roll?"

Lyle chuckled. "I don't think the musical talent you're going to see is very aware of rock 'n roll. He slightly predates Elvis."

"I figured it was going to be something like a big band or crooner from your era," I noted.

Lyle chuckled again. "All I can say is that you're going to be in for a very big surprise."

"Enough with the theatrics, Lyle," exclaimed Betty, with a smile.

Lyle looked at both of us, nodded, and emulated an orchestra conductor, using his cigarette as a baton. In an instant whoosh, we were standing in what appeared to be an antique, perfume scented parlor, sparsely decorated with a few pieces of heavy, austere furniture in dark wood: an armoire, two tables, and a large couch, lavishly upholstered in a simple green and black pattern. The floor was partially covered with a highly ornate rug in dark orange, brown, and rust foliage, and the single, white curtained window revealed that it was nighttime. Illumination was provided by a single, flickering oil lamp that made the many shadows seem alive. The effect was warm, but not overly friendly.

Then I heard it: a lonely piano note vibrating through the single open door. Another note. Then another. Then some muted conversation I couldn't comprehend. There was a long moment of silence followed by the shuffling of paper, and then a few more quick, seemingly angry stabs at the keys. This was obviously not what I expected. Music? A few stupid piano notes? Where had Lyle taken me? One thing was for certain: we weren't in Graceland. No hound dogs here.

Lyle motioned to Betty and me to proceed through the door. Instinctively, I began to tiptoe in, then realized I wasn't really there — just a silent, invisible, spectral presence, a distant memory. The room we entered was a much larger version of the parlor, with more of the same style furniture, and at least five large windows. One feature, however, defined the essence of the room, and the reason why we were here: a huge, magnificent piano dominated, and dwarfed, everything else.

As we slowly strolled to the side of this regal instrument, I saw a somewhat youngish looking man sitting at the bench, earnestly scribbling on some paper. Seated to his left was an older, severe looking woman in a flowing green dress, with a tight, dumb looking collar. From the looks of her, the words 'fun, friendly, and enjoyable' were not part of her vocabulary.

All of a sudden, he plopped the paper on a music rack, poised his long, thin fingers over the keys, and pounded out a few seconds of a melody that I faintly recognized. I was terrifically confused. Who was this guy and his bitch? Deep within, I suspected that Lyle had taken us to one of the grand masters. But I had no idea who it was. Not a clue.

Before his last note ceased to vibrate the piano strings, she waved her arms, and yelled something at him in a guttural language that I assumed was German. He halted her with his hand, held an acoustical horn to his ear (antique hearing aid), then beckoned her to continue. I issued a little nervous laughter, and felt Lyle poke me on the arm.

"Do you have any idea who he is?" asked Lyle.

"Not, Springsteen, Sinatra, or Elvis," I quipped.

"Seriously," said Lyle.

"I assume it's someone like Mozart," I guessed.

"Well . . . you're in the right neighborhood," he stated.

"Cut the crap, and just tell me who he is," I demanded.

"Ludwig van Beethoven," he declared with a flair.

"And who's the bitchy old bimbo?" I asked.

"Don't have the foggiest idea," he admitted. "But I doubt she's his girlfriend. Unless, of course, he was into a little dominance."

"Amen," I blurted.

Betty made one of those I'm annoyed sighs.

To say the very least, I was thrilled to be there. Beethoven. Obviously composing. What an experience. I was stunned. Elvis wouldn't have held a candle to this. Lyle and Betty were also held in awe, even though I suspected they had accessed this memory before.

Walking closer, I took a long look at him. He appeared to be around forty years old, good looking, with a medium build. His eyes were dark and intense, but very kind, and projecting a simmering intelligence. He had medium length, deep brown, wispy hair; long sideburns framed his compassionate face. A vivid blue, soft velvet suit contrasted with his bright white shirt and ruffled collar. I couldn't see his shoes beneath the bench, but I'm sure they weren't cowboy boots. All things considered, he didn't resemble the Beethoven I'd seen in paintings and sculptures.

Lyle knew what I was thinking. "He got stockier and sported the long, flowing grey hair he's famous for later in life. He's in his early thirties here; it's roughly 1802, and he was born in December of 1770."

"Where are we now?" I asked.

"Vienna," he answered. "And I'm sure you know why he's got that horn stuck in his ear."

"Yeah, he was deaf," I responded. "But this early in his life?"

"Not completely," Lyle assured me. "The history books claim that in 1796 he developed tinnitus, a very annoying ringing in the ears, that made it hard for him to hear and appreciate music."

"It's a friggin' miracle he was such a brilliant composer," I noted.

"Now . . . that . . . is a long, fascinating story," he exclaimed.

"One that you're not going to tell me now, I bet."

"Tomorrow. I promise," he said with sincerity. "You'll understand why."

"Can hardly wait," I exhaled. "By the way, when did old Ludwig make his little trip to your dimension?"

"Early in 1827," he answered. "Now . . . here's the big question — one I'm surprised you haven't asked. Do you recognize what he's composing? Did the few notes he played ring a bell?"

"Classical music has never been my thing," I sadly admitted. "But there was definitely something vaguely familiar about it."

"Moonlight Sonata," he said, closing his eyes.

"Wow. So this is definitely a proud moment in musical history," I said.

"One of the ultimate moments," he added.

"Hope you put this in your book," remarked Betty.

"Why not," I remarked, chuckling. "It's just as unbelievable as everything else. If I manage to write it, I'll become an honorary member of the Liars Hall of Fame, and a primary candidate for shock therapy."

"Sorry you feel that way," she sighed. "And . . . uh . . . will I be in your possible book?"

"What do you think?" I seriously asked her. "Couldn't be written without you. But . . . I'll have to change your character. You know, make you a nice, wholesome person. I mean ghost."

Kidding around, she pretended to smack me in the face. As I instinctively ducked, my ear must have gotten snagged on the edge of my pillow, and . . . I woke up. But not all the way up. Because I drifted back to sleep, with Beethoven's notes soothing my mind.

Chapter 25
Brain Drain

The first thing that crossed my mind when I woke up was that all this was going to be over, all too soon.

Well . . . not too soon.

It had been my own personal choice to put an end to these unbelievable dreams. Maybe I shouldn't say 'end.' Why not 'temporary reprieve?' No. I had to stick to my guns. If I left myself an inch, I'd take a mile. I was committed to getting my life back. And turning this experience into a book.

After absorbing my second coffee, I turned on my laptop, went to iTunes, and listened to Moonlight Sonata. What a magnificent achievement. Fucking genius. It's almost impossible to believe that Beethoven was nearly deaf when he composed it. And it's totally impossible to believe that I was there watching him do it. But it seemed so real. Even if it was purely an illusion, it was a wonderful experience.

The rest of my day flew by quicker than a warping starship. After a seriously mediocre Chinese dinner, I took a lengthy, energetic walk to assimilate all the monosodium glutamate that was crammed into my sweet & sour pork. Then I dragged my weary body into bed, chose an imaginary vegetable dumpling as my meditation focus, and softly wafted into the next world.

...

For a bunch of reasons, I expected to open my dream eyes in my favorite location. But that's not where Lyle had taken us. We returned to a much different location — a location I dearly loved, but for entirely different reasons. When I opened my eyes, I was staring at the barn in my old back yard where I grew up. Yes, it was wonderful being there again. Turning to look at Lyle, I wondered why he had made this decision. Then it crossed my mind that maybe he was just trying to be nice. Maybe he wanted me to be there at least one more time.

Lyle was walking around with his hands in his pockets, looking quite content and exceptionally relaxed. He was even whistling, which I had never seen him do before. Could be, he had been inspired by Beethoven. Betty, on the other hand, was frozen in place next to my old vegetable and flower garden. I walked over to her.

"See something you like?" I asked her.

"Something?" she shrieked. "How about everything. This is a great garden. You're lucky to have had this when you were a kid."

"Thanks. I really, really enjoyed it," I sighed.

Then I walked over to the tomato plants, and picked a handful of the cherries.

"Here. Try 'em," I said as I handed some to her.

"Shouldn't I wash them first?" she asked. "Any bug spray?"

"No," I answered. "But if there were, it wouldn't kill you."

I watched her put one in her mouth, close her eyes, and slowly chew it. She repeated that process three times before uttering another word.

"You know what I'm going to say," she announced. "These are delicious. Almost as delicious as the tomatoes from Wisconsin."

She picked herself a few more, and I loved watching her thoroughly savor every bite. While I had the time, I showed her all around the place, retrieving one emotionally charged memory after another. She encouraged me to let it all spill out, and listened carefully to everything I said. It was obvious from her kind expression that she sincerely cared.

Lyle walked over and cleared his throat. "John, I can hear you're taking her down memory lane."

"Every mile of it," I beamed. "I was thinking of running into my old house and getting a model plane to show her."

"Oh, that would be . . ." Betty said.

Lyle chuckled and interrupted. "Sorry. Not enough time. I've got lots to tell John before he wakes up."

"But can I get my plane after we talk if there's still time?" I asked, half seriously.

"Fair enough." he exhaled.

Within the blink of an eye, three, very comfortable director's chairs appeared right in the middle of the lawn. Following Lyle's nod, we sat down, and waited for his words of wisdom.

"John, I've got to apologize for something," he said, scratching his head. "The more I think about it, I shouldn't have waited so long to explain this brain/bundle thing to you. It would have helped you understand other things we've been discussing like Beethoven's abilities, for example."

"Honestly, it's probably better that you waited until now," I assured him. "I've had so much bizarre information overload that any more would have completely screwed up my head."

"You could be right," he muttered.

"Here and there, I've picked up disparaging remarks you've made about the brain," I reminded him. "I think you even said that the brain hinders our particle bundles. Limits their capabilities."

"Jesus, you really do listen to me," he declared. "But don't get me wrong; the brain, even with all its deficiencies, is a miraculous machine."

"You know, from the very first time you told me about these particle bundle thingamajigs, I found it very disconcerting. I mean . . . something from outer space imbedded in my brain. It creeps me out."

Lyle snickered. "Every last bit of you is from 'outer space.' Everything everywhere is made of stardust: fundamental particles."

"I realize that. It makes sense. But particle bundles are different; they're . . . uh . . . little devices, multi-faceted units with their own operational capabilities, maybe even their own power sources. And there's nothing random about them."

"Yeah," he exclaimed. "Not to bring up a sore subject, but, the more you think about them, the more you wonder about intelligent design."

"That again?" Let's just stick to science if you don't mind. Please."

"Won't mention it again. I promise," he stated with conviction.

"So . . . let me begin by refreshing your memory a little," he continued, as he lovingly lit a Camel. "Without a doubt, your brain controls just about everything. It's your central processor. Now, according to neurobiological theorists in my dimension, particle bundles control the higher brain functions like memory, communication, and everything that has to do with the senses."

"What about personality? And creativity?" I asked.

"Personality and individuality are a brain/bundle mix. You'll understand in a while. Creativity, however, is all under the control of your bundle. It's the undisputed king of your right brain."

"I'm confused about the control thing," I mumbled. "I thought the brain controls everything."

"In effect, it does. But, while the bundle is in control of specific functions, the brain has overall control over the bundle. That is the key to everything — from innovation to, believe it or not, civilization."

"Boy, do you have a lot of explaining to do," I blurted.

"No shit, Sherlock," he boldly responded.

"Somehow, I can't get used to you speaking like that. I mean . . ."

Lyle interrupted. "I'm just a person like you. I'm not some goody-two-shoes angel or some ethereal being spouting crap like thee and thou. I'm a smoker. I'm a joker. I'm a midnight toker . . ."

"Enough. I get it. I'm sorry. Sometimes I forget you're just a regular guy like every other asshole I know."

"Well . . . you don't have to go that far with it," he chuckled. "Now where was I? Yeah, your brain controls your bundle. Under the best of circumstances, it acts like a filter. Remember, your bundle enables you to see light in a very wide range of wavelengths; it allows you to hear a wide range of frequencies; and it radically increases your sensitivity for smelling, tasting, and feeling. Last, but certainly not least, your bundle provides photographic memory, plus access to the all-encompassing field of knowledge. Still with me?"

"Keep going. You're on a roll," I replied.

"But . . . your brain does not let you process most of that information. Most of what you see remains invisible. Same goes for your hearing and all your other senses. Your brain drastically narrows everything, literally smothering your particle bundle."

"Any theories why? I asked. "I take that back. There must be zillions of theories — from the sublime to the ridiculous."

"Believe it or not, there's only one general theory that everyone agrees on," he said, leaning forward to make a point. "To put it in highly technical terms, life would probably be pretty shitty if bundles weren't hindered."

I just gave him my best what-the-fuck expression.

Lyle continued. "You've got to remember that all particle bundles are identical — whether they're residing in the brain of a genius or a total moron. So, if bundles were given free reign, there's a good chance that everyone would have the exact same capabilities and very similar personalities. We'd all be geniuses, blasting through life, not stopping to smell the roses."

"But you all, in this dimension, are brain-free, and you seem relatively normal," I observed.

"Use your brain, John. Our individualities were formed when we were alive. We're continuations of ourselves, but with massively increased capabilities."

"I see."

"Let me continue," he said. "If bundles ran wild, so to speak, evolution would have been very different. What if cave men had been geniuses? And think about civilization? Would we have blown ourselves up hundreds of years ago? Everything would have flowed along entirely too fast. People would never have been content to do anything mundane like join the police force, or the fire department, or deliver the mail."

"Let me ask you this," I said. "If our bundles are all identical, and our brains have the same filtering controls, wouldn't we still be very much alike?"

"Now you're getting to the crux of what makes us us." he blurted with wild enthusiasm. "Our brains are dysfunctional. That's the beauty of it. That's what makes us all different. That's what's made it possible for humanity to progress in ways that are interesting."

"Dysfunctional in what way?" I queried.

"They all have different levels of control over the bundles," he explained. "Brains make mistakes because they're imperfect."

"Please take it slower," I advised him. "You're losing me. What do you mean by 'imperfect?'"

"Being as complicated and delicate as they are, brains are affected by everything: chemical imbalances, birth defects, genetics, bacteria, electricity, pollution, viruses, all diseases, environmental factors, magnetism, common accidents, hormone levels, meditation, radiation, eating habits, and thousands of more."

"In other words, what you're saying is that absolutely anything can have either a negative or positive influence on the brain's functioning capabilities, which determines its ability to either reduce or increase its filtering controls on our bundles."

"Essentially, yes," he replied. "That sums it up pretty well."

"I've got quite a few questions," I said.

"I bet you do," he quipped. "Fire away."

"Considering all these potential brain dysfunctions," I asked, "what happens to a severely retarded, I mean almost brain dead, person when they die? Are their bundles aimlessly floating around here?"

"All bundles are identical, no matter how severe the brain dysfunction," he coolly answered. "And bundles always perform flawlessly regardless of the situation. So, everything that person senses is recorded as a complete memory. When that person's bundle tunnels into this dimension and is brain-free, they become perfectly normal, but never ever forget the way they lived. Once here, they can begin a new life, experiencing all the memories they were deprived of. It's really heart warming."

"Amazing," I exclaimed. "For them, this really is heaven."

"It's heaven for anyone who's led a challenged or miserable life," he joyfully noted. "And that goes for people who've been severely crippled, blind, or deaf. Even if someone's been blind since birth, for example, their bundle and vibration have been seeing by accessing light frequencies. So, they go from the blackness of living to a dimension where they can finally see their loved ones, as well as the world they were stumbling through. They can relive all their memories in full visual detail."

"Even more amazing," I exclaimed again. "How about this: let's say someone dies at birth without having any memories at all. What happens in that situation? It must be completely disorienting."

"Hold that question, John. I'm going to answer it later in a very, very special way. It'll blow your mind."

"I can't wait," I said, taking a deep breath.

"I'm having trouble putting all this in an order that makes sense," he thought aloud. "There's a lot to explain. Many different angles to explore. I want to save the really good stuff for last."

"Don't worry. So far, it's all good," I strongly assured him.

Another question popped into my mind. "Is it possible for the brain to have too much control? I mean, if senses were restricted beyond the norm, could a person appear to be retarded or deficient in some way?"

"From what I've been told, that's usually not the case. Very, very rare, if ever," he replied. "But you can't rule out the possibility. It would seem to make perfect sense."

"Here's a question I shouldn't ask. It's about weirdos who see auras. Is this the result of a dysfunction or an enhancement?"

"You just hit the mother lode," he excitedly declared. "This is where the whole thing becomes amazingly fascinating. People who see auras, and experience other paranormal phenomena, are the victims of both dysfunction and enhancement."

"You've certainly got my attention," I said, rolling my eyes.

Lyle chuckled, then got dead serious. "As you know, the brain, for one reason or another, can be anywhere from mildly to drastically dysfunctional. Which can have effects on every part of the body. For now, we're only talking about the particle bundle."

"Of course," I agreed.

Lyle continued. "As the brain's control of the bundle decreases, the person gains more abilities — everything from sensory to what can be construed as overall intelligence. That's where dysfunction becomes enhancement."

"Holy shit," I exclaimed. "I know where you're going with this."

"Just hold your horses and listen," he stressed. "Thanks to these dysfunctions, countless numbers of people are enhanced from nearly imperceptibly to drastically. We'll talk about the drastic ones later: those are the really, really interesting ones. Now, getting back to your aura question, I think you know the answer."

"It's now plain as day," I blurted. "The brain is no longer blocking that ability. That's why lots of those people possess other paranormal abilities like ESP, divination, healing, telekinesis, and more of that metaphysical garbage."

"Garbage?" he asked. "I doubt you can call it 'garbage' any more. Or bullshit. Or hocus pocus."

"I wouldn't go that far," I asserted. "I still contend that those people are weird."

"Don't lose that thought," said Lyle, ready to make a point. "Let's talk about 'weird' people who can also be described as eccentric."

"There's a difference between weird and eccentric," I noted. "Weird usually applies to assholes, while eccentrics can be kindly old professors."

"That's your own warped perception," he snorted. "Wouldn't you admit that a highly creative, enormously talented guy like Michael Jackson was eccentric in his own way? His unique capabilities are typical of those with partially unrestricted bundles."

"He's a bad example," I grumbled. "The guy was an astonishingly gifted, weird asshole."

"You're impossible," he hissed with a smirk. "How about Elvis?"

"The King was definitely eccentric," I agreed.

"How about Salvador Dali?" he asked.

"Friggin' eccentric."

"How about Ernest Hemingway?" he asked. "And General George Patton? And Frank Lloyd Wright? And Martha Graham?"

"Brilliant eccentrics," I retorted.

"Here's the crème de la crème," he proclaimed. "Albert Einstein. He's the perfect example of diminished brain control. His unprecedented, astounding, theoretical abilities are proof of access to the universal field of knowledge. He was completely channeled into that."

"If his brain control was so diminished," I asked, "does that mean he also saw auras, possessed enhanced hearing, and had a photographic memory?"

"No," answered Lyle. "It doesn't work that way. You don't get the whole package. Brain dysfunction is selective: only certain bundle abilities manage to seep through."

"Hit or miss. Purely random. Reeks of quantum uncertainty." I mused.

"Excellent observation," he said. "After all, the brain is definitely a quantum machine."

"Let's not go down this road now," I advised. "We'll be straying too far from the main topic."

"Good thinking again, John. Now, where was I? Oh yeah, I was going to say that, generally speaking, all creative people are enhanced to some degree. They all have fewer restrictions on their bundle."

"Would you describe Patton as creative?" I asked.

"Absolutely," replied Lyle. "There's nothing more creative than brilliant military strategy, the ability to outthink the enemy under enormous stress. It's important to realize that creativity is not limited to the arts. Under the overall banner of creativity, you'll find medicine, politics, cooking, sports, finance, law, crime . . . you name it."

"What about . . . uh . . . Hitler?" I asked. "Would you include that monster in this special category?"

"Without a doubt," he exclaimed. "He's a great example. On one hand, he was an egotistical idiot when it came to military strategy. After 1939, his direction flushed Germany down the toilet. But, he was also a genius when it came to motivating people. His auditory skills, combined with facial expressions and body language, have never been equaled. His ranting speeches mesmerized people, whipped them into a frenzy."

"What confuses me about all this," I stated, "is that it's categorized as the result of brain dysfunction. There's nothing dysfunctional about it. The word 'enhancement' is far more appropriate."

"Point well taken," he uttered. "Dysfunction definitely carries a negative connotation, but it's, unquestionably, an accurate description. Remember, the brain will only lighten its control on the bundle when it's experiencing problems, even completely undetectable problems like very, very minor inflammations. If the problems aren't physically or mentally debilitating, we think of them as enhancements."

"What if a brain dysfunction gets healed?" I asked. "I've got to assume a person can lose an enhancement if the brain regains bundle control."

"You're one hundred percent correct," he answered. "People with special gifts have been known to lose them."

"I guess that's what happens with drug use," I observed. "Drugs create short duration brain dysfunctions that heighten senses and cause all types of hallucinations. When the drugs wear off, the bundle regains control."

Lyle nodded in agreement, then brought up an interesting point. "Many people who receive serious head injuries, especially to the left brain, experience heightened senses. Sometimes, yet rarely, their new abilities are confounding, especially to themselves."

"Reminds me of a movie with John Travolta that I think was called Phenomenal. All of a sudden, he developed mindboggling abilities like telekinesis, as well as radically enhanced intelligence. Turns out he had a terminal brain tumor that was causing it."

"Perfect example," beamed Lyle.

I sat back, methodically puffed on the pipe that appeared out of the clear blue, and let this stuff rattle around in my mind. He was right. These revelations were definitely fascinating and exceptionally thought provoking.

"Thinking?" he asked. "Got some more questions before I get into the really good stuff?"

"One thing I was wondering about: "Can someone be both physically and/or mentally debilitated, yet also positively enhanced? I mean can opposite conditions exist in the same brain?"

"Yes," he excitedly exclaimed. "Now this is where it starts to get more than astonishing."

"More than astonishing?" I questioned. "Didn't think that was possible. But, then again, up here in heaven . . ."

Clearing his throat, Lyle continued. "There are very special people who present a complete paradox. At the extreme, they can be severely retarded but have one ability that's extraordinary, beyond most human capabilities. They're astonishing and defy all logic."

"I think I once saw a movie about one of these people," I mentioned. "It's called Rainman."

"Precisely," he stated. "That was the first time most people were formally introduced to savant syndrome."

"You mean idiot savants?" I asked with sincerity.

Betty finally jumped in. "Only idiots call them idiot savants."

"How nice to hear from you, Betty," I quipped. "Sorry I woke you up."

"John, John, John," Lyle intervened. "To say 'idiot savant' is extremely politically incorrect. 'Idiot' was dropped years ago when the condition was better understood. And it just so happens that Betty is highly interested in the topic, and knows lots about it."

"Sorry. Correction noted," I said. "So you're an expert on this, Betty?"

"Not really an expert," she coyly admitted. "It's just that, to me, some of these people are the real miracles of this world. Lyle was understating it when he said they were 'more than astonishing.'"

"How long has this condition been recognized?" I asked her. "I wouldn't imagine it's something recent."

"As far as we know," she answered, "savant syndrome has been a human condition since the birth of consciousness and self-awareness. More recently, however, it was first described in medical journals as early as 1751. In 1887, the condition was coined 'idiot savant' by Dr. Langdon Down, the same man who had Down Syndrome named after him. During the twentieth century, savantism came into its own, and was studied throughout the world."

"You really are an expert," I gushed. "Now I know where to direct my questions."

Lyle was pointing at Betty with both hands, and nodding 'yes.'

"Here's a simple one: are all savants either retarded or mentally challenged in some way?"

"Not at all," she quickly responded. "Most savants are very mildly affected. You'd never know there was anything wrong with them. Wait a second, I should say 'anything right with them.'"

"What exactly do you mean by that?" I asked, puzzled. "Are you trying to give savantism a positive spin?"

"Very, very, very, very positive," she excitedly exclaimed.

"You've lost me," I sighed.

"Savants, the very mild ones, are the luckiest people in the world." she stressed. "And . . . they, to a large degree, have been the most important people in the world since day one."

"Now I'm even more lost," I said, rolling my eyes. "Would you please get to the point."

"Throughout history," she said, "many of the most brilliant people, those who've shaped the world, have been savants. They're the true thinkers — the creative ones — the risk takers. Without savants, the world would be a backward, dull place to be."

"If you can, please name a few savants. I'm curious," I stated.

Betty thought for a second, and appeared as though she was counting on her fingers. "Let's see: Einstein, Mozart, Nostradamus, Thomas Jefferson, Edison, Michelangelo, Isaac Newton, Mark Twain, Beethoven, and countless others."

"That's pretty unbelievable." I loudly stated. "But how the hell is it known that they were savants? How could it have been diagnosed way back then when they didn't know shit about brain function?"

"It's current knowledge," she answered "For the past few decades, scientists have made these observations by studying everything written about, and by, these people. They all possess undeniable savant traits."

"It's just that I would have never expected these incredibly influential people to be savants. I mean, I always thought savants were basically very dysfunctional, almost vegetative recluses who lived regulated lives."

"Unfortunately, that's what most people think," she assured me. "But the opposite is true.

"It seems to me that savantism is too extraordinary to be considered a brain dysfunction," I observed. "This mild version should have a different name."

"Not so," said Lyle, jumping back into the conversation. "Just bear with me for a moment, Betty. "It's definitely a brain dysfunction allowing particle bundle capabilities to filter through. It's not at all normal. On the other hand, some of the more severely retarded savants are the most gifted ones of all. They have mental abilities that run circles around their mildly effected counterparts. They're the ones who are truly astonishing."

"Excuse me," I said, "but I think I would qualify Beethoven as astonishing, not to mention Einstein, Michelangelo and the rest of them."

"Absolutely," affirmed Lyle. "Maybe I should have put it another way. Some of these savants are way beyond astonishing. You could say their mental skills are truly superhuman. They're also extremely rare."

"I've heard of some of their skills, but could you elaborate a little?" I asked.

Betty interrupted. "Lyle, before you describe some of these abilities, let me tell John about the different levels of savants — how they're classified. I think it might be useful."

Lyle nodded.

Betty continued. "The more profoundly retarded savants that have one or more abilities that exceed their normal level of functioning are called 'Splinter Savants.' The next group is called 'Talented Savants.' They are basically dysfunctional types, but with significantly higher abilities that exceed their level of functioning. And then there are the 'Prodigious Savants.' They're the absolutely spectacular ones who drive scientists crazy. No one has the wildest idea how they can do what they do. They perform impossible mental feats."

Lyle laughed and clapped his hands. "Impossible? Not when you consider the undeniable fact that aspects of their particle bundles are completely unrestricted. Their brains are free to access the field of knowledge. It's a severe dysfunction that produces an equally severe enhancement."

Betty took it from there. "Lyle's right. And scientists will continue racking their brains until they fully understand ability filtering, and the fact that bundles exist."

"But that might not be for hundreds or thousands of years," I added.

"Precisely," noted Betty. "It shall remain a mystery."

"Question," I announced. "Were any of these famous people you all mentioned Prodigious Savants? Oh . . . and, by the way, none of the famous savants were women. Any reason why?"

"Most savants at all levels are men," she answered. "It's six to one, male, female. To answer your other question, the famous people were all completely functional in every way, so they weren't your typical Prodigious Savants. And virtually none of them, except maybe Einstein and Newton, possessed mysteriously spectacular abilities. Remember, mere 'brilliance' doesn't adequately describe what most of these Prodigious types are capable of."

"Could you answer my earlier question now?" I asked. "You know, the one about these extraordinary skills."

Lyle spoke up first. "Yeah. First of all, I just want to say that one thing just about all these savants have in common is a fantastic memory. Fantastic memory? Sound familiar? Memory is such a powerful bundle ability that almost any reduction in filtering will enhance it."

"I think you've made your point about that. I'm convinced, I said, as I stretched my legs to relax.

"One last observation," he eagerly said. "Since what I'm telling you is completely unknown in your dimension, can't some of these revelations be construed as proof? Admit it."

"I guess you've got a point there," I reluctantly admitted. "I guess this isn't info that can be remote viewed."

"Bet your ass it can't," he proudly exclaimed. "Now I'll get back to the skills. Sorry about the diversion."

"I'm used to that," I laughed.

Betty strongly voiced her agreement.

Lyle cleared his throat. "Of the few Prodigious savants recorded in history, Kim Peek was probably the most famous, and the inspiration for the movie, Rainman. Talk about being spectacular, he spent most of his time in the library reading. He could knock off four to six books a day, and remember every last word. But . . . the most shocking thing about it is that he'd read two pages at a time: one with each eye."

"That's impossible to believe," I screeched. "You're jerking me around."

Betty responded to my disbelief. "It's true, John. He was able to do that. Pretty incredible, isn't it?"

"Thanks for bailing me out, Betty," Lyle muttered. "At least John believes you."

"After hearing that, I'll believe anything you tell me," I said with resignation.

"What a relief," he gladly commented. "Now I'll just quickly outline a bunch of other remarkable examples."

"Wait a second," I interrupted. "Before you get into that, I've got another quick question. Now that everyone in your dimension is completely brain-free, you must, at least to some degree, have these Prodigious savant abilities. Am I right about that?"

"Unfortunately not," he sadly remarked. "You'd think that would be the case, but it's far from it. From what I've heard, there are a couple of ways of looking at it."

"But you do have extraordinary abilities. I've witnessed them. I'd certainly classify thought construction as pretty freakin' astonishing."

"Agreed," he answered. "But . . . an ability like that isn't shared by any savants in your dimension. It's only a capability in my dimension. Likewise, Prodigious savants possess capabilities that don't exist up here in Heaven."

"What happens when a Prodigious savant dies?" I asked. "Don't their capabilities follow them here? I'd think they'd become even more spectacular."

"Once they tunnel here they become exactly like the rest of us," he answered. "They lose the spectacular stuff."

"I find this very confusing," I admitted, shaking my head.

"So does everyone else," he exclaimed. "The only sensible explanation I've heard is that the human brain is responsible for this mystery. Although it has lost considerable filtering control over the bundle, there's still a relationship between the two. And it's this chemical, electro, magnetic, or some other relationship, that creates this unique discrepancy."

"So . . . our brains, no matter how dysfunctional they are, still have ultimate control," I observed. "Regardless of any problematical condition, there's always a unique brain/bundle connection which permanently disconnects upon death. Makes sense in a non-sensical way."

"Let's leave it at that. You get the general idea," he muttered.

"No more interruptions," I faithfully promised. "Now you can get back to those examples you were about to reveal."

Lyle paced back and forth, thinking. Then he spoke. "Extreme mathematical abilities are evident in some Prodigious savants. For example, they can multiply and divide four and five digit numbers in their head instantly. Just show 'em the problem; they'll give you the answer. They, themselves, don't even know how they do it. The answer just springs into their mind."

"Keep going," I urged him.

"Savants have been known to hear a very complex, classical piano composition once, and then sit down and play it perfectly, note by note, chord by cord, with all the peculiar inflections. Amazingly, they had never played the piano before. The same goes for painting. Inexperienced savants have been able to look at a complicated, magnificent scene, and paint it with super realism. Their portraits of people can also be chillingly realistic, capturing their subject's personality. The same goes for sculpture. One savant I heard about does animals in bronze: magnificent works of art that are comparable to the most famous, world-class artists. This guy had no training in either technique or anatomy. He just sits down, knocks the sculptures out, then sells them through a gallery."

Lyle took a breath, did a little thinking, and continued. "What these miraculous people have in common is obviously a photographic memory, which, as you know, is a normal bundle ability. Listen to this example: there's a guy who can read a very thick phonebook once, and have it completely memorized. A researcher randomly chose a phonebook from this guy's extensive collection, opened it, and read a phone number aloud. The savant immediately rattled off the corresponding name and address, then proceeded to recite the names, addresses and phone numbers listed above and below. He even knew the page number. In a similar vein, there are savants who specialize in maps. They can recite any route and mileage between any towns, even obscure ones, in the world. But . . . they might not be able to tie their own shoes or tell you what day it is."

Betty piped up. "Lyle, tell him about the matchstick guy."

"Oh yeah. This is a good one," he excitedly announced. "You can take a handful of matchsticks, throw them in the air right in front of this savant, and, by the time they hit the floor, he'll tell you the precise number of how many you tossed. If I'm not mistaken, he was Kim Peek."

"There are more examples. Many more examples," he continued. "But keep in mind that the minor savants, those who seem completely normal, are the most influential ones — the ones who've had an impact on everyone in the world. The Prodigious ones are fascinating, but their contributions to humanity are nil."

"What you're saying doesn't make complete sense," I remarked. "Take Einstein, for example. You would consider him a mild savant, a normally functioning human. Right?"

Lyle nodded 'yes.'

"But, from what you've been telling me, I'd have to say that he was mild with Prodigious abilities. Just look at what he did. Letting his mind wander through the uncharted universe, he devised concepts that turned the world of physics, and most everything else, on its head. And it took scientists many, many years to conclusively prove that his ideas were right. His thinking abilities were astonishing. Spectacular."

"I'm not going to argue with you," he said, leaning back in his chair. "Einstein, and others, have definitely displayed Prodigious abilities, but they're still considered mild. It's all a matter of definition driving differentiation."

"That's a mouthful," I said with a laugh. "And, regardless of what you said before, I'd love to see what the world would be like if our bundles were unfiltered — free to operate at full capability level."

"I'll stick to my earlier observation," he stated. "The world would be incredibly dull, and possibly even more vicious than it is now. On the other hand, if the opposite condition was true, and brain filtering was perfectly efficient, the world would also be dull as hell, and probably uncivilized. Without mild savants opening new doors with their bold visions and creativity, the human race would be nowhere. Before I forget, I want you to hear a quote someone told me that sort of sums up the way savants were perceived long ago — before their abilities were accurately defined. The quote is from Socrates, who was probably a savant, himself. *The greatest blessings granted to mankind come by way of madness, which is a divine gift.* You have to forgive his inappropriate use of the word, madness."

"That's pretty damn observant and revealing," I seriously stated. "With that in mind, would you credit savants, mild and whatever, with all, if not most, major achievements throughout history?"

Betty interrupted. "I've got to add one thing about savants and history. The distant past was extremely cruel to them, actually, right up to the mid nineteenth century. They were tortured and murdered because religious, superstitious people attributed their amazing skills to the devil. Sorry to interrupt."

"No problem," I remarked. "I guess most everyone back then was religious and superstitious."

"Just back then?" asked Betty. "How about right now."

"Yeah," I quipped. "Tell me about it."

Lyle cut back in. "John, to answer your question about crediting mild savants with major historical achievements, I'd have to say 'yes.' Of course, it's my own opinion, and entirely subjective. But it simply makes too much sense. Just think about it: What level of mind power did it take to create the pyramids? Or forge Damascus steel? Or invent the telescope? Or write the Iliad? Or split the atom? Or organize the D-Day invasion?"

"For that matter, maybe what you call 'brain dysfunction' is no dysfunction at all," I asserted. "Maybe it's the norm. Maybe it was just meant to be."

"You know what you're getting at with that thought?" he chuckled.

"Yeah. Let's leave well enough alone," I firmly stated. "All I'll add to it is this: if, as you say, the universe is conscious and wants us to acknowledge it, the observational power of mild savants would have to be pretty remarkable."

"Amen," he declared, still chuckling.

On that note, Betty got up and strolled the short distance to the garden. She jauntily sauntered back, broadly grinning, with a bunch of cherry tomatoes in her hand. After offering some to Lyle and me, she said we had to touch on another aspect of reduced bundle filtering.

"There's a darker side to this, you know."

"I was waiting for you to point it out," interrupted Lyle.

Betty continued. "Not all people who experience brain dysfunction and so called enhanced sensory abilities are productive, balanced savants. In fact, they're not even considered savants."

"What are they called?" I asked with sincerity.

Betty answered unfairly. "Well, you'd undoubtedly call them lunatics, nuts, crazies, morons, idiots, psychos, and, God knows what else."

Lyle chuckled, shook his head, and grimaced. Realizing she shouldn't have taken a low blow like that, she apologized to me. I assured her that I didn't take it personally, and that she was probably right. I also said that I was confused and asked her to explain. But first I wanted to know what these people were called.

"They're commonly referred to as delusional, psychotic, paranoid, schizophrenic, and other labels, including lunatics and nuts," she informed me.

"There's at least one on every block in New York," I added.

Unamused, she continued. "Here's a very unfortunate, but typical, example: Let's say there's a guy who appears to be completely crazy, completely dysfunctional. Picture him rambling aimlessly down the street, holding his hands over his ears, and shouting at no one in particular. If a psychiatrist were to ask him why he was acting that way, he might say he was hearing and seeing all sorts of strange things, frightening things, things he perceived were out to hurt him. And he wouldn't be making this stuff up. It wouldn't be a figment of a disturbed imagination. Because of his heightened senses, due to reduced filtering, he might be seeing in infrared, and hearing a very wide band of frequencies. His ears would be pounded by everything from people whispering a hundred feet away to stray music from tons of MP3 player headphones to screeching brakes. This type of sensory overload would be enough to drive anyone nuts. But... a psychiatrist would think it was all in his head."

"On rare occasions, sensory overloads can be dangerous, even fatal." Lyle exclaimed. "Consider this, for example: A guy's speeding down an expressway, and, while passing under some high-tension lines, the electrical field causes his brain to momentarily release bundle powers. An instantaneous sensory surge could cause him to lose control of his car."

"Do you think this could explain why some people inexplicably commit suicide by jumping out of windows or off bridges?" I asked. "Or how about when people just snap, and slaughter the people nearest to them?"

"Entirely possible, and very probable," he sadly admitted.

"Sounds to me like brain dysfunctions and enhancements can be slightly less than a blessing." I announced.

"Yes. There's definitely a negative side, John," Lyle remarked. "But the positives absolutely outweigh the negatives when you consider how much the world has benefitted from savantism."

"So, I guess that, all things considered, the particle bundle is the most important part of our bodies," I added.

"Not at all," Lyle quickly answered. "Our brains are equally important because they're responsible for most everything the bundle will ever achieve. What's more, virtually all of our organs are also as important because they allow our brains to survive. We are complete, balanced systems."

"You know what, if I keep thinking about this, I'll have a million more questions," I said.

"No doubt," he remarked. "But I'm comfortable that, between Betty and I, we've covered all the most interesting and relevant aspects."

"I guess you're right," I sorely admitted. "But all this stuff about particle bundles, brain dysfunctions, and savants is just so fascinating."

"You know what else is fascinating?" he chuckled. "How long you've managed to stay asleep. This has got to be a record for you."

At that moment, right after he spoke, everything went dark. I was back in my bed, thinking very filtered thoughts about yet another intriguing conversation. In a couple of minutes, I wafted back to sleep for the rest of the night.

Chapter 26
Through Unborn Eyes.

I woke up as refreshed as ever, recalling every moment, as well as every word, of my dream. Just lying in bed with my eyes half closed, I thought about all the fascinating things I had learned. To find out if I had concocted any of that savant stuff in my mind, I decided to research the subject on my computer after breakfast. That would add yet another fatal blow to my enduring skepticism.

While reading all about the mysterious world of savants, I managed to actually think about my own book. Should I write it? Should I completely duck the subject? Would it be a waste of time? Would people, especially friends and family, think I was a liar? Or even worse, would they think I was delusional? I had very mixed feelings.

And if I did decide to write it, how would I proceed? I didn't have any notes — didn't need any because it was all in my head, ready to be put down on paper. I'd just have to logically break it into chapters. All it would take is a strong commitment, lots of patience, a shit load of perseverance, and some magical way to avoid procrastination.

That evening, I began to wonder what Lyle had up his sleeve for my upcoming dream. Where would I open my eyes? What would be the topic of our conversation? Would we be taking a memory trip? Then I realized how much I'd miss all the intrigue once this whole thing was over. On that note, I turned off my light, meditated on a twinkling acorn, and arrived at my destination.

• • •

Before I even opened my dream eyes, I knew exactly where I was. I had returned to my old back yard. All three of us were relaxing on the lawn, staring contently at the clouds. I knew Lyle had something on his mind, especially when he got up, lit a Camel, and began pacing back and forth. Just as I was about to break the silence, he began speaking in his, trademark, animated style.

"We're going to take a little trip that I've been looking forward to for a few days. It's an exceptional experience, another you'll never ever forget. Even Betty loves it."

"Are you going to tell me what this is all about, or are you going to stretch out the suspense until I'm ready to wake up?" I impatiently asked.

"I'll tell him, Lyle," she said with conviction.

Lyle smiled, nodded, and blew a series of three smoke rings.

Betty continued. "Tagging along with Lyle, we're going to do a bundle alignment with an unborn child in the mother's womb. It's incredible, especially for me because, as you know, I was never born. I've got sick Betty's memory of it, but it really isn't the same."

"I really don't know what to say," I readily admitted. "This sounds very, very strange to me. What's it going to be like? I mean, infants don't think. Or do they?"

"You'll see," said Betty.

"Just keep an opened mind," urged Lyle. "This is going to be a peculiar experience, some of which you won't understand until we discuss it later. Just let yourself go, and become part of the baby's nervous system. Try not to think about or analyze anything until we're through."

"When are we going to do this? And where will it be taking us?" I asked.

Lyle gave me an enormous grin, and hypnotically stared into my eyes. It was eerie. Without missing a beat, our location instantly changed from my backyard in Purchase to some cavernous room with lots of people methodically walking and pointing. Intensely looking around, it became immediately apparent that we were in some huge museum, surrounded by magnificent, ancient sculptures. I also detected many languages being spoken.

"Know where we are?" asked Lyle. "Anything seem familiar?"

"Obviously, we're in a museum," I answered. "But I have no idea which museum. It's not familiar at all."

"You haven't looked directly behind yourself yet," he excitedly stated. "Turn around, and you'll know exactly where you are."

So . . . I slowly turned around and knew precisely what Lyle had meant. Literally towering above me, dominating the entire room, was one of the world's most magnificent, let alone famous, statues: Michelangelo's David. Standing seventeen feet tall in gleaming white marble, this masterpiece was awe inspiring, to say the least.

"So," declared Lyle, "I take it you've figured out where we are."

"I was here a few years ago, but I didn't recognize anything until I saw good old Dave," I acknowledged. "Returning to Florence and The Accademia museum is something I've been wanting to do."

"Well, now you're back," he said, punching my shoulder.

"I'm not sure this counts as a trip, but I'll make the best of it," I remarked.

I simply stood there staring at that incredible statue. Everything about it was perfect. Every feature was remarkable. It was almost impossible to believe that it began as a huge chunk of marble, which, by the way, had been rejected by other sculptors because it was too big and flawed. Then I remembered what Lyle had told me about Michelangelo: he was a savant. And to think . . . I could have referred to him as an 'idiot savant.' Maybe I really was learning something from these ghosts.

Lyle snapped his fingers in front of my eyes. "Hey, you're in a trance. Come back to earth."

"Earth?" I asked. "You mean Nevernever land, don't you?"

"If that makes you happy then the answer is 'yes.'" he laughed.

"So what does all this have to do with an unborn baby?" I asked. "Is there a pregnant statue?"

"No." he said. "A pregnant goddess."

Then he pointed to a bunch of David admirers around twenty feet to our left. There she was: a tall, gorgeous, elegantly dressed pregnant woman with flowing, reddish blond hair, in her late twenties. A true, real-life goddess. But 'pregnant' was an understatement. She looked as though she had stuffed a large beach ball in her silk blouse.

Lyle continued, "We're going to walk up to her, and, in a blink, we'll be aligned with her baby's bundle. Oh... and that guy standing next to her is her husband, and the little girl holding her hand is her daughter."

"That really is some beautiful family," I remarked.

"Let's walk over to her now," he said. "Follow me."

There were a few people between us and the woman, and Lyle walked right through them. Right through them. Just like ghosts go through doors and walls in the movies. And I followed in his footsteps. Poooooft — right through them. I guess I'll never get used to these memory trip anomalies.

Once we were next to this stunning women, Lyle said, "Here we go. Remember to keep an open mind, and try to avoid thinking. Just become part of the child's sensory system, and experience things as they're processed in his mind. Also remember that he can't speak or understand language, so don't put your own words in his mouth."

I nodded that I understood, and braced myself for a weird, but probably very fascinating, experience. Betty gave me a gigantic smile, and my whole world went black, pitch black. As Lyle had advised me, I just let myself go, and became part of the baby's nervous system. But, the 'me' part remained extremely aware so I could process everything.

All at once, I was bombarded by many foreign sensations that I'll try to put into words. What I noticed first was the rhythmic throbbing that surrounded my curled body. It was almost like a gentle, touching massage that pressed lightly over every inch of me. It was one of the most soothing sensations I've ever felt. In perfect synchronization with the throbbing, I could easily hear the beating of the mother's heart. Basking in all these wonderful sensations, I realized that I couldn't feel any temperature variations. It was all neutral. I assumed that was due to the mother's body temperature being the same as the baby's.

All things considered, I felt extremely comfortable, happy, peaceful and secure. But more than anything else, I felt the strong sensation of love. Obviously, this wasn't in words, and it's almost impossible to describe, but the feeling was like nothing else in the world. I was surrounded by the deepest love I have ever felt. Now I knew why Lyle wanted me to have this experience, and why it was so special to Betty. Without wasting too much valuable time on thinking and analysis, I realized that this was the best, most emotionally driven experience to date. Then things slightly changed.

The mother must have somehow moved. Maybe she took a few steps, shifted her weight, or bent over to pick something up. But I felt a different orientation: a minor pressing on the baby's head. It wasn't bad, just slightly different. In an unconscious response, the baby gave mom a very healthy kick. Then another. And a few more. The feeling from my position inside was like kicking a firm, yet soft, spongy ball.

During the last few kicks, I felt an overall tingly sensation — almost like a very, very mild shock. But it wasn't uncomfortable at all, and added to my profound feelings of love and affection. Unable to stop myself, I went into my usual analysis mode, and couldn't figure out what the hell that was all about.

Then things drastically changed. Out of nowhere, I began to see some very dim light, and thought to myself that it was impossible. As the light became a little brighter, it occurred to me that, maybe, the baby was coming out in the museum. In the museum? No, that's impossible, I assured myself after assuming that they'd have to name him David. There was none of the expected trauma, just uninterrupted peace and comfort. But what was happening?

I got my answer almost instantly. It appeared as though Lyle had shifted our bundle alignment from the baby to the mother because the light focused into distinct images, and they were from the mother's point of view. She was looking down, watching her daughter's and husband's hands gently touching her bulging stomach. They were feeling the baby kicking. Her gaze shifted up into her husband's proud, adoring eyes, then back to her daughter who said something in what I believe was Italian. After reluctantly removing their hands, they walked around the sculpture for a different view.

But something was very wrong. Very strange. I tried to read what was on Mom's mind, and all I got were jumbled thoughts. It was as though mom didn't fully comprehend what she was seeing. But I did get a very powerful emotion: the mother's boundless love for the baby . . . and the daughter. It was all there, but all mixed up. Another thing that made no sense was that I still felt the peaceful throbbing all over my body, and, along with the droning museum sounds, I could still hear the dull thudding of a heart beating. It was as though the mother and baby had merged.

Then, everything changed again. The light and all museum sounds disappeared, and I was returned to all the original sensations. I assumed that Lyle had returned our alignment to the child. After what seemed to be several more wonderful minutes of floating in blissful nothingness, bathed in love and security, we left the alignment and snapped back to reality. Back to reality? You mean standing in The Accademia museum in Florence while in a dream of the afterlife? Well . . . I guess so.

Still standing beside the family, and still floored by the astonishing experience, I said, "Lyle and Betty, that was indescribably incredible."

"I knew you'd love it," declared Lyle.

"Now you can understand why aligning with unborn babies is so special to me," gushed Betty.

"John," remarked Lyle, "if you think it was incredible, wait until you learn what really happened. You don't know the half of it."

"Well . . . of course I have some questions," I admitted. "Like why you switched alignment from the baby to mama mia."

"Where do you want to go for a nice, long discussion?" asked Lyle.

I put a hand over my eyes and said, "I see monkeys. And treasure. And lots and lots of green."

By the time I put my hand down and opened my eyes, we were back in my favorite location. I felt very calm and content, ready for what I assumed would be an interesting chat.

"So . . . what was your overall impression?" Lyle asked me.

"It was thrilling. I mean really thrilling. But it was almost exactly what I expected."

"Elaborate a little on that, please," Lyle mumbled.

"Well . . . I mean . . . the darkness, the peaceful sounds and feeling of the mother's heart beating . . . you know."

"Any dominating emotions?" he asked, very seriously.

"Two," I answered after a moment's thought. "I felt extremely safe and secure. But, most of all, I felt my love for the mother and her love for me. Not in words or thoughts, but in some powerful way that I can't explain. It was almost like a sense in itself — a reason for being. Like I said, I can't adequately explain it."

"You just did a pretty damn good job of trying," he blurted.

"Lyle," I said. "You've been alluding to something very special about this alignment. Is there something I missed? I think I was aware of everything that happened."

"You missed something extraordinary," he loudly exclaimed. "But you couldn't have been expected to notice it. You'd never guess in a zillion years."

"Hold on," I remarked. "I bet your sudden alignment with the mom has something to do with it. Am I right?"

"What alignment with the mom?" he seriously asked.

I didn't expect that answer. It confused the shit out of me.

"What the fuck are you talking about?" I asked. "When pop and the kid touched mom's stomach to feel baby Guido kicking, I observed it through her eyes. You definitely aligned with her, and then returned to the baby."

"Now I'm going to tell you something unbelievable, and I beg you to keep an open mind."

"Christ, Lyle, that's been required for nearly everything you've ever told me," I uttered with exasperation.

"We never aligned with the mother," he firmly stated. "The fetus did."

"What do you mean by that?" I asked, completely startled.

"It's simple. While we were aligned with the fetus, the fetus aligned with the mother."

"What?" I asked with a nervous laugh. "The baby aligned with the mother? How does that even begin to be possible?"

"I'll assure you it's not just possible, but perfectly normal," he swore. "I'll be the first to admit that it's pretty hard to believe, damn hard to believe; however, it's just another one of life's amazing anomalies."

In a state of confusion, I asked, "How does a fetus even think to do this? What's the reason for it? Nothing's making any sense here."

Lyle shook his head. "Remember what I said; keep an open mind."

"Yeah, yeah, I know."

He continued. "Now pay attention. As far as anyone knows, the fetus does not think. The alignment is instinctual, most likely triggered by something environmental."

Betty interrupted. "It's got to be something that stirs or stimulates the baby's primitive nervous system. Could be a loud or intrusive noise like mom or someone yelling, a horn honking, pounding music, or any sudden change in frequency. Could be a radical position change, like if mom lied down, bent over to tie her shoes, or bounced around on a bicycle."

Lyle cut in. "What caused the alignment we witnessed was something all together different. John, did you feel anything odd before we began to see through mom's eyes?"

"Yes. I definitely remember a peculiar, tingling sensation, like an extremely mild shock."

"And what was the first thing you saw through the mother's eyes?" he asked with expectation.

I chuckled at the realization. "I saw the daughter's and husband's hand on her stomach feeling the baby kick."

"Exactly," he exhaled. "The baby was reacting to gentle, electrical stimulation: the life field emitted by everyone's hands. Babies can sense things like this because their brains have not begun to filter their particle bundles. As I once told you, roughly during the middle of the eighth month of pregnancy, the brain activates the bundle's signature vibration, which turns the fetus into an authentic human being. Then, towards the end of the ninth month, the filters are activated. So . . . there's a window of a few weeks where the fetus has extraordinary abilities."

"Boy, do I have a lot of questions," I said, with my head between my hands.

"Let me just add one thing to what Betty and I were telling you about before. There's another reasonable explanation why babies align with their mothers. It may be as simple as natural curiosity about life. That's one of the strongest human instincts known to mother nature."

"Regardless of any of your explanations, I'm still blown away by this whole thing." I earnestly remarked. "It was just so unexpected — nothing I could have ever imagined."

"We knew you'd react this way," chuckled Betty.

"Now, how about those questions of yours?" asked Lyle, as he lit a Camel and shifted position on his cushion.

"I was wondering about the effect on premature babies. Babies born as early as the sixth or seventh month, or maybe even earlier, have been known to survive without any ill effects. How's this possible considering that the vibration doesn't turn on until well into the eighth month?"

"Good question," said Lyle. "It's the same one I asked, myself, when I first learned about this. Unfortunately, the answer I was given sounds like a copout."

"Let's hear it anyway."

Lyle continued. "It seems as though our brains are far more resourceful than you'd imagine. Regardless of the traditional vibration turn-on timing, trauma can induce the brain to act earlier. The question of how much earlier is based on the level of brain development."

"I guess I'll have to buy that, just like you did," I admitted. "My other question is as basic as they come. Why? What's the whole point of fetus alignment?"

"By now, I would have thought you'd be able to figure that one out for yourself," he said, putting his hands out palms up.

"I've got some rough ideas, but enlighten me anyway."

"Let me explain this to him," Betty said to Lyle. "John, considering the way everything seems to be so well planned, fetal alignment makes all the sense in the world."

"Please . . . no intelligent design stuff . . ." I exclaimed.

"I'm not going there," she promised. "Planned, was just a slip. Getting back to what I was saying, fetal alignment allows the unborn child to familiarize itself with the overall environment in which it's going to live. The image of its mother through reflection in a mirror, as well as the father and any siblings, are etched into its mind. Of course, at this stage of the baby's development, it has no concept of what it's seeing . . . as far as we know, that is. But, when the baby is born, it's not shocked into existence. The baby has a foundation upon which it can develop its own perspective of the world and its own personality."

"I guess that's pretty straight forward," I remarked. "I want . . ."

"But, there's more," Betty interrupted. "Here comes the fascinating part — the part where the word, 'planned,' makes just too much sense."

"Ok. I'm listening," I said with a note of resignation.

Betty rolled her eyes and smiled. "Let's say, through some complication or disaster, a baby dies at birth or shortly before. By that time, the baby has a particle bundle with a fully activated vibration. That means it's going to tunnel into this dimension. But, since the baby already has a base of fully human memories, it can easily adapt to this strange new environment and acquire all the knowledge it would ever need . . . or want. So you see, it all goes back to the particle bundle being the essence of life, and this dimension, the afterlife, being the ultimate destination for all humanity."

"Taking that thought a step further," I said, "maybe your afterlife, as you define it, is really a stepping stone to the ultimate, ultimate destination, which could be where we all end up after our one hundred fifty years in your dimension. That would make the particle bundle the true instrument of genesis."

Betty and Lyle both sat there wide-eyed, just staring at me. I realized that I had just said something that was entirely out of character for me.

Betty broke the silence. "John, I can't believe that you, Mr. Narrow-minded, just said that. I'm proud of you, and I'm sure I'm speaking for Lyle, too."

"Just an observation," I quickly assured them. "Doesn't mean I've, all of a sudden, been converted into a believer of intelligent design."

"Why of course not," exclaimed Betty, laughing. "But at least it proves you have a somewhat open mind."

"Back to the original subject, please," I urged them.

"Yeah . . . you had a question you wanted to ask," said Lyle.

"I have absolutely no memories of anything before I was born. For that matter, I don't remember shit until I was about two or three."

"You remember absolutely everything." Lyle quickly assured me. "It's all locked in your subconscious. It's that way for everyone. Here's something else you'll find interesting. Psychiatrists have taken patients under deep hypnosis back to their pre-birth memories. They attribute this to past lives, and, of course, reincarnation."

I had a good chuckle over that one, but realized how this, apparently, very real phenomenon could fool almost anyone into believing in reincarnation. Then it occurred to me that if a French infant, for example, was adopted by an American family, that child could start speaking French during hypnosis, which could really point to a past life. I had recalled hearing instances like that. Jesus Christ, I thought to myself, these ghost friends of mine are really beginning to make sense.

"Any more questions, John?" asked Lyle.

"One more thing," I said, scratching my head. "Help me out with this: when you do an alignment, you're free to simply go directly into someone's head. I mean . . . you are a bundle and vibration separated from a brain. Following me so far?"

He nodded yes.

I continued. "But with a fetus, the bundle is within its brain. Does that mean that the fetus' bundle leaves its brain to join the mother? I assume that once a person's bundle becomes detached from their brain and body, they're a goner. A major stiff."

"Another good question," replied a smoke-surrounded Lyle. "Let me answer the second part of that first. Theoretically, it's entirely possible for someone to survive without their bundle. Never heard of it, but it's possible because the bundle doesn't play a major role with involuntary and very basic brain and body functions. At the very worst, a bundle less person might appear to be in a coma. Or they could just seem to be a very dull moron."

"That would definitely explain a bunch of people I've known."

Lyle frowned, cleared his throat, and continued. "Keeping the crux of what I just told you in mind, you can understand how a baby's bundle can harmlessly travel to its mother's brain and back. It's simply another wonder of nature that requires far more exploration."

"Lyle, you've got to give me a little time to think about this, and let it all settle in. I just want to lie back, smoke my pipe, and get my head screwed back on."

"You do that," he replied. "And when you're ready for some more ghostly bonding, I've got a little surprise for everyone. We're going to take a short trip that the David statue reminded me about."

"Are we going to watch him slay Goliath?" I mumbled, laughing.

"Not even close," he chuckled. "Now shut up, and enjoy your pipe."

Honestly, how was I going to relax after hearing about another trip? Come on. Really. It took a shit load of will power, but I was somehow able to push it into the back of my mind. Then, I remembered that I had been forgetting to ask about sick Betty.

Just as I was about to inquire, I was startled by Lyle. "Hey, snap out of it," he said. "Time to go. You're going to love this memory trip: it's short and unstressful."

I sat up and stretched. "Will we have the pleasure of Betty's company?"

"Sure. I'm coming," she quickly answered. "Just want to advise you; this is not exactly going to be an amazing trip, but it may give you a few goose bumps."

"Goose bumps are good," I replied. "But there's something I've gotta ask Lyle first. Unless I bring up the subject, and I often forget to, you never mention how sick Betty's doing. How's it going with her?"

"It's very frustrating," he sighed. "She has episodes where she comes out of her coma, and thinks normally. Then she lapses back. It's a terrible cycle, but it's probably what's keeping her alive. The hospital staff is more focused on her, which is also extending her life."

"Are there any signs of my observance?" I asked.

"Nothing significant. Nothing out of the ordinary for someone in her fragile condition," he solemnly answered.

"What about that poem you had mentioned? You know, the one that makes you feel she's trying to communicate with you."

"It's more than just a feeling, John," he noted. "I know it falls into the 'impossible' category, but she definitely senses my presence, and is trying to communicate with me. What's even more odd is that it's not in her own words or voice. She seems to have somehow heard a song that's expressing her emotions. Once in a while, they play a radio in her room to calm her, I assume."

"Can't you access the entire song from her memory?" I asked.

"You'd think I'd be able to," he exclaimed. "But it's jumbled, beyond my grasp. This is the one and only thing that leads me to believe that your observation may have set up some sort of interference with her vibration. Something has definitely been changed. It's premature to make any presumptions, though. Maybe that's why I don't talk about her too much these days."

"That's understandable," I said. "I hope I didn't create any additional problems."

"Don't worry about that for a second," he firmly declared. "We persuaded you to do the observance, and maybe it worked."

While Lyle was talking, I was observing Betty out of the corner of my eye. Her head was down, she was methodically kneading her legs with both hands, and she was obviously deep in thought. It was also obvious that she was exceptionally nervous. Considering that her whole future existence was dependent upon her namesake's condition, it was no wonder she was so distraught. Trying to relieve all the tension in the air, Lyle cleared his throat and spoke up.

"Ummm . . . on a more positive note, I'd suggest that we get on with our next little memory jaunt. Our distinguished guest," he said looking at me, "is going to wake up soon."

"Not that soon," I countered. "I still feel very awake. Or should I say 'very asleep?' Regardless, I guess we may as well get going."

"Say good by to paradise, John," he said, with a wink.

Just as I was about to open my mouth, I was jarred into a brand new reality, a place that, at first, seemed like some shithole. We were standing in front of a decrepit, one story stone building that, upon closer inspection, appeared simultaneously ancient and new. I could tell that there was sort of a courtyard within it. Puzzling.

The area, itself, was hilly, with lots more haphazardly placed buildings of a similar nature. The ground was rough: gnarly weeds and short, wiry bushes dotted the dusty, rocky land. Stubby, dense trees were also to be seen here and there. As usual, I was confused. But it began to dawn on me that we were most likely somewhere back in the Holy Land.

Lyle appeared to be quite amused by my obvious state of bewilderment. Just as he was about to speak, I cut him off. "Don't even think of asking me if I know where the hell we are. My only guess is that we're in Jesus' back yard, waiting for the dude to come out and perform some miracle. Maybe he'll clean up the area a bit."

Lyle found that very humorous, and remarked to Betty that I wasn't even close. "Wrong date, wrong location, wrong guy," he blurted.

"Enough of this bullshit," I announced. "Let's see what's inside. I suspect that's the point of this whole thing."

The next thing I saw was the tall door opening on its big, rusty, squealing hinges. Once inside, the only domineering sight was a huge rock sitting on the ground. So . . . I wondered to myself, what the fuck is this all about. Trying to determine the significance of this solid, whitish lump, I began to hear something peculiar. As it grew a tad louder, I realized that it was someone mumbling incoherently.

And then I saw him as he slowly sauntered around to our side of the boulder: a skinny, disheveled looking guy in his late twenties wearing a filthy tan robe.

As he stood perfectly still scrutinizing this rock, my mind started reeling off some possibilities. Maybe this gigantic white rock was some bizarre meteorite that had crashed into this schmuck's back yard, I wondered. Or maybe some local students had dumped it there as a practical joke. I bounced both of those ideas off Lyle, and he laughed, shaking his head in a very firm "no."

The guy walked back and forth, bending up and down, thoroughly examining every inch of his courtyard intruder. Pulling on his scraggly beard, I even saw him lick the fucking stone, then rub the wet area with his hand. Walking closer, I realized how ugly this guy was, but it was his eyes that really caught my attention. They were mean. Nasty. Kind of evil. I knew nothing about him, but I felt repulsion, and told Lyle.

"Funny you should say that," remarked Lyle. "Few people liked him at all. He was rude, offensive, disrespectful, vulgar, moody and quick-tempered."

"So who is this asshole?" I impatiently asked.

"Yes. He was all those things," said Lyle, ignoring my questions.

We both watched him toss his arms out and spit on the stone again, continuously mumbling again.

Lyle continued. "But ... despite all those rather negative qualities, he was, and is, one of the world's most profound, let alone famous geniuses — an amazing savant."

I was getting severely agitated. "Who the fuck is he, already? Sorry Betty."

"Who is he?" repeated Lyle, enjoying the damned suspense. "He's David's father."

"What in the fucking hell does that mean?" I yelled, losing my patience.

Betty laughed and said, "I can't take this any longer. John, the guy is Michelangelo. And that boulder he's so carefully inspecting is the hunk of marble that he'll magically transform into David."

I stood there speechless, with the most colossal, shit eating grin I've ever had. 'Michelangelo,' I kept saying that to myself over and over and over.

When my senses returned, I exclaimed, "Lyle, you're completely forgiven. And even though all your damn drama was a freakin' pain in the ass, I apologize for my impatience. This is definitely a great experience."

"Did you think I'd drag you hundreds of years into the past to observe some friggin' asshole?" he asked, chuckling.

"Speaking of that, what year is this?" I asked. "My . . . uh . . . history is a bit rusty."

"It's roughly 1501," he answered. "Since Michelangelo was born on March 6, 1475, that would make him around 26 years old. If you're wondering where we are, we're in Florence. In fact, Mikey here was commissioned to carve David for the Florence Cathedral."

"Since you seem to know everything about him, when did he die?" I asked.

"In 1564. About 53 years after he painted the Sistine Chapel."

"Honestly, I find that even more amazing than his David," I truthfully admitted.

"Obviously, they're both amazing, but there's more genius in the Chapel painting," he commented. Betty nodded in agreement.

"One last thing I've gotta ask," I said. "This might be a really dumb question, but don't laugh too hard. Is 'Michelangelo' a contraction for 'Michel Angelo?'"

Sure enough, Lyle ripped into what must have been a painful laugh. "Wrong," he shouted. "His real name just rolls off the tongue. Ready for this? His name was Michelangelo di Lodovico Buonarroti Simoni."

"What a mouthful," I exclaimed. "Sounds like a very involved main course at an Italian restaurant."

"You're all class, John. All class," he moaned.

We all stood there continuing to watch Michelangelo as he closely examined every inch of that humungous chunk of marble. But, now, for me, it was with the utmost reverence and awe. I kept trying to imagine how he was able to chip, grind, and polish that rough, cracked stone into what has to be the most precise, anatomically correct, and expressive statue in the world. Just amazing.

"You still with us, John?" asked Betty.

"I'm still stunned," I mumbled. "I'd love to know what's going through his mind right now: how he's envisioning David, how he's going to bring him to life. I wonder if he could predict exactly what the statue was going to look like, or if he played it by ear. Maybe the structure of the marble, all the faults and cracks, directed his hands. I've done a lot of wood carving, so I can appreciate what he's attempting to negotiate."

"Maybe you'll be able to return to Florence one day, and gaze at David from a whole new perspective," said Betty.

"God, would I love that," I declared.

"Let me know when you've seen enough of mad Mike," said Lyle. "We'll go back to the rain forest for what's left of your time. You're going to wake up momentarily."

"I'd much rather stay here until that happens," I said, as I watched Michelangelo pick up a small mallet, and expertly chip off a thumb-size piece of marble. He twirled the chip in his fingers, examined the spot where it came from, then tossed it over his head. I decided to take a few steps closer, but noticed that my legs were ridiculously sluggish and heavy. Then I realized that I was holding my arms at a really weird angle. As though someone flipped a light switch, everything faded to black. Good by Florence. Hello New York and the land of the living.

Chapter 27
Rocking Chair Revelations

Well . . . that was that.

Another astonishing dream.

And my time in that impossible dimension was quickly coming to an end. The more I thought about that eventuality, the more I wanted to prolong this whole crazy thing. I knew it was seriously fucking up my life, but, Christ, it was so incredible. So inspiring. How could I possibly want it to stop? No . . . I didn't want it to stop; I just wanted my life back, so it had to stop. There was no choice in the matter. The only consolation was a feeling I had that if I never needed a fix, Lyle would get me back. That I was certain of.

I made an attempt to read the New York Times with my breakfast, but my mind dragged me right back to good old, mean spirited Michelangelo.

Isn't it amazing how you can envision someone based on their life's work, and be so dead fucking wrong? I had always assumed that Michelangelo was a heroic looking, scholarly gentleman who drew praise from everyone he met. Just thinking so hard about this reinforced my decision to curtail these dreams. I mean I couldn't even concentrate on something as basic as reading the damn newspaper without drifting back to fantasyland. Shit. I was pathetic.

Knowing that I had limited time for more discussions with Lyle and Betty, I had to narrow down what I was going to inquire about. There were many things I still wanted explained, and at the top of the list was something Lyle had once mentioned: that stupid 2012 disaster dilemma. He had alluded to the possibility that it could be for real. If that was true, then so was seeing the future. Did that mean our destinies were predetermined? Was freewill an illusion? Yes... this whole thorny topic was on the top of my list. I just hoped that I wasn't going to get troublesome answers that would leave me filled with angst. My choice would be to end this whole thing on a positive note.

When I was through taking a long walk, I figured 'screw it,' I'll walk some more. My aim was to get as tired as physically possible so I could spend additional time in my deep dream state. Experience had taught me that this actually worked. By the time I had crashed into bed, I was thoroughly exhausted, but, instead of gliding into meditation, I pushed myself to read a novel, one of those page-turners you can't put down. After a few chapters, I was too pooped to keep my eyes pried open. So, I chose a mysterious agate marble as my meditation focus, and... zap; I was aboard the mind train to specterville.

• • •

Once I had arrived, I kept my dream eyes closed, and tried to determine where Lyle had chosen to take us. My first sensation told me that I was sitting in a rocking chair. It had to be outside because there was a cool, invigorating breeze carrying the distinctive scent of evergreens mingled with flowers. My ears picked up a variety of common bird songs, the squeaking of other rocking chairs, and the relaxing sound of water softly lapping against some unknown object. Believe it or not, I knew precisely where we were.

Smiling broadly, with my eyes still shut, I loudly exclaimed, "Great choice, Lyle. I'm thrilled to be back here."

"You know where we are?" he asked.

"Come on, you know full well that I know where we are. I'm sure you're reading my mind."

"Honestly, I wasn't before... but now I am," he giggled. "You actually guessed accurately. Mohonk. One of your favorite places, and, now, one of mine, too."

It was a magnificent, crisp, early fall day — the type of day that puts Mohonk in the category of Heaven. We were sitting right over the water on the long deck that surrounds most of the Lake Lounge, with a clear view of the mountains beyond. The leaves were just beginning to turn: vivid reds, yellows, and oranges would soon be dominating the entire area, creating one of the world's most spectacular art shows. I recalled sitting right here in these rockers many, many times, absorbing the unique ambience of this very special place. Mohonk could make anyone glad to be alive. Or . . . uh . . . dead — whatever the case may be.

"Why in God's name are we the only people here?" I asked. "It's not normal."

"We're in a memory compilation, where I've angled out all the other visitors," he answered. "I didn't want anything too distracting."

"Too distracting?" I moaned. "Everything about this place is distracting. It's all eye candy."

"So, what do you want to talk about?" asked Lyle, getting right to the point. "I know you've got a lot more questions."

"I've really narrowed down what I want to ask you about," I stated. "Otherwise, I'd be having these dreams for the next six months."

"At least," he retorted.

"I assume that, by this time, the universe has been thoroughly explored by millions of you all. This was one of the main questions on my agenda."

"I was wondering if you were ever going to touch on the subject of space exploration," he remarked. "I figured you would have asked me about that a long time ago."

"I assume," I said, "that being a virtually indestructible particle bundle must give you unrestricted freedom when it comes to exploring space. You can instantly go wherever you want to go just by thinking about it."

"I only wish it was that easy, that cut and dry," he admitted. "Honestly, we don't explore beyond our own limited solar system. We can't. It has proven to be far too dangerous."

That didn't make any sense to me. None at all. I'd never heard him use the word, 'dangerous,' and now I was really intrigued to learn more. Something told me that, as usual, this was going to lead to some incredible conclusions.

"Well . . . now you've certainly got my full attention," I declared. "Why is it far too dangerous? What could possibly go wrong?"

"This may be hard for you to swallow, but we don't have a definite answer. Within our own solar system, we can go anywhere without a problem. But . . . in deep space, something can destroy a particle bundle. It doesn't always happen, but it's happened enough to stop any sane person from exploring."

"I thought bundles were virtually indestructible," I asserted, quite confused.

"In theory, you're right," he answered. "Particle bundles float around the entire universe unscathed. However, some are probably unfortunate enough to get dragged into a black hole or get too close to some cataclysmic event. But, for the most part, they're constructed to endure forever."

"I don't . . ."

Lyle interrupted. "Please let me finish. Things will get slightly less confusing."

"Go ahead," I exhaled, thoroughly expecting a complete mind fucking.

Lyle continued after lighting his usual Camel. "Let's take this step by step. First of all, the four bonded particles in each bundle can withstand anything short of a black hole, a powerful collider's particle beam, an exploding star, and a severe electrical jolt. But, the bundle, itself, isn't the important factor here. It's the vibration. That's what makes us sentient beings. Compared with the physical structure of the bundle, the vibration component appears to be the weak link. If that gets destroyed, we're, for all intents and purposes, dead. Kaput. Forever."

"I was under the incorrect assumption that the vibration was permanently bonded to the bundle," I responded.

"The bond is incredibly strong," he reminded me. "But . . . there are mysterious, unknown forces in deep space that have proven to be deadly."

"Like what?" I asked. "Surely all the brain power up here must have figured this out."

"Our scientists are stumped," he admitted. "The universe is infused with an infinite amount of exotic, undiscovered particles, elements, magnetic anomalies, dark energy, and who knows what. It could take millions of years to figure it out."

"You must, at least, have some theories," I sputtered. "There never seems to be a shortage of those in this weird world of yours."

"Ok, here's a weird, yet thought provoking, theory," he said with a sly chuckle. "Maybe . . . we're not supposed to explore beyond our own solar system. Maybe, our intelligent, conscious universe is preventing us from learning about what's out there."

"That makes no freakin' sense," I declared.

"Of course it doesn't, but let me finish. It's very possible that the universe is filled with intelligent life, and each civilization has its own solar system—a private, protected area in which to thrive. If civilizations were to be intermixed, the result could be catastrophic."

"This smells of 'intelligent design' and a creator," I said, giving Lyle one of my best give-me a fucking break expressions.

"Yup. Sure smells like that," he agreed. "But . . . it's just a theory that nobody can disprove."

Deep in thought, I leaned back in the rocking chair watching leaves swaying in the breeze. My view was ideal: a dream within a dream. After a few seconds, I told Lyle that I just wanted to sit here for a while, and enjoy my pipe, just as I had done so many times before. I was so relaxed. And comfortable. Since it was sort of strange and unrealistic without all the people, I asked Lyle if he would let them back into the memory. He readily agreed, and, suddenly, it turned into the real Mohonk.

Just as I was marveling at the sheer intensity of this experience, Lyle interrupted my daydream.

"Sorry to yank you out of your moment, but Betty and I are going to vanish for just a few minutes. We're going to check out the original Betty at the hospital. Go ahead and wander around if you like. Don't worry about falling into a black, bottomless abyss. The memory base is continuous."

"Take your time," I exhaled, sinking even deeper into my chair. "I could remain right here for an eternity."

Now that I had some free time, I decided to spend it thinking about what was next on my diminishing agenda. Even though it was painfully tempting to extend my time here, I decided, once again, to curtail my visits to this astonishing place.

I wondered if this could possibly be my final dream. Just the thought of that gave me shivers. Jesus, I was hooked on these experiences. There were many more things I wanted to accomplish here: memory trips as well as answers to nagging questions. But I had to drastically narrow everything down or I'd be coming back for a few more days, then a few more weeks. No. This was it. One more night. Well, maybe two more nights. No. One more night at the very most. Thankfully, Lyle knew what I needed, what was best for me. I'd leave it to him to say "adios." He'd do it. Or would he?

Rocking steadily with my eyes shut, I heard some loud squeaking directly to my right. One glance showed me that my two spooky friends had reappeared in an instant and were also rocking with delight. Their hospital visit must have gone smoothly, considering their perfectly content expressions.

"How's Betty doing?" I quickly asked.

"Not well, at all," Lyle answered very matter-of-factly.

Very puzzled, I asked him why he and Betty seemed so content, considering what he had just revealed to me.

Lyle's answer made sense. "She keeps getting weaker and weaker, and rarely comes out of her coma. At least she doesn't appear to be in any pain. She's very close to passing away, which would be the best thing for her. And for us, to be honest. Look, she's lived a long time, and she'll get a new lease on life when she arrives in this dimension."

"I see your point. Makes lots of sense," I agreed

Lyle hesitated and said, "I heard it again, John."

"What?" I asked in surprise.

"The song. I now know it's a song that Betty's communicating to me. She must have heard it on the radio, and the whole thing — voice, words, and music — went into her memory. Subconsciously, she must have determined it was a message for me. It's hauntingly beautiful."

"Could it possibly be a coincidence," I asked. "Do you think it's something you just want to believe?"

"John, it's the only thing on her mind," he replied. "If I had decided to single it out of a continuous stream of thought, then I might agree with you. Between the lyrics, my past with Betty, and her current situation, the whole song is far too revealing. No. This is not a coincidence."

Lyle turned his gaze towards the lake, and sank back in his rocker. A strong breeze rippled the water and caused several bright yellow leaves to fall into the tiny waves. At that moment, an old man sat down in Lyle's chair, and both of their bodies seemed to blend together: one memory overlapping another. Lyle's head was right beneath the old guy's chin, right where his neck would be. If that wasn't bizarre enough, Lyle turned to talk to me right through the guy's collar. A couple of weeks ago, I would have been freaked out. Now it was just comical.

"There's only one way I can make you understand what I'm talking about," he said with sincerity. "I want you to hear some of this song for yourself, just as I've been hearing it. Only then will you fully realize what's going on. So sit back, close your eyes, open your mind, and listen. I'll transfer it directly from my memory, just as I, myself, heard it at the hospital."

I was thrilled that Lyle was going to share this with me. Very recently, he had mentioned several passages of the song, but now I had absolutely no idea what I was in store for. To say the least, what I was about to hear brought some serious tears to my eyes.

Just as I had blocked out as many of the Mohonk sounds as I could, I focused all my attention on the magnificent music I began to hear. The song began with a chillingly beautiful, piano melody that led to a soft, woman's voice that can best be described as heavenly. She brought an uncanny level of emotion to the following lyrics:

*"Who can say for certain
maybe you're still here
I feel you all around me
your memory's so clear.
Deep in the stillness
I can hear you speak
you're still an inspiration, can it be?
That you are mine forever, love,
and you are watching over me from up above.
Fly me up to where you are
beyond the distant star,
I wish upon tonight to see you smile.
If only for a while to know you're there,
a breath away is not too far from where you are."*

• • •

I was simply stunned. I couldn't believe what I had just heard. This was magnificent beyond anything I could have possibly expected. Everything about it gave me the chills. But, most importantly, Lyle was right. Betty was definitely trying to communicate her feelings to him. After all these years . . . he was still hers. She had to know that he was with her in spirit. Or maybe she actually saw him.

"Lyle, I . . ."

He put a finger over his lips as if to say 'shhh' "John, you needn't say anything. It's written all over your face. You now know, beyond a doubt, how I feel. For the first time in too many years, I can finally describe something as being incredible."

"Have you ever heard of anything like this happening before," I quickly asked.

"No, not in all my years here."

"Do you think there's a one in a million chance that this could be at least partially due to the observation," I asked. "Could we have enhanced her abilities by over-stimulating her vibration?"

Lyle shrugged his shoulders. "I don't have the slightest idea," he reluctantly admitted. "But I can't rule anything out. It's entirely possible, but I don't want to get my, or Betty's, hopes up. It may be too good to be true. The anticipation is killing me."

"Absolutely understandable," I commented.

"Doesn't anyone care about what I think," interrupted Betty.

"I was going to ask your opinion about this whole thing," I said, "but I wasn't sure about your frame of mind. Didn't want to make you any more nervous than you already are."

"Thanks for your concern," she said, with a note of enthusiasm, "but I can handle it. Actually, your remark about her vibration makes me optimistic. Gives me some hope. Believe it or not, I'm in a good mood."

"What did you think of the song, itself," I eagerly asked her.

"You described it perfectly," she answered, smiling. "It made me tingle. Now, more than ever, I want the transition to work . . . want to become her, not just pretend to be her."

"You are her," Lyle boldly asserted. "You're everything she was, and everything she ever will be. I can feel it. This is going to work."

"But what if it doesn't," she asked as calmly as she could.

Lyle shifted his position in the chair, just as the old guy got up and walked away. "If it doesn't work, we'll figure something out. You will always be with me. Count on it. Now, let's change the subject. Speculating about this is painful and useless. The future is in the hands of the creator . . . and/or fate."

After Lyle's last remark, we were all overcome with silence — a chance to reflect on his straightforward, sensible comments. Sitting way back in my rocker with my feet braced against the railing, I looked out over the lake. As I watched several Mallard ducks make a graceful landing, I recalled the last words Lyle had just uttered. His mention of the words 'future' and 'fate' made me remember that I wanted to touch on that subject. Maybe not just touch on it, but dive into it. The same goes for the 2012 shit, I decided.

There were a few moments of uncomfortable silence, then Lyle and I broke into hysterical laughter for some reason I really couldn't determine. Maybe it was just to take the edge off all our thoughts. I was laughing so hard that I couldn't catch my breath. The harder I tried to breath, the more I realized that my pillow was partially blocking the airflow.

Pillow?

Blocking airflow?

I was awake.

Shit.

I didn't want to come home so soon.

As I gradually wafted back to slumber land, I realized that the following day was going to crawl by excruciatingly slowly. When I woke up again, I hit the snooze button on my faithful Casio several times. When I finally dragged my ass into the bathroom and began to brush my teeth, I laughed at my reflection in the mirror. Boy, did I need a shave, and my hair, what little I had left, was sticking up at weird angles. I wondered if this was how I appeared to Betty and Lyle. No, if I didn't want to look this disheveled, then I didn't look this disheveled. No wonder they call it heaven. Imagine spending one hundred fifty years appearing young and slim, with a full head of perfectly combed hair. Keep dreaming.

No, I couldn't keep dreaming, and that's what I had to continuously tell myself the entire day. Fighting the temptation to prolong my evening visits was as difficult as fucking hell. The only thing that calmed my nerves was the possibility of visiting Betty and Lyle every now and then in the future. Yeah, they'd welcome me back for a few reunions.

My single goal for the day was to get as tired as humanly possible so I could stretch every last second out of my final dream. That translated into miles of brisk walking with as little relaxation as I could muster. By the time I was finished with dinner, I was ready to collapse, but I pushed myself to do some more walking. Torture. Couldn't move my legs. Couldn't keep my eyes open. Before meditating, I actually tried to read. Despite the fact that I was at a critical point in a spectacular thriller, I couldn't focus on the words. And I was yawning so wide, a car could have driven into my mouth. So that was that. Good bye New York City; hello wherever Lyle was going to take me.

Chapter 28
Destined to Dream

As usual, I made a perfectly smooth transition. Upon my return, I found myself sitting comfortably on a cushion with my eyes firmly shut. Where was I? I wanted my senses, other than sight, to answer that question. The previous day, I had had a feeling that Lyle might take us on one of his short, but astounding, memory adventures. Or maybe he'd bring me back to Purchase for another model plane ride. Or give me one last spin in that ferocious 427 Cobra on the twisty road to Mt. Lemmon. Any of those would have provided a fitting finale to my dream adventures.

After sitting there for a fleeting moment, my ears betrayed our location. Well, I certainly wasn't at Mohonk any longer, not unless there are wildly chattering monkeys.

"Thanks, Lyle," I said with sincerity. "Glad to be back here."

"You know, I find it hard to believe that this might be your last dream adventure with us," he said in a low voice. "But . . . we'll be back in touch with you when sick Betty passes away. You'll find out if the observance was successful. Of course, that could happen tomorrow or in six months. Who knows?"

Betty tapped me on my knee. "When you finish your book, we'll all get together and discuss it."

"Hey, that's great. I'll really look forward to that. You've just given me the perfect kick in the ass to actually write it."

After blowing a rather lame smoke ring, Lyle said, "John, keep going into a deep meditation when you fall asleep. Use that special acorn. It'll make it easy for me to get you for the Betty thing, and who knows what else."

"Yeah, yeah . . . I know. Now I've got one last question on that subject. If, let's say in two years from now, I wanted to return for another evening, would that be possible? Just spend a few minutes catching up?"

"We'd welcome it," he quickly answered. "Just focus on that thought when you meditate, and I'll make it happen. But it can't become a habit."

"Great. I may never do it, but it makes me feel good knowing I can."

Just as I was about to say something else, I was rudely interrupted by a loud commotion from way above: all kinds of squawking and hysterical chattering. A bunch of monkeys was taunting a large, colorful bird with a squirming insect in its beak. The defiant bird wasn't about to relent to these mischievous creatures and fly away. It just perched on a swaying branch making a deep guttural sound.

"Don't want to disrupt your heavenly gaze, but I bet you've got a few profound questions to ask," remarked Lyle.

I hunched my shoulders. "There's a virtual shitload of stuff I'd like to ask you and Betty about. But, you'll be glad to hear, most of it's not too profound."

"That's a relief," Lyle and Betty said in unison.

"The other day, you mentioned a troublesome four letter word that begins with F.

"Never thought you'd find anything like that troublesome," snickered Lyle.

"The word was fate," I announced. "What do you all up here, especially your scientists, think about that? Is everything in our lives predetermined or do we have free will?"

Lyle looked at Betty, then turned to me. "That very subject is debated a lot, but I'm afraid to say there are no new answers or revolutionary theories that make any sense."

"Oh. I kind of knew you'd say that."

"Look, whether we have free will or not doesn't matter, doesn't make a damn bit of difference," mused Lyle. "Knowing one way or the other won't change your life. As far as most of us are concerned, we all have free will to think we have free will."

"Not the same thing," I retorted. "I want to know whether I can control my future."

"You absolutely can," blurted Lyle. "People can do anything they desire to control their futures. Let's say you want to be a lawyer . . ."

"Perish the thought," I interrupted.

Lyle smiled, shook his head with frustration and continued. "As I was saying . . . you plan your future by going to law school, and securing a job at a law firm. You meet a girl there, fall madly in love, marry her, and have a family. Everything you do is carefully planned. And you can change your plan at any point in your life: run away with some bimbo, open a bar in Cancun, become a Buddhist . . . it's all up to you. The only catch is that all those plans and decisions may have been predetermined. What's the difference? You can't see, feel or even sense destiny."

"So you mean the future could all be there, just waiting for all of us to catch up and run through our lives."

"Like I said, who gives a flying fuck," he exclaimed. "Just do what you're going to do, and don't think about destiny. Maybe you were destined to have these dreams, and destined to write a book about them. Maybe someone dying in a hospital was destined to read your book, and it made him or her feel wonderful. That one event could be why you were born."

"If the future is there, is that why people can predict it?"

"I suppose so, but most of those clairvoyants are frauds and assholes," he spouted.

"Now you sound like me," I noted. Of course, Betty got a good laugh out of that.

"Just for the hell of it," intoned Lyle, "I'll mention a theory, or maybe I should just call it a bold thought, about this topic."

"Understood," I said.

Lyle lit yet another Camel, quickly blew three trails of smoke, and told me that the future could happen like that. I was as confused as all fucking hell, but knew I was going to get an explanation. This was certain to be a mind blower. What in God's name was he going to tell me?

"Ready for this one," he asked. "It'll make you feel better. It's kind of like free will on crutches."

"Just spit it out," I said, blowing my own trail of smoke. "Is the future filtered or unfiltered?"

Lyle actually stood up to talk. "Multiply my streams of smoke by a million. Each stream represents a potential path to the future with every moment of a life fully predetermined. When you're born, you're destined to follow any one of these paths, but since they intersect at various points, you can shift between them, thereby altering your future. It's been theorized that the strength of your thoughts and actions in life can direct you to any one (or many) of these paths. Obviously, that means you may have a level of free will."

"That sounds preposterous," I said, wincing.

"Hey, don't shoot the messenger," he remarked. "This ain't my theory."

"But it makes absolutely no sense," I stammered.

"What does?" he retorted. "Science is getting weirder every day. At first, people thought quantum concepts were insanely absurd. Now, that's all taken for granted."

After a few moments of silence, he continued. "Major events in history, events that radically alter lives and thoughts, occur at points where all futures cross paths. For instance, World War Two was one of these events. So was the French Revolution. And the Crucifixion. And the sinking of the Titanic. And the fall of the Berlin Wall. And Einstein's announcement of E=MC2. And 911. And so on."

"Any basis for this part of the theory," I asked.

"Of course," he said with flair. "All these events, and many more, presented paradigm shifts that sent out information ripples along all the destined paths. That's why so many serious prognosticators and psychics have been able to predict these events with a fair degree of accuracy. Remember, picking up and interpreting vibrations is a special gift shared by very few. And keep in mind that all these people were on their own predetermined paths, which adds credibility to the theory that the paths cross."

"I think the paradigm shift and information ripples ideas are very interesting, but offer absolutely no proof that life paths cross," I said, being proud of my response. "If there was only one predetermined path that everyone followed, those psychics would still be getting their signals loud and clear."

"No one could argue with that assessment," he replied. "Makes perfect sense. But look at it this way: being able to predict inescapable events in the future is a strong indication—more appropriately, a frightening indication—that the future is predetermined. So, the multiple path angle gives people hope that they possess at least a semblance of free will."

"Yeah. I sure as hell agree with that," I exclaimed. "While we're on the subject, I want to ask you about this whole ridiculous 2012 disaster, end-of-the-world thing. Several evenings ago you alluded to the fact that there may be some truth to the predictions."

Lyle laughed, then got serious. "It's probably true. But nothing to worry about."

"Nothing to worry about? Are you kidding? How can you make a statement like that?"

Lyle laughed even harder. "Let me attempt to explain. First of all, considering the strength of the so called '2012' predictions, there most likely will be some event that can be classified as an influential paradigm shift, something that will have an effect on everyone with a pulse. But it doesn't necessarily mean there's going to be a disaster, and it probably won't occur in 2012."

"Well, once again, you've managed to thoroughly confuse me," I stated, squirming on my cushion.

"I figured as much," he readily admitted. "Now I'll try to clear things up. The books and most of the articles you see about 2012 present disaster scenarios. People love disaster scenarios. They get under your skin, not to mention that they sell lots of books. How many movies have you seen about one kind of disaster or another? That shit really sells tickets. And as far as the 2012 date, itself, is concerned, no one could have predicted long ago with that level of precision. 2012 could have happened years ago, could happen tomorrow, or in twenty years from now. But it only works as a sales tool if there's a specific year. 2012 could have been 911: that sure changed the world. Or it could have been Obama's election. Look at the positive effect that's having on the black community all over the world. What a paradigm shift."

"But there still could be a disaster. Right? Something terrible could happen," I offered.

"Of course, that's a possibility. That's always a possibility. There could be a monstrous earthquake or a massive undersea volcano that could generate ferocious tidal waves; we could be pulverized by an asteroid, or some stinkin' Arab could detonate a dirty bomb in a major city. Just use your imagination."

"I'd rather not use my imagination," I exclaimed. "It's simply too friggin' scary to think about."

"Then think positively. There are many possible paradigm shifts that don't involve crumbling buildings, cataclysmic explosions and massive loss of life. You know, paradigm shifts can range from the sublime to the ridiculous."

"Give me a ridiculous," I said, feeling a little better, a little calmer.

"How about this: in 2012, 2014, 2020 or whenever, we could be contacted by an alien civilization. That would have a rather profound effect on everyone, don't you think? Or maybe a fossil could be found that would turn all theories of evolution on their head. Here's an idea you're sure to love: maybe there'll be the second coming of Christ."

"Ok, ok. I get your point. Let's bury the whole 2012 thing," I said. "I want to ask about another subject that's always intrigued me: time travel. If the future is just sitting there waiting for us to catch up, maybe it's scientifically possible to jump ahead . . . you know . . . take quantum leaps."

Lyle cackled in sheer amusement about that. "Time machines? Portals? Not that I or anyone else know of. And there are no theories that I want to dredge up. You're getting into an area that attracts too many nuts."

"What about traveling into the past," I asked, realizing precisely how he was going to answer that.

"We do that all the time when we experience memories. In fact, we live in the past most of the time."

"I know that, but it's not at all what I meant. I'm asking about *real* travel into the past where the theory of causality comes into play. You know what I'm talking about. If someone traveled into the past and killed their grandfather, how would they have been born in the first place?"

"There's a somewhat simple, way to explain that," he carefully responded. "Anyone who could or would potentially do that wouldn't be here to talk about it. In fact, they never ever would have been here. Their existence would have been erased along the whole timeline."

"I see what you're talking about. That's a real mind fucker if I've ever heard one. Sorry Betty. Betty? Are you awake?"

"Just listening," she softly answered. "This stuff is really Lyle's territory, so I'm quietly paying attention and watching the monkeys. They're very entertaining."

I decided to bring up an entirely different topic. "You know what's been troubling me lately? I've never written anything down about all these dream experiences. Not one freakin' note. I can't even begin to imagine how many things I've forgotten."

"I'll assure you that when you sit down to write up your experiences and reactions, you'll remember absolutely everything."

"That's easy for you to say," I sternly responded. "You've got a freakin' photographic memory."

"So do you. Or have you forgotten everything I've jammed into your head about memory? Everything you've experienced, everything we've said, and everything you've thought about will come back to you. Don't think too hard about it, and don't create your own self-doubts. During this whole period of time, your memory has been enhanced and so has your ability to access it. If you experience normal writer's block, just relax, clear your mind, and it'll all start flowing again."

"Thanks for all the reassurance," I said. "That makes me feel a whole lot better. Does this mean that, from now on, my memory will be better?"

"That's hard to say. If you believe it will be, and you concentrate on that thought, there's a good chance you'll retain an enhanced memory. Now I know that you don't like hearing this, but when you get here in the, uh, normal way, the memory of every last detail in your life will be as clear as a movie."

"At this point, all I can say is that I hope you're right. I hope all this hasn't been my imagination on steroids."

"There's no more proof I can offer until . . . well, you know," he assured me.

"Yeah . . . I know."

"One more thing about your book," he said, grinning. "Don't get creative. Don't embellish anything. No matter how much you want to, don't give me wings and a halo."

"You needn't worry about that. You'll get horns and a tail; Betty will get the whole angel outfit."

"I'd love that," Betty said, perking up.

"Don't encourage him," Lyle answered.

"So . . . where do we go from here," I cautiously asked. Suddenly, I was beginning to feel as though my mystical journeys had really come to an end.

"Honestly, I feel bad about your leaving. I'm experiencing a sense of loss," he said with total sincerity. "Right about now, I'd be scheming about your next evening: planning our next memory trip, or thinking about some astounding revelation that would amaze you. Watching your range of expressions when I attempted to explain something seemingly impossible was always enjoyable. And I always respected your honesty. You never pretended to understand something when you didn't."

"I'm also distressed about John's leaving," said Betty. "It's going to be like losing a friend . . . for a while."

"Now you're making me feel even worse," I said with a half laugh. "Fucking ghosts. I'll always be haunted by your memory. Oh, and, while I'm gone, don't screw up my 427 Cobra. When and if I return, I'm going to take Betty for a frightening ride up and down Mount Lemmon."

"Don't forget you said that. I'm taking it as a promise." She was more emphatic than I'd ever seen.

"Let's get away from all this soppy shit. I actually have a serious thought I'd like to express."

"We can't wait to hear this," commented Lyle, fully expecting some tasteless joke or remark.

"This really is serious," I assured the both of them. "It concerns a thought I had right after we were discussing free will and the future. If our whole lives are predetermined, I will assume that includes our deaths and so-called rebirths. You with me so far?"

They both nodded "yes."

"Regardless of whether or not I've chosen my own paths to the future, my being here with you in this dimension was determined by fate. And that means all of our fates. All of our paths have crossed for one purpose: for me to perform my observance and assure Betty's future. Come on folks, why else am I here? The odds against it are what? A trillion trillion to one?"

"The odds are probably even worse than that," he remarked.

"So you see what I mean? Destiny didn't make our paths cross so I could fly model planes, or watch monkeys. It was for a far more important reason. I know it. I can feel it."

There was a pause in our conversation that seemed to take forever. Lyle and Betty were staring at each other, communicating in a silent language that went far beyond my comprehension. But, I was relieved to see that they both looked ridiculously happy.

"Amazing, John. Truly amazing." Lyle was almost stammering. "Neither Betty nor I ever thought of that. But it's very possible that you're right. Jesus, what a positive, powerful, perceptive suggestion. You've really stunned us."

Betty added, "You've renewed my hope."

"Listen guys," I said, carefully choosing my words, "Truthfully, I don't really know where my thought came from. The whole thing kind of just popped into my mind, and found its way out my mouth. It's got me pretty damn confounded. It's almost like I witnessed it rather than thinking and saying it. Can you understand what I mean?"

"I understand it completely," stumbled Betty.

"Look, I don't care about any of that," proclaimed Lyle, slapping his hands together. "What was said, no matter how it was said, made a whole lot of sense. It simply leaped out of your subconscious mind. Who gives a shit how those ideas got into you head. All I want to say is that I'm thrilled with these new thoughts and the obvious implications. I can't wait to tell my friend about this."

I looked at Lyle and Betty and shrugged my shoulders. "Well, this has been an interesting evening if I must say so myself."

"Like many others," Lyle reminded me. "Which leads me to a question. Do you have a favorite experience, John?"

"No. Really, I don't. Everything we've done has been exciting and very informative in its own special way. I loved it all, except for that one accident when I stepped into the memory void."

"I've got another question, but before I ask it, I have to remind you that you could possibly wake up at any moment. I'm not sure when we'll see you again; it all depends on the Betty situation and the completion of your book. Whichever comes first."

"It's hard to imagine falling asleep at night and simply waking up in the morning. You know: like normal people do. Nothing will ever really be normal for me again, not with these impossibly incredible memories bouncing around in my head. To be sure, I'll get my life back, but it'll be a different life, a more aware life. I mean, how could it be otherwise?"

"I guess you've got a point there. I think I know the answer to this, but if you had the option to erase this whole thing from your mind, what would you do?"

"Come on, Lyle. What the F do you think? How could you even ask me that? I won't even dignify it with an answer."

"Hey, I just had to ask. You know that I already knew the answer."

"Guess so," I admitted. "I'm just a little touchy."

"Getting back to my logical questions," continued Lyle, "I realize that you don't have a favorite experience, but does anything you learned, any piece of knowledge, stand out above the rest?"

"Christ, I've learned so many extraordinary things. But the most fascinating and provocative of all is the concept of particle bundles and their astonishing role in life at every level. Their significance is overwhelming.

There's another thing you've taught me that you probably don't even realize. Tolerance. I'll never look at crazy people the same way again because, just possibly, some of their bundle abilities may be unfiltered, and they're reacting to strange, unworldly stimulation.

And here's something you'll find hard to believe. I'm not going to perceive the metaphysical section of my bookstore as a repository for annoying gibberish. Well, not all of it, that is. After everything I've seen and heard, thanks to you and Betty, I'll have to assume that others have, in one way or another, been in touch with this dimension. Even if they're just conversing with an unknown presence, or they've slipped into a memory trace, it would radically change their views on reality."

"Congratulations. Those are major steps for you," chirped Lyle. "You really have been altered. Positively."

"Anyone with half a brain would be," I responded.

"You strongly asserted that, of all the revolutionary concepts we've touched on here, particle bundles offer the most important, let alone radical, paradigm shift. Right?"

"Without a doubt," I quickly responded.

Lyle continued. "But . . . aren't you forgetting one little thing? A piece of knowledge powerful enough to shake up anyone's foundation in reality? Even someone who doesn't give a damn about science and physics?"

I looked at Lyle and shrugged my shoulders. Then I glanced at Betty for maybe a hint. She was playing along with him, waiting to see if I knew what he was talking about. What on earth was I missing?

Right in the middle of my quandary, we were all interrupted, and rather startled, by a very loud screech from close above. It was another monkey, but unlike any I had ever seen. The thing was damn big, at least twice the size of any of the others, and it swung directly overhead. Mottled brown fur covered its body, but it was the face that really took everyone's breath away. It was menacing looking: a long, protruding mouth was wide open, revealing some serious looking teeth. And beneath its reptilian-like, dead black eyes were evil stripes in multiple colors. Fortunately, it was gone as quickly as it had come.

"As you were saying, Lyle, there's something I missed? Instead of torturing me, just spit it out. No drama. No suspense. Please."

"I was beginning to allude to the most basic premise of all: the reason all of this has been happening. You've got to attribute it all to the undeniable fact that death is a misnomer. You don't die. You just make a transition to another world. Life goes on."

I kept hearing his words over and over: "Life goes on, life goes on, life goes on, life goes on." As his words slowly faded away, so did everything else. The cushion I had been clutching turned into my pillow, and the tomb became my bed. I was up. No, I was half up, already beginning to doze off again. In my mind, all I could hear was Lyle's final statement: "Life goes on." That's when I realized my book had a title.

• • •

When I woke up to a bright new day, I could still hear Lyle uttering "life goes on." As I stretched the sleep out of my back and arms, I realized that what I needed more than anything was a steaming cup of brutally strong coffee. In record time, I was sitting at Juan's enjoying an invigorating breakfast. Sitting back, fully satiated, I realized that I was attempting to forget about the awful fact that my spectacular dreaming had reached its finale. Shit, it was hard to believe. Of course, the skeptic in me found it even harder to believe that it had ever happened.

I could have written off one or two of the dreams as pure imagination. Not all of them, though. Time and again I had received knowledge that was verifiable. Stuff I hadn't previously known. That was certainly no illusion. Could all this have been a combination of remote viewing and unbridled imagination? Maybe. Who knows? At that point I made myself a promise to stop questioning my otherworldly experiences. That was it. Period.

Sitting there, relaxing with my second coffee, I began thinking about my massive new project: the book I had to write. Now that I had my normal life back, I had no more excuses to procrastinate. Somehow, knowing that I wouldn't be visiting my favorite dimension anymore had begun to clear my mind. I was ready to begin my endeavor.

When I first sat down to write, I anticipated a long, painful, frustrating process. But I was wrong. Dead wrong. The whole thing went surprisingly smoothly. All my thoughts, all the dialog, and all the related visuals flowed with ease. It was all in my memory, precisely as Lyle had assured me. I wrote as quickly as I could, trying in earnest to keep pace with my thoughts. If I stopped to think about what I was writing, I'd hit a roadblock. Lyle was absolutely right again; analysis was my enemy, but one I conquered with ease.

After several weeks of writing my ass off, I decided to print out what I had so I could experience the reality of reading it on paper. Honestly, I could hardly believe what I had written. It all seemed absurd, surreal, and completely insane. It was also sort of embarrassing. This was me I was writing about? Me? Dreaming? Who would believe this shit? But it all sounded fascinating. Especially all the sciency stuff, which was a bit difficult to understand. But, as Lyle had advised, I didn't change a word.

A few more very productive weeks went by, and one afternoon I suddenly felt extremely tired, couldn't keep my eyes open. So I figured, fuck it, I'll take a well deserved nap. Out of habit, I cleared my mind, brought my acorn into focus, and meditated myself into oblivion. It turned into the snooze of a lifetime, an experience that shook me to the core. Lyle had once again reached out and grabbed my subconscious being.

CHAPTER 29
THE REBIRTH

I had woken up from a very deep sleep completely disoriented.
    Was I sick, I wondered?
    Or emerging from a bad dream?
    I felt weary. And sad. And my legs ached.
    My breathing was heavy and labored.
    The air had a medicinal odor
    There was an odd taste in my mouth.
    A cold lozenge. Right.
    I heard it click on my teeth.
    But were they *my* teeth? In *my* mouth?
    Why were my eyes shut?
    Why couldn't I move?

• • •

Then I felt my eyelids gradually begin to rise.
    I sensed a trickle of light.
    I saw a book in my hands. *My* hands?
    My hands aren't all wrinkly and gnarled.
    These were the hands of an old man. Not mine.
    Like the blotchy hands, the book was old and worn.
    The cover was creased and scratched black leather.
    I saw no writing. No title.
    Just a faded and stained red ribbon draped over the front.
    The experience was beginning to upset me.
    I wasn't awake, but locked in some bizarre dream.
    Then I felt my head start to gently rise.

My gaze shifted from the book to . . . to what?
To a very old woman lying motionless on a bed?
She seemed very familiar.
Why? Who was she? Why was she in my dream?
And why did I hear music? Sweet, quiet music?
I've heard that music before. Somewhere.
But where?
I strained to listen.

• • •

There was a voice. Heavenly.

And the most enchanting words.

The words whispered in my ear telling me exactly where I was, and what I was about to witness.

Who can say for certain, maybe you're still here

Out of what seemed to be a mist, Lyle appeared. He was sitting on the hospital bed, leaning over Betty. His hand rested on hers. Beside the bed, the Betty I knew so well was sitting on a chair, intently watching her future unfold. She appeared intense. Expectant.

I feel you all around me, your memory's so clear.

It was finally happening. The moment of truth had arrived much sooner than I expected. And Lyle had brought me back, just as he had promised. I realized immediately that I was observing this event through the eyes of a priest who, I assumed, had delivered a solemn last rights. Now he just stood there in silent contemplation.

Deep in the stillness I can hear you speak.

Lyle had aligned me with the priest so I could witness the transition from his perfect point of view. What I was about to see was invisible to him, but not to his particle bundle which recorded every detail. Through his deep faith, he was probably imagining her soul taking flight. One day in the very near future, his own dreams would come true.

You're still an inspiration, can it be?

The miracle began to unfold. I could hardly believe my eyes. Or should I say *his* eyes? A ghosted image of Betty began to slowly rise from her lifeless body, angling itself towards Lyle. My whole being within the priest was chilled. Absolutely shivering.

That you are mine forever love,

Lyle didn't budge an inch. Betty leaned forward in her chair, tears streaming from her eyes. She was shaking with emotion. The diaphanous image rose higher towards Lyle, taking on more detail. Now I could see a pronounced difference. Her features were changing, becoming far more lifelike. Younger.

and you are watching over me from up above.

Lyle tried as best he could to put his arms around her intensifying image. It was difficult. She wasn't really there. But she *was* there, rapidly gaining detail. And changing.

Fly me up to where you are beyond the distant star.

Shifting my perspective, I took a fleeting look at the other Betty, still seated beside Lyle. Was it my imagination, or was she slightly fading? Or was she getting blurry? Maybe the priest's eyes were playing tricks on me. That was out of my control.

I wish upon tonight to see you smile

My gaze quickly shifted back to the scene on the bed. Now it was very apparent. Sick Betty no longer looked like sick Betty. She appeared much younger, much healthier and decidedly more solid. And real. Real? Yes, real. I had to accept that now. Her soul, or whatever it was, had left her body and was curling into Lyle's arms. Now he was crying too.

if only for a while to know you're there

This was completely, astonishingly unbelievable. It was really happening. I was watching a human being pass from one dimension to another... one existence to another. But... was it working? Were the two Betties merging? Were two signature vibrations becoming one. I couldn't tell. Or could I?

a breath away is not too far from where you are.

The tighter Lyle held this dreamy apparition in his arms, the more she began to respond. When she placed her head on his shoulder, she appeared as solid as Lyle himself. And much younger. In fact, she looked exactly like the Betty in my dreams.

Are you gently sleeping here inside my dream?

It was then that I realized that spooky Betty was seriously fading away. I could still see her transparent image perched on that ugly, yellow vinyl chair. What a lousy place to spend the last moments of a wondrous life. Or . . . was it the beginning of a new life? I didn't know. Yet. But I would soon find out. The anticipation was nearly unbearable. Fortunately, the Priest remained frozen in place. I was afraid he was going to walk away when I realized that, in real time, he may have been standing there for all of a second.

And isn't faith believing a power can't be seen?

Lyle seemed to tighten his grip on Betty, and, now, she was hugging him, as well. I wondered how long this was going to take. How long is a miracle? As it turned out, not too long. Because Betty opened her eyes, and kissed Lyle on the cheek. She was radiant with life, a far cry from her gray, shriveled, former self in permanent repose on the bed.

As my heart holds you just one beat away,

As I intensely watched Betty's rebirth, I didn't immediately realize that the other Betty had completely vanished. Gone. I felt absolutely horrible. But after a moment's thought, I began to feel amazingly wonderful. It made sense that, if the union of vibrations hadn't worked, both Betties would still be present. But there was only one Betty. Both Betties in one? Maybe. Must be.

I cherish all you gave me every day
'cause you are mine forever love,
watching over me from up above.
And I believe that angels breathe,
and that love will live on and never leave.
Fly me up to where you are . . .

That magnificent song was instantly replaced by the sound of a splash. And that dreary hospital room was replaced by Lake Mohonk.

The three of us were out on the water in a rowboat. I was stunned. Completely stunned. And jammed with joy. Could it be?

I could see that things were back to normal. Before so much as a word was uttered, Betty began to laugh at me. And so did Lyle.

"John," exclaimed Betty, "couldn't you have at least dressed for the occasion? I mean, really, red striped underpants?"

All of a sudden, I realized that I had forgotten to think on some clothing, just as I had done during my earliest dream experiences. And Lyle hadn't helped a bit. He just let me thoroughly embarrass myself, wearing only my sleep attire. Good thing I don't sleep in my birthday suit.

Once I was in my jeans and blue striped shirt, I could only think of one profound thing to say: "Well?"

"Well, what do you think," asked Betty. "Am I me?"

"Since you seem happier than a pig in shit, I'll have to assume that you're Betty. But you'll have to prove it to me."

"So ask me something," she said, laughing up a storm.

I thought for a few moments then replied, "Ok. What's your favorite car?"

She stared at me with a devilish grin, just lapping up the suspense.

"For Christ sake," exclaimed Lyle, "just tell him."

"Honestly, I have two favorite cars," she playfully announced. "One is a 1937 Cord. Just adored that car. The other is a dumpy little thing with a funny name. It's called a 427 Cobra. And you faithfully promised to take me for another ride in it on the road to Mount Lemmon."

No sooner did she utter those words than I jumped up and gave her a big hug, nearly tipping the boat over.

"I don't know what to say. This is just too good to be true. It's way beyond my comprehension.

"Doesn't surprise me," quipped Lyle. "I always knew this would happen."

Betty shot him a look. "As John would say, you're a friggin' liar. You were as nervous as I was. Admit it."

"For the answer to that, we'll have to wait for John to finish his book. Which, in itself, will be a miracle."

"You'll see," I responded. "Before you know it you'll be eagerly reading every word, biting your nails. Then I'll be back for all your fucking criticism. Oh, sorry Betty."

Lyle chuckled as he lit a Camel. With the smoke whirling around us, the scene disappeared, and I was comfortably back in my bed. I would awake knowing I had had the best dream of my life.

• • •

I drifted back to a drowsy, semi-awakened state in my own dimension late in the afternoon. For some reason, it was always more difficult to get my senses in order after a nap. And, as emotionally charged as this one had been, it's surprising I was able to get up at all. Actually, I was half up, leaning on my elbows, trying to absorb my most miraculous dream yet. Witnessing a rebirth was simply too astonishing for description, let alone belief. I was drunk with joy and excitement. It had finally happened. After all the doubts, worries, heartaches and speculation, the two Betties had become one. And I had been an active participant, not just a student and spectator.

Over the next few weeks, I got up every morning in a fantastic mood, ready to plow into my book. These were probably the most productive days of my life. Every here and there, I'd print out what I had written so I could review every word. Without fail, I always had the same reaction; I was shocked, amazed, perplexed, often confused, and always in total disbelief.

Then it happened. Something more exciting and unbelievable than anything I had experienced: I was done. Finished. My book was just about complete. All that was missing was my review with Lyle and Betty.

That night, after two slices of pepperoni pizza, an hour or so of tv, and several hours of reading, I was ready to hit the sack. Hoping that Lyle was on my wavelength, I attempted to communicate through meditation that my book was done. I was dying to see them. Dying to hear what they had to say. But, that evening, it didn't happen. All I got was a refreshing, good night's sleep. Shit.

The next day, I just fuddled around in a daze, unable to accomplish anything. But what was there to accomplish anyway? My next steps were entirely dependant upon my ethereal friends. There was nothing more I could do until I had heard from them. That afternoon I was tempted to reach them via a nap, but I decided against that. It would, I knew, be smarter to get exceptionally tired and do my usual late night ritual. That turned out to be a very wise thing to do.

Chapter 30
Happy Trails

Gently roasting logs.

The most fragrant scent in the world.

A gift from nature, more enchanting than any flower.

At least to my nose, that is.

That's what I smelled before I opened my dream eyes.

My meditation had worked.

Lyle had taken my consciousness across dimensions into the marvels of the afterlife. But where was I? I knew I was sitting on a wooden bench before a soothing fire. But where? Was I at a Viking celebration? Or in Mohonk's magnificent Lake Lounge on a chilly winter day? Too eager to learn the answer, I opened my dream eyes, and found myself in the lodge at the summit of Mount Lemmon. The fire was as welcoming as the mug of hot cider waiting for me at the table.

Lyle and Betty were sitting across from me, looking more calm and relaxed than ever. Betty radiated more warmth and happiness than I had ever seen, but that didn't surprise me, considering her new lease on life. As expected, Lyle's whole head was partly obscured by a thick cloud of cigarette smoke. "So . . . happy to be here?" he asked, waving the smoke away from his face.

Enjoying a mouth full of the spicy cider, I simply nodded "yes."

"We've been discussing locations for a week," said Betty. "Your favorite tomb was a strong possibility. So were Mohonk and your old back yard in Purchase. But we knew you loved this spot as well, and it offered us an opportunity to give you a very special surprise."

"Surprise?" I asked.

"No more about it now," continued Betty. "You'll find out soon enough when we're through discussing your book."

"Well, do I have a masterpiece here or not?" I asked enthusiastically.

"What can I say?" answered Lyle. "There were no surprises; you reported everything with complete accuracy, just as I had predicted you would. Your own separate thoughts and analysis are insightful, honest, and interesting. Yeah, you did it. I'm proud."

"So am I," added Betty. "I had fun reliving our experiences with you. And it brought back my own pains. Gave me more insights into what I was going through before my miraculous transition. It also reminded me of how astonishing and unbelievable everything is in this dimension, and made it clear that I should never take anything for granted."

Lyle was getting fidgety, and I could tell he had something profound to say. "I also learned something about myself. I'm a great teacher."

Betty shook her head, and looked up at the ceiling.

I did too. And started laughing.

"My only regret is exposing you to all those Viking shenanigans," he said.

"Shenanigans?" I asked. "That's how you describe the torture and mutilation of women?"

"You know what I mean," he muttered. "Should I have avoided showing you what those people were really like? The experience, as extreme and horrendous as it was, accomplished just what I wanted; it got under your skin, made you think, illustrated many of my points about humanity."

"In retrospect, I don't think you were wrong in exposing me to this. I'm glad you did. And I'm not going to change one word of it."

"Honestly," he said with a chuckle. "Do you think anyone's going to believe anything you've written?"

"No, I don't. But maybe I shouldn't go that far. Some people will definitely believe every word of it, and it'll make them feel great, give new meaning to their lives. But that'll be a very select minority. Look, as you know, I'm having a rough time believing any of it myself."

"You'll always wonder about it until you know for sure," he reminded me. "If you had never doubted any of this, Betty and I would have thought for sure that you're nuts. Plus, if you weren't such a skeptic, your book wouldn't be anywhere near as interesting or authentic."

"I'm happy you see it that way." I was gleaming.

Lyle stood up, stretched, and said that we had accomplished everything on his agenda. He seemed genuinely pleased. I requested one last mug of cider, which he gladly created, along with my favorite pipe. "God, am I going to miss these dreams," I sadly announced.

"You've got a lot of work ahead of you," he said. "Getting your book published will take quite an effort. But it'll be worth it."

"Don't remind me now. I'm trying to enjoy my last minutes here."

"Not another word about it. I promise," he said.

"I have one more request," I said, almost whispering. "Do you think I could possibly finish my cider in the rain forest? That would be the perfect end of a perfect evening."

Betty answered. "But we've got a better perfect ending in store for you. Remember, we've got a very special surprise for you."

"And it's waiting right outside," added Lyle.

"I completely forgot," I admitted. "I'll save the birds and monkeys for another time. If there's another time, that is."

Lyle and Betty glanced at each other, giggled, and led me out the door. The air was exactly how I remembered it: crisp, dry and clean. You know what they say about a mountain breeze. Well, I followed them into the parking lot, and nearly fell to the ground when I saw my surprise. Sitting before me in all its glory was my 427 Cobra. I really, really couldn't believe my eyes. There it was, without so much as a drop of dust on it, its gleaming blue finish reflecting the puffy, white clouds.

"What do you think?" asked Betty, with her biggest smile yet.

"I'm at a loss for words," I answered. "Can I take it for a spin?"

"Can you take it for a spin?" exclaimed Betty. "You can take it and me for a spin down the mountain. Remember, you promised me."

Then I heard a jingling sound. It was Lyle. Holding the keys out to me. Before I slid into the car, he gave me a whopping swat on the back and said, "See you soon. But not too soon."

Once I was seated in the car with Betty beside me, I inhaled the intoxicating scents of new leather and a trace of oil. With unbridled exhilaration and anticipation, I slipped the key into the ignition and firmly twisted it. The engine immediately came to life with a belching roar, and as I slowly revved it up to 2000 rpms, the torque made the whole car rock to the side. Once the oil pressure and engine temperature gauges were within their safety zones, I depressed the clutch, grabbed the shift knob and snicked into first gear.

Gliding out of the parking lot, trying not to kick up too much gravel, I felt that I really was in heaven. If you looked up dream in the dictionary, this would have been the definition. For the first quarter mile or so, I took it very easy, getting reacquainted with the car again. But the beast wanted me to give it more gas. Lots more gas. Only then could it do what is was born to do: eat the asphalt and shatter the wind.

When I slammed into my first turn, downshifting from third to second, the staccato engine noises were lovelier than any music I had ever heard. Yup. I was undoubtedly in heaven. Then I heard a sound just as charming: Betty's voice. "This is fun," she screamed. "Too much fun."

After rounding another curve at an irresponsible speed, I spotted a car in the distance coming in my direction. It had also shot through a tight curve, but was dangerously fishtailing all over the road, kicking up a haze of sand.

"What an asshole," I shrieked, as I applied my brakes.

"Yeah." shouted Betty. "What a complete asshole."

At that moment, as the careening car settled down, I could have sworn it was a Triumph TR-4A, just like the one I had in Tucson. And it was white, just like mine. As we got closer, I noticed that it had bright blue racing stripes on the hood, just like mine. When we finally passed the car, I couldn't believe my eyes. I was nearly in shock.

It was my old car. And the "asshole" driving it was me at 20 years old. "Holy fucking shit," I screamed. To make matters even more astounding, Lyle was in the passenger seat waving like a mad man. This was just too much. I was speechless. Could hardly catch my breath. Of course, Betty was laughing hysterically.

I hollered, "How did he do that? That was me. From the past. And he was in my friggin' car."

Betty hollered back, "By this time you should know how easy that was to do. Just think about it."

I realized that she was right. Then something else captured my mind: that strange feeling of déjà vu. I distinctly remembered passing a Cobra on this very road when I was driving my Triumph. Was it blue, with white stripes? Was it a 427? That much I couldn't recall. But the memory was absolutely there: vivid as hell. I had passed a Cobra right here over forty years ago. But was this the one, the car I was currently driving? Had I caught a glimpse of my future, a stroke of fate already embedded in my memory?

Betty knew exactly what I was thinking, and before I was able to verbalize anything she gave me a winsome smile and shrugged her shoulders. Coming out of another slippery corner I said, "Honestly, Betty, tell me what just happened. You've got to let me know."

Looking back and forth between the road and her, I noticed the sky begin to dim and my engine sounded fainter. Betty brushed a tuft of hair from her eyes, peered into my soul, and whispered, "Until we meet again." Then I woke up. My dreams had come to an end. Maybe.

About the Song

I learned through internet research that "Betty's song" is actually titled, "To Where You Are." Lyrics and music are by Richard Marx and Linda Thompson, and it was initially performed in 2001 by Josh Groban. Since that time, there have been 50 versions of this hauntingly magnificent song by different artists. The version that Betty communicated to Lyle was sung by Chloe Agnew in 2006. As you can well imagine, I purchased the song for my iPod, and I've been playing it to death. Shit. Did I just say what I thought I said?

About the Author

In a nutshell, I was born in New York City, and at the age of four my family moved to Purchase, a bucolic suburb about 30 miles North of Manhattan. This was a wonderful place to grow up! After high school, I went out to Tucson, Arizona to attend the University of Arizona where I graduated with a degree in Journalism. While I was out there, my family moved back to the city after having lost our home to eminent domain. Upon my return, I joined an advertising agency, and began a successful career that spanned many many years. In addition to being an award-winning copywriter, I developed marketing skills that led to my becoming an independent consultant. In my spare time, I dabbled as a toy inventor and developed two product lines that met with tremendous success. Then, after a long bout with cancer, my life went from the relatively ordinary to the extraordinary when I had my afterlife experiences. Today, I still reside in NYC, and I have a wife, two great kids, and the cutest dog in the world.

Made in the USA
Middletown, DE
10 August 2017